T0265639

LAWLESS

ALSO BY ILYA SHAPIRO

*Supreme Disorder: Judicial Nominations and
the Politics of America's Highest Court*

*Religious Liberties for Corporations? Hobby Lobby,
the Affordable Care Act, and the Constitution*
(with David H. Gans)

LAWLESS

THE MISEDUCATION OF
AMERICA'S ELITES

ILYA SHAPIRO

BROADSIDE BOOKS
An Imprint of HarperCollins*Publishers*

LAWLESS. Copyright © 2025 by Ilya Shapiro. All rights reserved. Printed in the United States of America. No part of this book may be used or reproduced in any manner whatsoever without written permission except in the case of brief quotations embodied in critical articles and reviews. For information, address HarperCollins Publishers, 195 Broadway, New York, NY 10007.

HarperCollins books may be purchased for educational, business, or sales promotional use. For information, please email the Special Markets Department at SPsales@harpercollins.com.

Broadside Books™ and the Broadside logo are trademarks of HarperCollins Publishers.

FIRST EDITION

Library of Congress Cataloging-in-Publication Data has been applied for.

ISBN 978-0-06-333658-2

24 25 26 27 28 LBC 5 4 3 2 1

To the memory of my parents and the promise of my children

And when the last law was down, and the Devil turned 'round on you, where would you hide, Roper, the laws all being flat?

—Robert Bolt, *A Man for All Seasons*

Contents

LAWLESS

Introduction

"So ideally if you could go back in time, how would you have reworded your tweet to convey what you were intending? . . . When you were posting the tweet that evening, was that in your personal capacity or was that professionally? . . . Was there anything different or unusual in that moment in how you posted that tweet? . . . When you read it yourself, do you think it sounds offensive? . . . Are you aware that other university community members, including students and alums, staff, and faculty have expressed that they were offended by your tweet?"

Those were the questions I faced one morning in February 2022, on a Zoom call with university bureaucrats. Two Georgetown offices were conducting a joint investigation into off-the-cuff comments I had posted on social media a few weeks earlier. Would I be allowed to start my job as the head of a prestigious law school center or terminated for wrongspeak? That was the bizarro world I found myself in. I didn't think I was naive about higher education, but still my eyes were opened to the institutional rot in academia—most alarmingly at law schools.

When I accepted a position with Georgetown Law, one of the most prestigious law schools in the most credential-focused profession, I thought it would be an opportunity to have a big impact. After nearly 15 years at the Cato Institute, ultimately directing the think tank's center for constitutional studies and rising to the level of vice president, I was open to a new challenge. Having developed Cato's nationally renowned amicus curiae (friend of the court) brief program and published a best-selling book on the Supreme Court, I needed to consider what else I could do in my career. Having been invited to apply to be dean of the University of Tennessee's law school the previous summer—which process included a required diversity statement, about which more later—I had begun thinking outside the box.

And so when Randy Barnett, the esteemed law professor who had revolutionized constitutional interpretation, offered to make me the executive director of the Georgetown Center for the Constitution, I had to take it. The center was renowned for advancing originalism, the idea that constitutional provisions should be interpreted according to their original public meaning. So that was a chance to do something different, to have more of an academic profile while expanding the center's footprint in the world of legal policy and practice.

Well, if I wanted a new challenge, that was what I got—but it wasn't quite what I'd imagined when Randy and I started discussing the possibility over dinner at a Capitol Hill bistro.

On January 26, 2022, five days before I was set to start at Georgetown, Supreme Court Justice Stephen Breyer announced his retirement. Or rather, because his press conference didn't happen until the next day, it was announced for him. Rumor has it that it was White House Chief of Staff Ron Klain who had leaked the news, to lock in Breyer's decision and ensure that there would be a vacancy for President Joe Biden to fill while Democrats had control of the Senate (which wasn't assured past the 2022 midterms). Indeed, we haven't had a Supreme Court confirmation process under divided government since 1991, when then-Senator Biden presided over an explosive set of hearings for Clarence Thomas.

I was on a plane to Austin, Texas, when the news broke. Upon landing, my phone blew up, and I spent the rest of the afternoon writing press statements and fielding media queries about Breyer's legacy and the search for his successor. My bottom line was that it was unfortunate and unseemly that Biden was narrowing his candidate pool by race and sex—he had promised during the presidential campaign that he'd pick a black woman—but that whoever he picked would be a reliable vote on the Court's left wing. After all, it has long been the case that Democratic-appointed justices vote much more in lockstep than their Republican-appointed counterparts do.

At a certain point, the immediate media cycle ended and I went to a dinner celebrating a friend's new job. Walking back to my hotel from the restaurant, I was feeling festive and feisty. As I doomscrolled Twitter before going to bed—not recommended—I became increasingly upset about the criteria being applied to the Supreme Court nomination. I asked myself: If I were a Democratic president, whom would I tap? I got it: Sri Srinivasan, the chief judge of the US Court of Appeals for the DC Circuit—the second-most-prestigious court in the country—an Obama appointee who had argued 25 cases in the high court and was universally respected for his intellect and legal acumen. He had been born in India, to boot, and emigrated to Kansas with his parents, so he combined "diversity" and the American dream. Judge Srinivasan had the potential to have a huge impact as a justice and had been considered for the 2016 nomination that had ultimately gone to Merrick Garland but was now preemptively disqualified because of his race and gender.

So I fired off a late-night hot take on Twitter:

> Objectively best pick for Biden is Sri Srinivasan, who is solid prog & v smart. Even has identify [identity] politics benefit of being first Asian (Indian) American. But alas doesn't fit into the latest intersectionality hierarchy so we'll get lesser black woman. Thank heaven for small favors?

> Because Biden said he'[d] only consider black women for SCOTUS, his nominee will always have an asterisk attached. Fitting that the Court takes up affirmative action next term.

In other words, I argued in stilted Twitter prose that Judge Srinivasan was the best candidate, meaning that *everyone else in the entire world* was less qualified. So if Biden kept his promise, he would pick a less-qualified—or, given the platform's character limit, "lesser"—black woman.

Then I went to bed.

Overnight, a firestorm erupted on social media, particularly over those three words: "lesser black woman." I deleted the tweet and apologized for my inartful choice of words but stood by my view that Biden should have considered "all possible nominees," as 76 percent of Americans agreed in an ABC News poll released a few days later. Many politicians and legal commentators made the same point.

But it was too late. My ideological opponents were out for blood, or at least my new job, even before I assumed it.

The day after the tweet was the second-worst day of my life, after another January day nearly 25 years earlier, when my mom died. I thought that I had blown up my life and killed my career. Everything I had worked hard for over decades—the sacrifices my parents had made in getting me out of the Soviet Union, the earnest striving of an immigrant kid to get to the Ivy League and work in the halls of power, the life my wife and I were building for our two young sons—all of it was crumbling. Over a tweet.

Never mind that no reasonable person could construe what I said to be offensive. It's willful miscomprehension to read my tweet to suggest that "the best Supreme Court nominee could not be a Black woman," as Georgetown Law dean William Treanor did in a statement that afternoon, or that I considered black women to be "lesser than" everyone else. Although my tweet could've been phrased better, as I readily admitted, its meaning that I considered one candidate to be best and thus all others to be less qualified is clear. Only those acting in bad faith would misconstrue what I said to suggest otherwise. Only those trying to get me fired for my political beliefs would campaign for my banishment from polite society.

Thanks to friends and allies with public platforms and private back channels to Dean Treanor—ranging from Bari Weiss to Kmele Foster and the organization on whose board he sits, the Foundation for Individual Rights and Expression (FIRE), to various other public figures and alumni—I wasn't fired during those initial four days of hell. Instead I was onboarded and immediately placed on paid leave pending an investigation into whether I had violated any university policies. That investigation continued for more than four months of purgatory, during which I was banned from campus.

It's clear now that the "investigation," led by HR and an office with the Orwellian title of Institutional Diversity, Equity and Affirmative Action (IDEAA), and advised by the very prestigious (and expensive) Washington law firm WilmerHale, was a sham. The process was the punishment. It doesn't take months to investigate a tweet—or to look at a calendar. Any junior law professor could've applied the law (the short policies at issue, particularly Georgetown's vaunted Speech and Expression Policy) to the facts (an even shorter tweet) and come up with a quick answer—specifically that I had engaged in protected speech that wasn't discriminating against or harassing anyone. But that didn't happen, and as the process dragged on, it became abundantly clear that university officials were just stalling until students left campus.

And indeed, on June 2, 2022, about a week after the semester ended,

I was reinstated on the technicality that I hadn't been an employee when I had tweeted and so wasn't subject to discipline under the relevant policies. I celebrated that technical victory in the pages of the *Wall Street Journal*, as one does, but soon saw that Georgetown had made it impossible for me to fulfill the duties I had been hired for. After digesting the IDEAA report that hit my email inbox that afternoon—a "confidential" document that has *never before been published* but appears in the appendix here, with my annotations—and after consulting with Randy, my lawyer, and other trusted advisers, especially my wife, I concluded that remaining in the job I was hired for was untenable.

I won't rehash the explanation here—my resignation letter is also in the appendix—but suffice it to say that Georgetown implicitly repealed its free-speech policy and set me up for discipline the next time I transgressed progressive orthodoxy. Instead of participating in that slow-motion firing, I quit.

Ever since, I've been using the platform I've been given to shine a light on the rot in academia—and at law schools in particular. Because alas, as it turned out, my saga was no freak exception. You'd think that future lawyers would have greater appreciation for spirited and open engagement with provocative ideas. After all, they'll be facing much harder situations in their legal careers than bad tweets. You'd think that legal faculty would be at the vanguard of protections for free speech and due process, given their deep understanding of the importance of the rule of law. But it's at law schools in particular that academic freedom is under threat, free speech in retreat, and civil discourse a thing of the past. The illiberal forces of woke justice are on the march.

***

Legal education used to be a staid and intimidating enterprise. Think of *The Paper Chase*, the 1973 film set at Harvard Law and featuring the old-school teaching style of Professor Charles Kingsfield. The classroom scenes there have all the standard themes: teaching students how to think, probing the weaknesses of an argument, differentiating fact patterns to apply precedent. Kingsfield's idiosyncrasies represent the demands of law school, where the most important skill is logic-based communication. Student acculturation into professional norms began with their being addressed as Mr. and Ms., updated from Miss as the profession modernized. All took the same rigorous curriculum (torts, contracts, property, criminal law, civil procedure) their first year before getting into doctrinal classes (constitutional law, corporate law, administrative law) their second year and more specialized or esoteric electives (securities, international law, Roman law) their third year.

What "extracurriculars" there were also related to professional training, such as participation in law reviews and moot court competitions, plus clubs for those interested in going into particular legal fields and "fun" things such as intramural sports and film societies. That cursus honorum produced what people want in their lawyers: the ability to see all sides of an issue, navigate complex rules, and work with people they don't like to achieve their clients' goals. The law was an esteemed profession because its practitioners were responsible for upholding the rule of law—including leveraging their skills and savvy to advocate for changes in the law as required.

Although the basic subjects taught in law schools, particularly in the first year, are largely the same as they were decades ago, much about them has changed, often radically. By this I don't mean the leftward slant of the faculty, a tendency that began in the 1960s and has continued such that it's now essentially impossible to become a law professor, especially in "public law" areas such as constitutional and criminal law, if you're to the right of Bernie Sanders. Faculty activism, accelerated by the growth of clinical education—where practicing lawyers "teach," with some notable exceptions, crusading social-justice litigation—and the generational change of Boomer liberals being replaced by Millennial progressives, is certainly a problem. But even more, nonteaching bureaucracies have grown to enforce a rigid ideological orthodoxy and student cultures have shifted to avoid even a hint of conflict with prevailing (left-wing) views. And "affinity groups," divided by race, ethnicity, sexuality, and other signifiers, have balkanized the student body and inculcated identity-based advocacy.

Thus there have been, in just the last few years, numerous attempts to "cancel"—shame, ostracize, and threaten the careers of—anyone who deviates from a "safe" discourse. In April 2023, FIRE released a comprehensive report, "Scholars Under Fire," that explored cancel culture in colleges and universities across the country. It examined attempts to punish or otherwise professionally sanction scholars from 2000 to 2022 for speech that is—or would be in public settings—protected by the First Amendment. Its findings are staggering, with 1,080 scholar sanction attempts, almost two-thirds of which (698) resulted in sanctions, including 225 terminations. Alarmingly, the annual number of attempts at cancellation has increased dramatically over time, from 4 in 2000 to 145 in 2022. Here are some highlights:

- More than one-third of attempts (37 percent) were initiated by undergrads, while graduate (including law) students accounted for 8 percent, fellow scholars 16 percent, administrators 28 percent, the general public 7 percent, and government officials 7 percent.

- Many more attempts to cancel or sanction have come from the targeted scholar's left than his or her right, especially regarding attempts originating on campus. Indeed, 75 percent of attempts by undergrads, 82 percent by fellow scholars, and *94 percent by graduate students* came from the left.

- More than a quarter of sanction attempts (27 percent) came from something the scholar had said in the classroom, 19 percent on social media, 19 percent in public, and 18 percent in scholarship. The social media figure is striking in that this forum developed only midway through the study.

- Scholars were most often persecuted for speech about race (39 percent). Other controversial topics included gender (18 percent), religion (11 percent), sexuality (9 percent), and protests against the police or military (9 percent).

- The top schools with cancellation attempts were Harvard (23), Stanford (22), UCLA (19), Georgetown (16), Columbia (14), and the University of Pennsylvania (14). Indeed, scholars at elite schools are targeted more often. The top 10 schools according to *U.S. News & World Report* have had 113 attempts, more than 10 percent of the total.

- Ninety of the top 100 universities have had at least one sanction attempt since 2000.

What's most telling is that law professors were targeted more than any other discipline, 95 times out of 1,080 documented instances. The next two subjects are also central to the maintenance of our civic institutions: political science (79) and history (71).

For example, Professors William Jacobson of Cornell Law School and Thomas Smith of the University of San Diego (USD) Law School were condemned for politically incorrect commentary. Jacobson, the founder of the popular Legal Insurrection website, criticized the Black Lives Matter movement, after which students and alumni called for his firing. A large group of clinical faculty—including the directors of the First Amendment Clinic!—in consultation with the Black Law Students Association (BLSA) chapter denounced "defenders of institutionalized racism and violence." Eduardo Peñalver, the dean of Cornell Law School, ultimately declined to take any action but issued a statement that supported the clinical professors and criticized Jacobson. Smith, meanwhile, posted on his personal blog an excerpt from a news article about the origin of Covid-19, adding that those who believed that the coronavirus hadn't been created in a lab in Wuhan, China, are "swallowing . . . Chinese cock swaddle." USD started an investigation, with Dean Robert Schapiro accusing Smith of reflecting "bias" that "demeans a particular national group." The university ultimately determined that the blog post was protected by its academic freedom policy, but, again, the process itself is the punishment.

Then there are the cases of Professors Amy Wax of the University of Pennsylvania Carey Law School and Scott Gerber of Ohio Northern University (ONU) Law School, both of whom have won teaching awards at their respective institutions. They've both been persecuted and may yet lose their long-tenured positions for criticizing progressive shibboleths. Wax is a macrocosm of what happened to me, in that she's facing cancellation for an entire body of work rather than a stray tweet. It all began in September 2017 after she wrote in an op-ed that the decline of bourgeois values has contributed to social ills and that not all cultures are able to prepare people to be productive members of society. She later argued that the cultures of countries to which people migrate are superior—but not for racial reasons—as well as criticizing Penn's racial preferences for leading to black students' ending up in lower tiers of achievement. Dean

Theodore Ruger announced that Wax would no longer teach mandatory first-year classes because she had allegedly violated policy by discussing student grades. In April 2018, a university trustee emeritus, Paul Levy, who was also on the law school's board of overseers and who had donated millions of dollars to the school, resigned in protest. "Please reconsider this illiberal ban on Wax's pedagogy," he wrote to Penn's president, Amy Gutmann.

A couple of years later, after Wax said at a conference that the United States should take immigrants from countries with similar values to our own, students held a town hall at which Dean Ruger said her comments were racist and had caused "harm." He also said that it "sucks" that Wax "still works here." In April 2021, law school alumni filed a complaint about her 2017 comments, arguing that minority students could "reasonably assume" that she had violated the school's anonymous-grading policy. The report of an outside investigator report found that the charges against Wax were baseless, and Penn doesn't appear to have considered these findings actionable. The law school sat on the report for months, neither notifying Wax of its completion nor initiating any disciplinary process. Then in December 2021, after she said on a podcast that "the United States is better off with fewer Asians and less Asian immigration," in the context of a broader argument about the challenges of demographic change, Ruger abandoned his defense of academic freedom to launch an official disciplinary process. He didn't provide Wax the report that had exonerated her for some time, even as the disproved claims were incorporated into a final list of charges. Ruger asked the faculty senate to impose "major sanctions" in a process that had been used just a handful of times: the last time Penn had acted to get rid of a tenured professor, it was because he had killed his wife. In June 2023, the faculty senate's hearing board indeed recommended a public reprimand, a one-year suspension at half pay, the removal of Wax's named chair and summer pay, and a requirement for her to note in public appearances that she doesn't speak for Penn Carey Law. The university confirmed those sanctions in September 2024. Wax's case raises intense concerns about the future of academic freedom—particularly since it's an illiberal persecution led by lawyers.

But at least Wax has been fully aware that she's under the gun for her speeches and writings. Scott Gerber is undergoing a similar "investigation," but in a Kafkaesque process that's both secret and won't reveal the charges against him. In January 2023, Gerber received an email telling him that ONU had opened an investigation of him, without being given any details. The professor and his counsel repeatedly explained that without being given specifics, he could not adequately defend himself against what allegations there might be. A month later, an outside lawyer notified Gerber that his lack of cooperation could bring career-related consequences—and so, in April, campus security officers entered Gerber's classroom and escorted him to the dean's office. Armed town police followed him down the hall. Dean Charles H. Rose III immediately removed him from all "teaching, service, and scholarship duties" and banished him from campus. Rose told Gerber that if he didn't sign a separation agreement and claims release in the next week, ONU would begin dismissal proceedings. When a gobsmacked Gerber pressed for reasons, the only reply was "collegiality."

Gerber is no fool and surmises that his resistance to aggressive DEI initiatives—those that don't include viewpoint diversity and would lead to illegal employment or admissions practices—had ruffled feathers. Still, he wasn't exactly a pariah, either on campus or in broader academia. His teaching evaluations were excellent, and his courses were filled to capacity. In September 2022, he was elected vice chair of the University Council by acclamation. Cambridge University Press published his tenth book in 2023, and he was reappointed to the Ohio Advisory Committee of the US Commission on Civil Rights. His lawyers asked for the specifics of what he's supposed to have done wrong many times, as have FIRE, the Academic Freedom Alliance, and the American Association of University Professors (AAUP). AAUP is notable; it's no ideological group but a hybrid organization that's part think tank, part advocate, and part labor union. Its stated mission is to "advance academic freedom and shared governance; to define fundamental professional values . . . and to ensure higher education's contribution to the common good." When such institutionalists argue that "an absence of collegiality ought never, by itself, constitute a basis for . . . dismissal for cause," they can't be ignored out of hand. ONU eventually moved to start a termination process, which led Gerber to ask a state court for a temporary restraining order, which the judge granted. The judge also ordered ONU to produce its charges, including any formal complaints or grievances. However that process turns out, Gerber is well-positioned in his lawsuit for defamation and a host of other torts and employment law violations. By the way, the school's motto is *Ex diversitate vires*: Out of diversity, strength.

Nearly all these cases follow the same pattern: Students weaponize hurt feelings—which are often performative, not genuine—to demand the obliteration of a political opponent's career. Institutional cultures are so weak, thanks to a bureaucratic explosion and increase in academic activists, that administrators are easily overwhelmed by these moral panics and either engage in performative denunciations of the accused or actually terminate them. This pernicious dynamic is reminiscent of the Chinese Cultural Revolution, in which students publicly shamed and otherwise humiliated professors to scare them into ideological obedience.

There's some resonance here with my case, where the campaign against me had more to do with my ideology than my tweets. "I've talked to many left-leaning friends here in private who admit freely that the BLSA demands go over the top or concede they only want Ilya fired because of his conservative political views," one Georgetown student who chose to remain anonymous told *National Review*. "One person told me they didn't like his views on masks. Another told me they thought he was racist because he advocates for conservative policies. . . . People worry about losing journal spots, jobs, or letter grades if they aren't woke enough and so aren't willing to say anything." But during my suspension, Georgetown Law hosted Mohammed El-Kurd, who accused Israel of "unquenchable thirst for Palestinian blood"—literally, he said, Israelis "harvest organs of the martyred" and "feed their warriors our own."

And then there's the disruption of outside speakers. Indeed, one "fun" aspect of my Georgetown purgatory was being shouted down at a long-planned event at the University of California Hastings College of Law (since renamed UC College of the Law, San Francisco, because of Mr. Hastings's political incorrectness). That experience was no isolated incident, not even in that one month of March 2022. The week after, a similar thing happened at Yale, ironically over a panel bringing together lawyers from the left and right who agreed on the importance of free speech. Dean Heather Gerken basically buried her head in the sand. Then it happened again at the University of Michigan, when students obstructed a debate on a Texas abortion bill. I learned of that event only because I was due to speak there the following week. Then it happened a year later with the shutdown of US Court of Appeals Judge Kyle Duncan at Stanford, with the mob egged on by the dean of diversity, equity, and inclusion (DEI). Remember, this is going on at law schools, having migrated from the craziness that we've seen for some time on the under-graduate campuses, from which we even have a word—*sophomoric*—to describe youthful immaturity.

That's why this is so worrisome. If an English or sociology department is led astray—if an entire academic discipline goes off the rails—that's unfortunate and a loss to the richness of life and the accumulation of human knowledge. But the implosion of legal education has much more dire consequences, as I told the *Wall Street Journal*'s Tunku Varadarajan when he interviewed me for that newspaper's "weekend interview" feature in March 2023. Law schools train future lawyers and politicians and judges, who are the gatekeepers of our institutions and of the rules of the game on which American prosperity, liberty, and equality sit. An illiberal takeover of medical schools might be more immediately dan-gerous, in that you wouldn't have the best doctors treating people, but law students who police their professors' microaggressions and demand the "deplatforming" of "harmful" speakers will eventually be on the fed-eral bench. Even before that, they'll be occupying positions of authority, bringing legal cases, occupying corporate general counsel's offices, and filling the partnership ranks of big firms. Without any understatement, it would be a disaster for the American way of life to have future genera-tions of lawyers think that applying the law equally to all furthers white supremacy or that the strength of one's rights depends on one's level of privilege—or that due process and freedom of speech protect oppressors and perpetuate injustice.

The problem isn't limited to canceling professors and treating speak-ers differently based on their viewpoints. The illiberal takeover of law schools involves the clash between the classical pedagogical model of legal education and the postmodern activist one. This dynamic was crys-tallized in Stanford DEI dean Tirien Steinbach's memorable question to Judge Duncan, "Is the juice worth the squeeze?" It's just a cute way of giving ideological opponents a heckler's veto—not just on speakers, but on class materials, extracurricular activities, whatever. If they hate an idea enough, surely it isn't worth exposing students to a person who espouses that idea. Progressive students in particular envy the protest culture of the 1960s and think their every cause is akin to that of the civil rights movement. Well, apply the juice-squeezing notion to Selma, Alabama, and see where you end up; it's not with the people marching across the Edmund Pettus Bridge. What an associate dean of a top law school was advocating is the exact opposite of freedom of speech and association, equality, and due process of law, let alone the development of lawyers capable of understanding all sides of a legal issue to be able to zealously advocate for their clients and uphold the rule of law.

Then, law schools got more than their fair share of attention during the eruption of antisemitism following Hamas's attack on Israel on October 7, 2023. The president of NYU Law School's student bar association circulated a schoolwide newsletter blaming the Jewish state for the attack. Later in the school year, protesters disrupted a graduating-student dinner at the home of Berkeley Law School dean Erwin Chemerinsky. (For more on antisemitism at Berkeley, see chapter 7.) And after the NYPD cleared out the anti-Israel encampment at Columbia in May 2024, the student editors of the *Columbia Law Review* claimed to be "irrevocably shaken" and demanded that their school cancel final exams and pass all students, or at least move to "mandatory Pass/Fail during this horrific time for our campus." Later that month, the same journal published an inflammatory article arguing that Jews "capitalized on the Holocaust to create a powerful narrative that monopolizes victimhood"—after an unusually secretive editorial process that excluded Jewish students and others who might object—causing the *Law Review*'s board of directors (alumni and professors) to temporarily suspend the publication's website.

How did all this happen?

Well, like a lot of stories of decline, this one happened first gradually, then suddenly. This book uses my "lived experience" as a jumping-off point to discuss how the growth of bureaucracies generally, and DEI offices in particular, have fueled a monstrous shift in the legal academy. The Covid pandemic and "racial reckoning" provoked by George Floyd's killing accelerated those pathological trends such that critical race theory, once thought to be a relic of the 1980s and early '90s, returned with a vengeance. Radicals went on the march as intolerant faculty and weak administrators let them. The at-best mealymouthed response by university leaders to the explosion of antisemitism after Hamas's barbarism—and indeed the fomenting of that terrorism apologia by DEI ideologies instructing that Israel is an "oppressor"—opened people's eyes to academia's moral corruption, including at the nation's top law schools.

These are systemic issues. What we're seeing isn't the age-old complaint about liberal professors—the ideological ratio among either faculty or students hasn't changed much since I was in college 25 years ago or law school 20 years ago—but careerist administrators who placate the radical left. Whenever deans and presidents stand up for free speech and the core truth-seeking mission of any academic institution and enforce long-standing rules against disruption and intimidation, the mob disperses, but most university officials are amoral but ambitious bureaucrats. They're spineless cowards.

Even white-shoe law firms—no bastions of rectitude—blanched at the pro-genocidal sentiment unleashed last fall, warning deans that they won't hire graduates who engage in "discrimination or harassment" against Jewish students. More than 100 firms ultimately signed an unprecedented joint letter scolding law school leaders for failing at their most basic jobs: "As educators at institutions of higher learning, it is imperative that you provide your students with the tools and guidance to engage in the free exchange of ideas, even on emotionally charged issues."

Is there anything we can do to stop or reverse these illiberal tendencies? Should we—those of us who care about universities' traditional truth-seeking mission and law schools' commitment to the American constitutional order—just throw up our hands, gird our loins, and regroup to fight elsewhere? Surely we need to develop novel responses to heterodox challenges, ones that involve culture, legislation, and institution-building.

I cover all that here. I've long been an advocate for free speech, constitutionalism, and classical liberal values—including in educational settings—but only by living through this crucible did I truly understand the urgency of the task.

CHAPTER 1

Law Schools Shape Our Society

Law schools are different from academic departments. They train future lawyers and politicians and judges, who are the gatekeepers to our institutions, about the rules of the game. That game has the highest of stakes: the rule of law, upon which American prosperity, liberty, and equality sit. An illiberal takeover of medical schools might be more immediately dangerous, in that you don't want doctors selected for their identity over their merit and then discriminating against patients in the name of "equity." But the sorts of students you see on the news who rage against anyone who slightly disagrees with them are people who, in 20 years, are going to be joining the federal bench. Even before that, they'll be holding important government positions, bringing lawsuits, and advising Fortune 500 companies.

Already, law firm partners cower in fear of their associates, who question their firms' representation of certain types of clients and demand that statements be made after Supreme Court decisions and political developments.

For example, a friend of mine who's pro-life was a partner in the Houston office of a large global law firm and ran into trouble after the Supreme Court overturned *Roe v. Wade* in the *Dobbs* case. Various firm leaders asked her to handle some pro bono clients who were advocating for abortion rights. She said she was too busy and didn't make a stink over it. Eventually, the managing partner of the Houston office said, "Well, I guess you're pro-life. What a waste of a female equity partner." She now practices independently.

In late 2022, another big firm, Hogan Lovells, fired a senior partner,

Robin Keller, for positive comments she had made about *Dobbs* during a conference call advertised as a "safe space" for female lawyers. Keller was called a racist for referring to what some have called a "genocide" regarding the disproportionately high rates of abortion in the black community. Other participants in the call said that they had "lost their ability to breathe." The firm cut Keller off from its email and document systems within hours, suspending her pending a three-week investigation that resulted in her termination.

And it's not just unfashionable opinions on abortion or "social" issues of sexuality or identity that Big Law finds objectionable. Take the case of former solicitor general Paul Clement, whom many consider to be the best appellate lawyer in the country, along with his colleague Erin Murphy. After they won a landmark Second Amendment victory before the Supreme Court in June 2022, their firm, Kirkland & Ellis—which had long been thought of as being among the more conservative large firms—ordered them to drop their politically incorrect clients or resign. They walked away, announcing their departure in the *Wall Street Journal,* just as I did. Kirkland claimed that it was purely a business decision, that its clients felt uncomfortable with the ideological valence of Clement's litigation practice. Blaming clients is a classic dodge, reminiscent of the firms that said in the 1950s that they'd hire black lawyers except that their clients wouldn't go for it.

Cancel culture has been a pox on the body politic for years now, but this censoriousness and moral panic—far from mere "accountability," as its proponents claim it is—can exist in certain places with minimal harm to society as a whole. It's probably good for our thinnest-skinned citizens to cluster away in ivory towers distributing niche liberal arts degrees. But again, law schools are different. Their graduates aren't going to shuffle off, as gender studies majors do, to similarly academic and inconsequential jobs. No, law graduates, an increasing number of whom have undergraduate degrees in activism that masquerades as education, will end up running the country. They're the elite in training.

Contrary to popular perception, corporate law firms haven't been dominated by Republicans (let alone conservatives) for quite some time. That means the conflict is largely an intra-left purity battle, as liberal partners live in fear of activist associates who want to burn the place down—and still be paid $200,000 to do so. Lawyers at top law firms in New York, DC, LA, and elsewhere constantly worry about saying the wrong thing or proposing to take the wrong client.

It's not a new development for law firms to shy away from representing controversial clients, but what used to be a sporadic occurrence has become more commonplace. Younger lawyers often consider representing a client to mean supporting that client's actions or agreeing with its beliefs. Even amicus briefs are one-sided as far as Big Law is concerned; in *Dobbs* and the Harvard/University of North Carolina affirmative action challenges, the highest-profile Supreme Court cases of the last few years, not a single brief was filed by the Am Law 200 (the top 200 American law firms by revenue) on the winning side. I've experienced a microcosm of this myself; even as major firms are still willing to file briefs on behalf of the Cato and Manhattan Institutes in certain types of cases—typically in regulatory areas, nothing that approaches hot-button political issues—certain lawyers remove their names from their own briefs lest they be doxed in future for such unsavory associations.

Then there's the worry about losing corporate clients, which have become as narrowly ideological as many other American institutions. Law firms feel pressure to stop representing (or not to represent in the first place) many kinds of politically incorrect clients: oil companies and gun manufacturers, Republican-controlled legislatures, anyone challenging the Biden administration's environmental or vaccine regulations, or anyone associated with Donald Trump. If representing tobacco companies can cost them business, they reckon, imagine the financial harm from defending a "transphobe" or "racist." Even religious-liberty cases that have nothing to do with abortion or LGBTQ-related issues are off the table. The same white-shoe bar that fell over itself to represent Guantánamo detainees in the wake of 9/11 and that bristled at accusations of being "pro-terrorist" now looks askance at a group of nuns who just want to be left alone to practice their faith even if it runs afoul of some bureaucrat's interpretation of Obamacare. The Overton window shift we've seen in law schools has graduated into the real world.

According to a summer 2020 survey conducted by the National Association of Law Placement (discussed in chapter 12 with reference to law schools), 99 percent of the 240 law firms responding implemented new antiracism and/or DEI initiatives after the murder of George Floyd, 93 percent have at least one DEI committee or staff member, 76 percent issued a statement about racial justice, 69 percent increased racial-justice-related pro bono commitments, 63 percent required new or increasing antiracism training, 58 percent offer diversity scholarships or fellowships for law students, and 52 percent developed new partnerships with organizations focused on racial justice or DEI. These numbers have undoubtedly increased since then.

Much of this seems self-defeating. Would you hire a lawyer who claims to be made to feel "unsafe" by a court ruling? Shouldn't a lawyer who heckles a judge in court go to jail for contempt? Is a lawyer who constantly needs "personal days" to get over perceived social slights cut out for the billable-hour-obsessed world of corporate practice? You would think not—but the jury's still out, as it were, on what the legal culture will be like if the current trends continue.

After all, professors have long been shying away from entire topics, not just conservative perspectives on those topics. Rape and hate crimes, for example, are too sensitive. Too many professors have been tripped up when, say, writing exam questions. Yet law school faculties do their students a real disservice by not training them in how to advocate in the real world. Litigation is not a conversation between the left and the far left.

Fundamentally Transforming American Institutions

Except when it is. Canada, for example, provides a glimpse into the future. Legal activists there don't simply seek to address unjust decisions but also to attack the very pillars of the rule of law in a liberal democracy.

The first bedrock principle to come under attack was equality under the law, with a movement to racialize the law in a way that treats people differently according to their skin color or ethnic background. Canada has instituted the use of Impact of Race and Culture Assessments (IRCAs), presentencing reports that allow "Black and racialized Canadians" to show how systemic racism motivated them to turn to crime. First used in an attempted-murder case in Nova Scotia in 2014, IRCAs encourage Canadian judges to give more lenient sentences to nonwhite crimi- nals on the ground that they've been subjected to historic and systemic racism—without even the need to establish concrete instances of racial discrimination in the life of the specific defendant. This is all built on previous innovations that required judges to "pay particular attention to the circumstances of aboriginal offenders," which in the last quarter century has led to lighter sentences for Native Canadians, who are vastly overrepresented in prisons.

That racialist approach to criminal law has already moved into the United States. In 2020, California passed the Racial Justice Act, giving felons the right to challenge their convictions as being racially biased. And in 2023, the California State Assembly passed a bill explicitly re- quiring judges to consider a convicted criminal's race when determining his or her prison sentence. Even without legislative change, some judges now see themselves less as impartial adjudicators and more as agents of social change. During the 2020 Black Lives Matter protests, the state of Washington's Supreme Court put out a letter opining that "[a]s judges, we must recognize the role we have played in devaluing black lives" and reminding courts that "even the most venerable precedent must be struck down when it is incorrect and harmful." Massachusetts Superior Court Judge Shannon Frison, meanwhile, promised to "never be silent or complicit again, in any courtroom or any context." As the *Washington Free Beacon*'s Aaron Sibarium has observed, "Such statements are not mere virtue signaling. They reflect sincerely held beliefs with real-world consequences."[1]

Another wrongheaded attempt to address racial disparities in the law has led, predictably, to making the justice system *worse* for minorities. In the past few years, the Arizona Supreme Court eliminated the ability of trial attorneys to strike jurors without giving a reason, in response to a petition claiming that these "peremptory challenges" were racist. Elite liberals cheered, while defense attorneys who actually represent ra- cial minorities were aghast, because the ability to eliminate jurors with

1. Aaron Sibarium, "The Takeover of America's Legal System," *The Free Press*, March 21, 2022.

perceived bias (of any kind) is of much greater benefit to minority defendants than are protections against prosecutors' potential dismissal of minority jurors.

Even the fundamental principle that one is innocent until proven guilty beyond a reasonable doubt is under attack. Making the prosecution carry the burden of proof is part and parcel of that concept. In 2019, however, the American Bar Association nearly passed a motion urging legislatures and courts to adopt the trendy "affirmative consent" standard for sexual assault cases—already in place in California on college campuses—which would shift the burden of proof onto the accused. Fierce opposition from cross-ideological legal scholars and defense lawyers sank the measure at the last minute, but nearly 40 percent of delegates voted for the proposed model rule. The motivation behind the change is that the existing social stigma for making sexual assault claims is already so high that it does enough to disincentivize false accusations.

Making the accused establish his innocence, the logic goes, promotes justice far more than forcing victims to relive their violation again and again. While one understands the emotional appeal of this argument, the history of racism in this country shows abundantly how often false accusations have been weaponized against nonwhite men. Look no further than *To Kill a Mockingbird*, in which Atticus Finch defends, against the overwhelming weight of community sentiment, a black man falsely accused of raping a young white woman. At the end of the day, again, the original principle of due process is a far better bulwark for vulnerable minorities than the trendy new legal activism.

As Sibarium wrote, "we don't need to speculate about how temper tantrums in New Haven will reshape American institutions. The ideas underlying these outbursts have already spread to boardrooms and government agencies," as well as to courts and legal regulators. In 2021, NASDAQ implemented gender and race quotas for new listings. Food-delivery companies waived fees for orders from black-owned restaurants during the Covid pandemic. New York City employed racial considerations in medical treatments, while several states gave racial minorities earlier access to vaccines. Some such programs were blocked, like the federal government's distribution of pandemic relief such that minority-owned businesses would get more funds sooner. Litigation continues over other Biden administration applications of "equity" to engage in race-based policymaking, but the fundamental principle of equal treatment under the law is fraying.

Rebecca Slaughter, one of five members of the Federal Trade Commission, which oversees consumer protection and antitrust enforcement, posted on Twitter in September 2020, "There's precedent for using antitrust to combat racism. E.g., South Africa considers #racialequity in #antitrust analysis to reduce high economic concentration & balance racially skewed business ownership."

What that meant was that government should step in if a company board didn't fit a diversity quota. Slaughter, who's a former counsel to Senate Majority Leader Chuck Schumer, is saying that her agency should throw out its legislated mandate to ensure competition and protect consumers, in favor of an ideological goal that Congress did not authorize. Her proposal is environmental, social, and governance (ESG) standards—an evaluation of companies that goes beyond their financial bottom line—on steroids. It's bad enough for private-equity firms to evaluate investment targets based on how progressive their corporate policies are. But when a regulator might treat a company differently based on its board's racial makeup, it's a recipe for societal balkanization and ethnic tribalism. The Securities and Exchange Commission might approve or disapprove a securities registration based on social justice criteria. The FTC, Sibarium noted, "might even block a merger if the resulting conglomerate would be insufficiently diverse—something that has actually happened in South Africa" (not exactly a model of either good governance or racial harmony). Jobs, companies, investments, commercial and industrial development: all economic understandings are subject to massive reorganization that go far beyond the conventional arguments between left and right on how to regulate the market.

What could motivate such an extreme anti-institutional argument? It all comes down to a philosophically anarchic belief now common on the far, *illiberal* left: the idea that neutrality is impossible. "I want to be working to promote equity, rather than reinforce inequity," Slaughter said on CNBC soon after posting her Twitter comments. She decided that "it isn't possible to really be actually neutral, nor should we be neutral in the face of systemic racism and structural racism." It's Ibram Kendi dressed up for the C-suite. This "antiracist" opposition to legal neutrality is infecting more and more of the legal profession. The idea that lawyers' duty to confront (a particular definition of) injustice must supersede all else has eroded the norm that every American deserves legal representation and even the norm that the law should treat everyone equally. As Noah Phillips, another member of the FTC, explained, "Deliberately attempting to apply the law in an unequal fashion, based on the preferences of those in power, is inimical to the rule of law." Still, in the strategic plan that the FTC adopted in late 2021, the agency listed "support equity for historically underserved communities" as one of its four objectives for each of its missions regarding consumer protection and competition, respectively.

Attacking equality and neutrality under the guise of supporting equity isn't just a niche bureaucratic fad. The Biden administration also got into the act. On January 20, 2021, on his first day in office and as his very first official act, President Biden signed Executive Order 13985 (Advancing Racial Equity and Support for Underserved Communities Through the Federal Government), which established that "affirmatively advancing equity, civil rights, racial justice, and equal opportunity is the responsibility of the whole of our Government." The order asserts that converging economic, health, and climate crises exposed and exacerbated inequities that can be remedied only by a comprehensive approach to advancing equity for all, especially by fighting structural racism. Accordingly, each unit of government must evaluate "whether, and to what extent, its programs and policies perpetuate systemic barriers to opportunities and benefits for people of color and other underserved groups."

Note the slyness of the language. Who could possibly support "perpetuat[ing] systemic barriers"? But those barriers are bulwarks against identity-based rules, which are now to be replaced with race essentialism. That's why Biden's order also revoked President Trump's Executive Order 13950 of September 22, 2020 (Combating Race and Sex Stereotyping), which, among other things, blocked federal agencies and contractors from giving workplace training based on "divisive concepts." Apparently it was unacceptable to the new president that the government be unable to advance a "vision of America that is grounded in hierarchies based on collective social and political identities rather than in the inherent and equal dignity of every person as an individual."

Five months later, on June 25, 2021, Biden issued Executive Order 14035 (Diversity, Equity, Inclusion, and Accessibility in the Federal Workforce), which "establishes that diversity, equity, inclusion, and accessibility are priorities for my Administration and benefit the entire Federal Government and the Nation" and tasks various high officials with developing a governmentwide DEI strategic plan. All federal agencies must now report on their progress in implementing that plan to make "advancing diversity, equity, inclusion, and accessibility a priority component of the agency's management agenda and agency strategic planning."

Then, on February 16, 2023, Biden signed Executive Order 14091 (Further Advancing Racial Equity and Support for Underserved Communities Through the Federal Government), which, after praising his administration for delivering "the most equitable economic recovery in memory," doubles down on "an ambitious, whole-of-government approach to racial equity and support for underserved communities and to continuously embed equity into all aspects of Federal decision-making."

To wit, the order established a White House Steering Committee on Equity and requires each cabinet secretary or agency head to "have in place an Agency Equity Team within their respective agencies to coordinate the implementation of equity initiatives and ensure that their respective agencies are delivering equitable outcomes for the American people." One of the order's provisions, titled "Embedding Equity into Government-wide Processes," requires the Office of Management and Budget to "support equitable decision-making, promote equitable deployment of financial and technical assistance, and assist agencies in advancing equity," while also "designing, developing, acquiring, and using artificial intelligence and automated systems in the Federal Government . . . in a manner that advances equity."

There are too many of these kinds of executive orders, actions, and proclamations to include here, at least one for every demographic subgroup plus others that focus on specific parts of the government. Each one recites a litany of claimed achievements on diversity, equity, social justice, and other related measures, whether through seemingly unrelated legislation or previous executive actions. For example, on March 8, 2021, the socialist/Soviet-originated International Women's Day, the Biden administration created a Gender Policy Council, which soon rolled out a National Strategy on Gender Equity and Equality. It all makes previous efforts, even those by the Obama administration, such as the October 2016 Presidential Memorandum on Promoting Diversity and Inclusion in the National Security Workforce, seem like child's play.

The upshot is that, in no uncertain terms, the federal government has now fully adopted the DEI agenda and, through its army of lawyers and bureaucrats, is implementing and reinforcing it throughout every nook and cranny of its increasing reach into our lives. So even if the only kinds of jobs that law school graduates who spew epithets at federal judges may be qualified for are in corporate DEI offices and the Biden administration's equity commissariats, those jobs now have real power. It's the road to regime change.

I've seen firsthand exactly how hellish such a society would look.

CHAPTER 2

The Online Mob Takes No Prisoners

On the morning of January 27, 2022, I woke up in my Austin hotel room refreshed and ready to take on the world, knowing that I would now be spending the week before I joined the Georgetown Law faculty discussing Justice Breyer's legacy and succession. But when I checked my phone, my heart sank and I realized I'd be taking on the world in a completely different way.

My tweets from right before bed—saying that, given President Biden's race and sex criteria, we'd end up with a "lesser black woman" on the Court who'd always have an affirmative action asterisk attached— had gone viral. And not in a good way. That morning after the night before began one of the worst days of my life.

A Twitter troll named Mark Joseph Stern, *Slate*'s legal correspondent and my longtime self-appointed antagonist, had taken advantage of my inartful phrasing to go after my head—or, more precisely, my job. Screencapping my tweets, he commented, "I hate to draw attention to this troll because attention is what he craves. But now that @GeorgetownLaw has hired him, I feel an obligation to condemn his overt and nauseating racism, which has been a matter of public record for some time. I am deeply ashamed of my alma mater."

Before Stern's salvo, my tweets hadn't been getting that much attention. But afterward, the mob piled on. In addition to the usual collection of bots and anonymous accounts, left-wing activists and intellectuals who were already upset about my hiring pounced. Most notably, law professor Aderson Francois, who directs the civil rights section of Georgetown's Institute for Public Representation, asked me to "clarify": "Mr. Shapiro, as one of your future Georgetown colleague[s], I am curious: is your phrase 'lesser Black woman' meant to describe a particular Black woman or do you intend 'lesser Black woman' to encompass the general set of Black women under consideration for the seat?"

To her credit, another Georgetown law professor, Rosa Brooks, also the associate dean for centers and institutes, emailed with advice and support. We ended up talking on the phone later that morning, and she counseled me about what to do to get ahead of the growing controversy. Nobody would accuse Rosa of being anything but on the left politically, but she showed grace, compassion, and professionalism to me from day one.

I had my online defenders, to be sure. Still, I quickly realized that things were getting out of hand and that a debate about what I had actually meant—even if those who were against me were disingenuous—was both professionally unhelpful and a distraction from my point about judicial nominations. So I deleted the tweets and responded to Professor Francois by quote-tweeting his question and saying the following: "I apologize. I meant no offense, but it was an inartful tweet. I have taken it down."

Stern also got some social media backlash, causing him to backpedal and insist that he wasn't out to get me fired. Charles C. W. Cooke, who's a friend, skewered Stern's facetious posture in *National Review*:

> There he was on Twitter, minding his own business, when he came across some tweets he disliked from Georgetown's Ilya Shapiro, screenshotted and shared them, condemned their author as a racist troll in tweets that tagged his employer, insisted dramatically that he was "ashamed" of his "alma mater," solicited and published a reproaching comment from that alma mater's dean, and . . . well, for some inexplicable reason, the people watching this saga concluded that Stern was trying to get Shapiro *fired*. . . .
>
> When Stern said that Shapiro was a "troll" and a "racist" whose "overt and nauseating" bigotry made him "ashamed" of Georgetown, he was simply confirming that overtly racist nauseating trolls are precisely the sort of people whom Georgetown should *keep on staff*— and maybe even give a promotion and a raise.

Many others in the media would also come to my defense with both reported and opinion pieces.

But on that first morning, the damage had been done. As Cooke noted in the piece quoted above, Dean Bill Treanor, having been apprised of the brewing "scandal," put out a statement a little after lunchtime mischaracterizing what I had said as a "suggestion that the best Supreme Court nominee could not be a Black woman" and labeling that idea as "appalling." He also said that my tweets were "at odds with everything we stand for at Georgetown Law and are damaging to the culture of equity and inclusion that Georgetown Law is building every day."

"As soon as I read the dean's email, I thought, 'Oh my gosh, this is gonna make it so much worse,'" said Luke Bunting, the editor of the *Georgetown Journal of Law and Public Policy*, in a media interview. The dean's email, he said, "took an already volatile situation and made it worse by inferring that students should adopt the worst possible reading of Mr. Shapiro's tweets."

It wasn't at all clear what would happen to me, though it was certainly within the realm of possibility—perhaps more likely than not—that I'd be fired later that afternoon. I had repeated conversations with Randy Barnett, the founder and faculty director of the Georgetown Center for the Constitution and thus my boss-to-be. He was actually much more than that; as an academic leader of the libertarian legal movement, he had also long been one of my mentors and heroes.

Randy and I discussed whether I should just resign to save both of us from being dragged through the mud. Although he was concerned about his center's reputation and disappointed in me for being so loose with language as to give our ideological enemies an opening for attack, we decided that this simply wouldn't be the right course, that it would show weakness and damage the ideals of free speech and academic freedom that were already under attack on university campuses.

Damage Control

So it was time to move into damage control and crisis public relations. I would need both an "outside" strategy of media and public statements and an "inside" strategy working behind the scenes in private communications to push Treanor not to fire me.

I emailed Greg Lukianoff, whom I'd known for a long time, with the subject heading "My Twitter storm crisis." Greg is the president and CEO of what was then called the Foundation for Individual Rights and Education (FIRE), the nation's premier organization dedicated to the freedom of speech and expression in the academic world. (That summer, FIRE would rebrand itself as the Foundation for Individual Rights and *Expression*, expanding its mission to defend and promote "the value of free speech for all Americans in our courtrooms, on our campuses, and in our culture.") I was no stranger to FIRE, having worked with the organization's lawyers on Supreme Court and other appellate cases over the years, either supporting them with amicus briefs or joining together on filings.

Never had I expected that I would ever personally be in need of the organization's services, as the target of potential disciplinary action in response to something I had said or written. But then nobody does—or should. It's a sad testament to the state of the academic world, and the world beyond, that FIRE continues to exist, and expand, 25 years after it was founded.

A basic question about how I should deal with media queries quickly evolved into an A-Team thread regarding all aspects of speech-related crisis management and legal action. Greg didn't hesitate to involve all of his top people. In the next 48 hours, that core group exchanged so many emails that we had to start a new thread several times.

The day was drawing on, and I needed to get dressed, check out of my hotel, and eventually take a flight home. The day before, I had made lunch plans to meet an old friend, Judge Don Willett of the U.S. Court of Appeals for the Fifth Circuit, along with a few of his current and former clerks. I texted him to say that I was running late because of "a Twitter-related personal crisis." The fact that I was meeting that particular federal judge made the episode seem scripted; Don had gained national acclaim for being the most active judicial Twitter user when he was on the Texas Supreme Court. (I hasten to add that his feed was all dad jokes and civics lessons.) He had paused his tweeting upon being nominated to the Fifth Circuit in 2017, and it might well have been seeing me going through this experience that made his Twitter recusal permanent.

When I arrived at the highly recommended Tex-Mex place Serranos, my eyes glazed over as I looked at the menu and my stomach really wasn't into it.

I spent the rest of the afternoon strategizing with friends and allies, dodging media queries, and trying to settle my nerves. Randy offered that we were in a "wait and see" period and there wasn't much to be done unless things escalated. Just in case, and with FIRE's help, I drafted several statements, some combative, some conciliatory, eventually settling on a short one regretting my choice of words but doubling down on the point about colorblind judicial selection. I learned all about the need to screen-capture ("screencap") written statements before posting them on Twitter, both to be able to evade the character restrictions and so nobody can misquote you. But I didn't tweet or send anything out yet.

Seeing that the furor wasn't dying down on either social media or the Georgetown faculty listserv, however, Randy strongly advised me to prepare an apologetic letter to the dean and faculty—apologetic with regard to my language, not my message. The FIRE brain trust was uniformly against my issuing any further apology, because in its experience with academic persecutions, apologies are taken as admissions of guilt and capitulation and never achieve a beneficial result.

At 11:03 p.m.—still on day one of the initial "four days of hell"—I sent a statement to the faculty listserv, again expressing regret for my communication failure. Here's what I wrote:

I sincerely and deeply apologize for some poorly drafted tweets I posted late Wednesday night. Issues of race are of course quite sensitive, and debates over affirmative action are always fraught. My intent was to convey my opinion that excluding potential Supreme Court candidates, most notably Chief Judge Srinivasan, simply because of their race or gender, was wrong and not good for the long-term reputation of the Court. It was not to cast aspersions on the qualifications of a whole group of people, let alone question their worth as human beings. A person's dignity and worth simply do not, and should not, depend on any immutable characteristic. Those who know me know that I am sincere about these sentiments, and I would be more than happy to meet with any of you who have doubts about the quality of my heart.

In seeking to join the Georgetown community, I wanted to contribute to your worthy mission to educate students, inform the public, and engage in the battle of legal ideas that lead to justice and fairness. I still want to do that. Recklessly framed Tweets like this week's obviously don't advance that mission, for which I am also truly sorry. Regardless of whether anyone agrees or disagrees with me on a host of legal and policy issues, I can and will do better with regard to how I communicate my positions.

There was no immediate response, but the next day, around lunchtime, the Georgetown Black Law Students Association (BLSA), joined by many other groups and individuals—some of whom felt social pressure to sign or whose organization joined without consulting them—issued a letter criticizing Treanor's "bare-bones email" for offering "no apology or action plan" and arguing that I was undeserving of "a space as a leader and educator in the Georgetown community." It also made a series of demands, including, of course, that my employment contract be revoked. Other demands included expanding the diversity office, giving BLSA a voice on the faculty hiring committee, and funding an endowment for black students. One interesting allegation was that my comments "pit South Asian communities against Black communities in furtherance of white supremacy."

Numerous members of the faculty joined in the attacks. Joshua Matz called my statement "despicable, ignorant and racist"; Josh Chafetz accused me of "perpetuating racism and sexism." The faculty listserv began sounding like a Maoist struggle session as activist academics smelled blood in the water. One professor sent out an email condemning the "racist tweets" and offering to hold a Zoom session for students to process their "pain and anger."

Studentwide group chats were also buzzing. "Now is not the time for debate," one member of the class of 2023 wrote, adding that "instead we should be supporting our incredibly talented black female law students." Another quipped, "Some of y'all still think you belong in the Confederacy I see."

Rafael Nuñez, who told a *National Review* reporter that he "tends to lean a little more liberal," was thrown off the group chat after being called "privileged" for defending students who questioned the cancellation mob. "That's what really got to me," he said. "Like, my mom was undocumented for 35 years. I grew up on food stamps and welfare and had to dig myself out of a hole to get to go to Georgetown Law. My life has been difficult, but I don't complain. And it just bothered me that these kids that didn't even know me—you know, a fellow person of color— were telling me that I'm privileged. Like, you don't know the things that I had to see growing up and what I had to do and struggle to get here." Nuñez was also kicked out of a separate group chat for first-generation law students. "Some people encouraged me to go to the administration, but like, you've seen the administration's response," he explained. "They're not going to be on my side. . . . I'm on a scholarship. I don't want to get kicked out, you know?"[1]

Other students and alumni organized counter-letters. Georgetown Law's Conservative and Libertarian Student Association (CALSA) bravely put out a strong statement of support. FIRE organized a nationwide faculty letter that was ultimately signed by more than 200 academics. The Academic Freedom Alliance, spearheaded by Princeton Professor Keith Whittington, issued a similarly powerful letter. Nadine Strossen, a former head of the ACLU, wrote a particularly strong statement, concluding that my case "provides an especially compelling context for Georgetown to abide by the important constitutional norms that it has committed to honor." She also wrote a pointed personal missive to Treanor.

Peter Kirsanow, a member of the US Commission on Civil Rights and former member of the National Labor Relations Board who happens to be black, wrote in support of me and my "mainstream opinion" that "deserves to be heard at a law school, which is supposed to be a place of free expression and intellectual inquiry." Eugene Volokh and other academics at the influential *Volokh Conspiracy* blog took up my cause. Nicholas Quinn Rosenkranz, one of the very few heterodox thinkers at Georgetown Law, as well as a longtime friend and professional collaborator, expressed on the faculty listserv his personal disgust at my treatment.

---

1. Nate Hochman, "Inside Georgetown Law's Campaign to Cancel Ilya Shapiro: 'This Is Melting Down,'" *National Review*, February 2, 2022.

Thanks to both public and private efforts by my allies and supporters—most of whom acted without my asking—I survived that second day. Treanor let the campus community know that Friday afternoon that there would be no decision made about my situation until Monday.

That was a reprieve of sorts; surviving the first 24–48 hours is key in cancellation campaigns. But I wasn't out of the woods yet, and the emotional toll was beginning to manifest itself physically: not just sleepless nights, but I lost my appetite and developed gastrointestinal issues. My wife, Kristin, was also, of course, affected. There were tears—from both of us—and she told me over and over, "Fix this, fix this." Kristin had prophetically warned me over dinner a few days earlier, before my trip to Austin, that at Georgetown I would have to be particularly careful about issues of race and sex. And now I had stepped into that exact quagmire because I wasn't yet in the mode of thinking of myself as being in academia. We tried not to convey our worries to our two young sons (then six and almost four), but kids can sense when something's not quite right with Mommy and Daddy, so they displayed some unusual behavior and even mild vomiting.

The End of the Beginning

On Saturday, January 29, after discussing where I stood with Randy and my good friend Libby Locke, one of the premier plaintiff-side First Amendment lawyers in the country, I asked to meet with Treanor. The meeting was arranged for the next day via Zoom. It would have been better to meet in person, but Georgetown was maintaining extreme Covid measures such that masks were required even for small gatherings, so that would've been even more surreal and impersonal.

When I entered the Zoom, Treanor was joined there by Rosa Brooks, the associate dean who had shown me grace the last few days. I opened with the following remarks, which I drafted in the wee hours that morning:

> Thank you for meeting with me. I wanted to do this to clear the air, because I think it's unfortunate that this whole surreal episode has been unfolding without any dialogue between us.

First, I want to personally reiterate what I wrote to you and the faculty: I sincerely and deeply apologize for my tweets. One in particular, and especially three words there, were sloppy, careless, inartful . . . many adjectives. I unwisely wrote those words late at night Wednesday, and quickly deleted and apologized for them in the sober light of Thursday morning. I recognized my mistake immediately and tried to remedy it, and I thank Rosa for the compassion she showed in reaching out and advising me on just that course of action.

Rosa, and many others, reached out to me empathetically without necessarily agreeing with my underlying view about the propriety of Joe Biden's selection criteria. That's the definition of intellectual honesty and goodwill, the epitome of grace—all values that the Law Center and University stand for, which is why I want to join this community.

It's the opposite of what my online (and offline) enemies have done, willfully misconstruing my ill-chosen words, seeing them, unreasonably, in the worst possible light. Twisting my mistake to accuse me of what in our world is perhaps the greatest sin of all. I hope you can appreciate that I've been acting in good faith throughout this whole ordeal, trying not to further inflame things. I've turned down numerous requests for media interviews, including on Fox News this morning.

But second, regardless of all that, and as I wrote you in requesting this meeting, I'm keenly aware that this roiling mess has created a difficult situation for you, one that appears to be a no-win. That's what I want to work on with you today. Is there a solution we can find to move Georgetown (and me) beyond last week's events in a way that maximally preserves our reputations? I very much do still want to join this community, and am willing to make extraordinary efforts, across the various platforms you and I have access to, to allay the concerns of faculty and students and indeed to move the national conversation in a positive direction.

After all, you hired me for a reason, and that reason was a record of rigor, excellence, and integrity in support of the Constitution's protection for individual liberty and legal equality. I hope you can agree with me that that reason wasn't destroyed by one bad tweet.

So where do we go from here?

Treanor, who was in shirtsleeves with an open collar, looked pained and asked for *my* suggestion of where we should go. I said that free-speech principles and the university's own policy protected my expression, so I should be allowed to take up my job. I said that he had muddied the waters by mischaracterizing my tweet and thus advancing the notion that a maliciously unreasonable reading of my tweet as racist was its best reading. Nonetheless, and despite that unfortunate start to my Georgetown tenure, I said that I was prepared to do my job and be a better communicator in the future.

Brooks asked whether I could be effective given the offense I'd caused. I explained that I could because I still had my professional skills, networks, and media contacts and students and faculty who didn't want to interact with me wouldn't have to. (The inquisitors would eventually use that point, which I reiterated when they interviewed me, to claim that I would be denying "access" to some students' educational opportunities.) She asked whether I was open to issuing a further apology, perhaps in the context of "structural racism." Biting my tongue about the reference to critical race theory, I explained that I'd already said enough and that any further statements would have to be issued jointly in the context of the continuation of my employment.

The Zoom meeting lasted less than half an hour. That evening, I was in touch with two prominent members of the Georgetown Law board of visitors, who were appalled at my treatment. It could be that their entreaty was the last straw that allowed me to survive past the initial decision-making period, to force Treanor to punt.

The next day, Monday, January 31, Treanor declined to take my suggestion and vindicate the values of free speech and grace, but also declined to take BLSA's suggestion to cut ties with me and pay reparations. Instead he announced that even as I would be onboarded the next day—as I was supposed to be under my contract—I would be immediately placed on paid administrative leave pending an investigation into whether my social-media comments had violated university policies on harassment, antidiscrimination, and professional conduct.

My personal hell had ended, only for my purgatory to begin.

CHAPTER 3

Campus Inquisitors Aren't Interested in Truth, Just Convictions

Once the acute pain of the immediate "scandal" ended, a period of chronic annoyance began in which pain ebbed and flowed. Dean Treanor launched the next part of my Georgetown journey with a letter on January 31, 2022, saying that because I had "potentially" violated Georgetown's "non-discrimination [in education and employment], anti-harassment, and professional conduct policies," I was to be put "on paid administrative leave until the current investigation is concluded" even though he said that such an act was "nondisciplinary."

The phrase *banality of evil* raises the specter of Nazi clerks and Soviet apparatchiks, but I think it's also apt for an evil that can result "merely" in career death rather than loss of life. My experience with the diversity office was precisely of encountering bureaucrats—call them diversicrats—enforcing a ridiculous and sadistic regime that expects people to bend the knee to established orthodoxy or suffer the consequences. This office, and the DEI offices that have metastasized across academia, go far beyond merely preventing discriminatory practices and ensuring that everyone has access to university facilities. They are the apotheosis of what those warning about political correctness in the 1990s feared: thought police.

Initially, I didn't think that the "investigation" would last long—Associate Dean Rosa Brooks suggested that it might take a month or six weeks because "there's still a process, but here there's not much to look at"—so I took it seriously because, after all, I wanted both to keep my job and to stand up for free speech.

What I didn't understand was that the values I was expecting to be applied—reason, good faith, professional courtesy—had long since been abandoned by Georgetown's bureaucracy. There's a difference between an investigation and an inquisition. The first is trying to find the truth, and the second is trying to assemble evidence for a predetermined result. Bureaucracy is about order, tidiness, and obedience. Academia is about growth, challenge, and debate—or it should be. As you can imagine, the growth of the first is deadly to the survival of the second.

What should have given me a clue that the investigation was farcical from the outset was that its very genesis patently contradicted George-town's Speech and Expression Policy, which is actually quite good on paper and worth quoting from:

> It is not the proper role of a university to insulate individuals from ideas and opinions they find unwelcome, disagreeable, or even deeply offensive. . . .
>
> It is for the individual members of the University community, not for the University as an institution, to judge the value of ideas, and to act on those judgments not by seeking to suppress speech, but by openly and vigorously contesting those arguments and ideas that they oppose. . . .
>
> . . . [C]oncerns about civility and mutual respect can never be used as a justification for closing off the discussion of ideas, no matter how offensive or disagreeable those ideas may be to some members of our community.

Given that my speech alone was being investigated—and that I wasn't harassing or discriminating against anyone, except possibly President Biden for having a racist and sexist employment policy—the case should've been open-and-shut. Even the left-wing literary critic Jeet Heer tweeted that my comments "were vile but well within the param-eters of academic free speech. The university is betraying fundamental principles here." Notorious critical race theorist Nikole Hannah-Jones, the founder of the 1619 Project, which aims to recenter America's story around racism and slavery, joined the criticism of Treanor's decision to "investigate" me, however "nondisciplinary" my leave might be framed. "I agree," she quote-tweeted Heer.

And recall that all that took place at a law school, where any faculty member could've applied the above policy to the discrete set of facts and closed the case before the last sleepy-headed students rolled in for morning class. That's what would've happened in a sane world.

In the real world, something different happened. It quickly became apparent that the true priority for those campus bureaucrats was not implementing due process but pleasing everyone who had an opinion about the matter—and there were plenty of those. On February 1, my first official day as a Georgetown faculty member, students held a sit-in, calling for "the immediate termination of Ilya Shapiro and for the administration to address BLSA demands." Treanor and three other administrators attended, fielding questions in an apologetic manner for more than an hour. Student activists floated the idea of defunding the Center for the Constitution—"I really want you to defend why we really need it, beyond, like, you know, free speech, and beyond diversity of opinion"—and demanded everything from "reparations" to free food to . . . a crying room. "Is there an office they can go to?" one student asked. "I don't know what it would look like, but if they want to cry, if they need to break down, where can they go?"

"It is really, really hard to walk out of class or a meeting in tears, and you should always have a place on campus where you can go," the dean of students, Mitch Bailin, replied. "And if you're finding that you're not getting the person that you want to talk to or not getting the space that you need, reach out to me anytime—*anytime*—and we will find you space."

The pained Treanor defended the center as "important" but added that he wanted to "draw a line between conservatism and things that are racist." He reiterated that he was "appalled" by my tweets and promised to "listen," "learn," and ultimately "do better." "I know how painful and awful it is for you, and I know what a terrible burden it is," he told the students. He was trying to placate the students without committing to any action. "Since we're a private institution, the First Amendment doesn't apply to us," he said. But "on the other hand, the university does have a free speech and expression policy which binds us." It wasn't exactly a profile in courage.

Another student demanded that school officials make a statement defending BLSA. "Something that's important is to remind our classmates that are attacking us that they are only here because our ancestors were sold for them to be here," she said. "What I hear today is that you lost our trust as an institution," interpreted Sheila Foster, the associate dean for equity and inclusion. "And we get that. And we take that. And we take accountability."

Treanor maintained a deferential tone but remained noncommittal about taking concrete steps: "I'm grateful for you taking the time to talk; I'm grateful for your insights. I heard a lot today that I won't just be reflecting on but that I'll be moving forward with, and I will be in dialogue with you about what we're doing."

The students, far from being mollified, were defiant. "A lot of eyes are on you right now," one said. "That's very powerful," Treanor replied. At the same time, the law school's "bias reporting" hotline fielded complaints about a student who had defended me in a national publication—taking particular issue with the article's headline (which of course the editor, not the student, had written). While sitting in class later that week, that student received a letter stating that law school administrators were evaluating a potential violation of the same policies under which I was being investigated. The student had to contact a lawyer to push back; Georgetown ultimately decided not to pursue an investigation. But there, too, the process was the punishment: in addition to unnecessary anxiety and distress, the episode cost the student upwards of $10,000 in legal fees.

While those sorts of spectacles were taking place on campus, I began the virtual "onboarding" process: setting up direct deposit for my hard-earned paycheck, signing up for benefits, figuring out email and other computer systems, going through HR training that definitely absolutely weeds out actual racists and harassers, and other standard procedures. I was contacted by both the Office of Human Resources and the Office of Institutional Diversity, Equity, and Affirmative Action (IDEAA) to arrange my investigatory interview. We set it for February 17 at 9:00 a.m., via Zoom again because of the whole masking thing and also because my presence on campus could be "triggering" and "harmful." For me, the virtual meeting would actually be at 6:00 a.m. Pacific time, because I was on the West Coast that week, speaking to chapters of the Federalist Society (the conservative and libertarian legal organization) and participating in an academic conference. That was all in my personal capacity, because Treanor's letter also specified that I was "not to perform work for the University."

And so I prepared to face my inquisitors. I was staying with a friend in San Diego, which was where, in the wee hours that Thursday morning—three weeks after the tweet that shook the world—I fired up my laptop.

The Zoom Inquisition

The reason that bureaucrats have eschewed all of the virtues undergirding the rule of law is that they've accepted the new orthodoxy that what matters is not the objective meaning of a given statement or even its intent but its effect—not the facts but the feelings. In retrospect, it's obvious that IDEAA's questions weren't about understanding me or what I had said but instead about getting me to agree with a bad-faith reading of the situation. It was a struggle session in which I was supposed to "do the work" and admit my guilt. If others perceived what I said as bad, it *must be* bad. No wonder we got nowhere; we were in a pitched epistemological battle.

I had three interlocutors: Bisi Okubadejo, associate vice president of equal opportunity, affirmative action, and compliance; Kay Bhagat-Smith, senior civil rights investigator and compliance manager; and Roberta Paul, senior director of employee and labor relations. Okubadejo clarified that "as part of our process advisors are really present as support persons. So to the extent that there are questions they should be coming directly from Mr. Shapiro." The kangaroo courtiers really didn't want the subjects of their "interviews" to have legal assistance, but at least they let my "support person" attend. So I had that going for me, which was nice.

They questioned me for an hour, almost exclusively asking variations of three questions:

1. What did you mean by your tweet?
2. What was the context of your tweet?

3. Do you think you can still be effective in the job for which you were hired?

I answered 1 and 2 in the last chapter. As to 3, I said that I still had all my knowledge, skills, and contacts and would apply those to teaching, writing, speaking, and mentoring students. This book opened with several of the more salient questions, and here's a fuller taste of one exchange:

Kay Bhagat-Smith: So ideally if you could go back in time, how would you have reworded your tweet to convey what you were intending?

Ilya Shapiro: I mean, ideally, I wouldn't have been tweeting right before bedtime. . . . It's not a good practice when you're upset about something. I'd been stewing in my thoughts, I put out a blog post, a press release earlier in the day as part of my Cato job to comment on the process and Breyer's retirement. So ideally I would not have been tweeting at, I think it was 10:30. . . . I was traveling. If I had been at home, then we wouldn't be here. But had I reworded it—and again, Twitter's generally not the best place to engage in serious discourse—I would've said something like what I've said since . . . that I abhor discrimination based on immutable characteristics. I think it's inappropriate for the president to limit his pool of potential Supreme Court nominees by race and gender.

KBS: I'd love to talk more with you about the process that led to this tweet. I know you've characterized it as being a product of being upset and being on the road. Can you tell us a little more about what led you to post that tweet that evening?

IS: There's really not much to tell . . . there's not much to investigate here. My statements speak for themselves, and I think it's unreasonable and generally in bad faith to read them as being derogatory or racist or misogynist—but that's the nature of the Twitter mob and the way that social media operates these days. It's unfortunate that there's even an investigation going on.

The questions were repetitive; she wasn't really focused on my answers but waiting on me to say the magic words "I was completely wrong." She then tried another tack: pointing out that other people had *felt* harmed by my words. How, then, could I not concede that I was wrong?

> **KBS:** So I would love for you to sort of explain how you will perform each of those responsibilities that we just touched upon given the concerns. When I say given the concerns, you said that you were aware of a lot of the concerns. There's a letter that I have seen signed by 70 black alumni and allies. There's another letter . . . that's signed by more than 1,000 students and 38 student organizations. . . . So, given this large opposition, how will you be able to perform those duties?
>
> **IS:** Well, there's a large support network for it as well. Lots of prominent people and not so prominent. There are letters of various kinds by students, by alumni. I get bcc'd on assorted emails to the dean expressing support for me and expressing disgust at the process, the fact that there's even an investigation. Because make no mistake: if an error in wording, if a failure or mistake in communication results in an employment action, then that's a huge chilling effect on speech, on the freedom of expression, on academic freedom—which would sorely harm the university and the law school. So I think we should be wary of giving a heckler's veto to anyone, whether an alumni letter, whether one particular prominent alumnus, whether a student group or student groups. And by heckler's veto, I mean shutting down a speaker because the listeners don't like the speech or don't like the anticipated speech.
>
> So how will I be effective? I mean, look, I'm happy to meet with students, with faculty, with alumni. I don't know why people sign letters. . . . I'm not going to get into people's heads to think about their motivations, but, ultimately, I've always treated people fairly, decently . . . without regard to immutable characteristics. There are plenty of letters [saying] that I simply do not have a record of racism and sexism and misogyny and all the rest of it. So if students don't want to deal with me, they don't have to.

I'm not going to be teaching required classes. I'm not going to be giving required lectures or writings.

. . . all I can do is continue to operate in an ethical way, showing integrity and intellectual rigor and an openness to academic debate and engaging in the world of ideas, and just hope that people approach things in good faith. . . .

It was all rather straightforward and, dare I say, easy. It was not a lawyerly deposition. There were no gotcha games or sharp questions. The inquisitors were incredulous that I didn't back away from my explanation that I had just imperfectly expressed a sentiment by which I stood, but there was nothing that they gleaned that would affect what in retrospect was a predetermined judgment that I was guilty of creating a "hostile educational environment" because some people were offended (or claimed offense). It was clear that, even if I had fallen on my sword and pledged fealty to critical race theory, the outcome—a technical victory with the promise of discipline for future speech crimes—was preordained.

In any case, the inquisitors gave me time for closing thoughts, and here's what I said:

Look, I wish none of this had happened. I really do. But I stand by everything I've said publicly about these tweets. My email to the faculty, my public statements since. I apologize for the inartful phrasing. I still sincerely regret that. I regret causing offense. . . . But at the end of the day, this is about poorly communicating a very standard idea and being part of the intellectual discourse that's essential to any university and certainly Georgetown—and certainly the Law Center's mission. Punishing me, or taking an adverse employment action based on erroneous wording, would have a significant chilling effect. . . .
I hope that the law school, that Dean Treanor, will use this moment as an exemplar of how to move, not just our respective institutions or us as individuals forward, but to move the country in a positive direction and show that even on very fraught issues that we will never agree upon. . . . We can still be civilized and

understand each other's comments reasonably and fairly. . . . We can improve as long as we just don't hold double standards. And as long as we do treat people as individuals who are not infallible and who are deserving of fair and equal treatment.

With that, the Zoom meeting adjourned. My counsel was ecstatic and said he'd use my performance as an example of how to behave in a witness chair. I breathed a deep breath and, at around 7:45 a.m. local time, split a bottle of champagne with my friend.

On Monday, February 21, I filed my written submission with HR and IDEAA. The upshot was that I urged Georgetown to uphold its values and live up to its ideals. Ironically, the day before, Georgetown professor Paul Butler, who teaches criminal law and civil rights and is also a legal analyst for MSNBC, had published an op-ed in the *Washington Post* titled "Yes, Georgetown Should Fire an Academic for a Racist Tweet."

The following week, on March 1, I headed back to California to speak at the law school formerly known as UC Hastings, which would mark another bizarre twist in the saga.

CHAPTER 4

Cancellation Is About Power, Not Accountability

By the time I flew back to California, my lawyer and I decided that I should resume a normal schedule of public events and writings. The thinking was that it would help my case to show that I was still capable of performing as a communicator and exponent of my area of expertise. That course of action would also address the investigators' concerns about my being able to do my job. And it would be a psychological balm, because I was beginning to get antsy about being bottled up and "inside my head" about the surreal situation I was in. Moreover, the publisher of my last book had decided to release *Supreme Disorder* in paperback—I had begun working on an epilogue that would update the narrative to include Amy Coney Barrett and whomever Biden would pick now—so being "out there" would help sales.

What I was about to discover was a truth that contradicted the most prominent defenses of cancel culture. Cancel-culture apologists like to claim that cancellation is about accountability for bad actors. Who could oppose that? Every society needs a way to chastise those who have broken its rules. What puts the lie to the "accountability" defense, however, is that cancellations aren't specific; they're blanket punishments. Accountability is designed to seek truth and *then* punish, but cancellation seeks to isolate its victims without investigation—and to isolate them in every way across their careers. That's simply an exercise of power. Presumption of innocence? Forget about it. Grace? That's for chumps. Such an atmosphere is particularly detrimental to the development of lawyers.

The only way to dissipate the toxic cloud is for courageous leaders to stand up and call it what it is.

As it happened, the day before I flew to San Francisco to speak at the University of California Hastings College of Law—which has since been renamed UC College of the Law, San Francisco, because its founder didn't abide by 21st-century mores in the 19th century—President Biden announced the nomination of then-Judge Ketanji Brown Jackson to the Supreme Court. Great, I thought, Professor Rory Little and I will be able to discuss not just the role that politics plays in judicial nominations or my ongoing Georgetown travails, but the merits of this particular nominee. But it was not to be; we didn't get to discuss anything at all.

"Shut up." That was the response, cleaned up for publication, that I got from students when I tried to speak on March 1, just over a month after my fateful tweet. There were signs and placards—with criticism that wasn't constructive, to say the least—and I was expecting tough questions, because that's what the freedom of speech is all about. But I wasn't able to say anything. The activists chanted and banged tables as if it were Occupy Wall Street, preventing the event from taking place at all.

It was the first I time had been protested in more than a thousand speaking events.

Although the school's Federalist Society chapter had duly booked a room and—even before Justice Breyer announced his retirement—invited me to discuss my book, a heckler's veto prevailed. Applying a bad-faith lens to my poorly phrased tweet, activists adjudged me a racist misogynist and my expertise illegitimate. So many people showed up that the meeting was moved to a larger room. But the move was pointless, because there didn't end up being an event, at least not one involving civil discourse.

The vocal students who shut me down wanted to hear neither my reasoning about President Biden's selection criteria nor my broader analysis of the confirmation battle now that there was an actual nominee. And they did so in the vilest language imaginable, several times getting literally in my face or blocking my access to the lectern.

The protesters also castigated their own law school for allowing me to speak and in a concurrently circulated letter called for "a committee of diverse student representatives" to approve speakers, among other demands about mandatory training in critical race theory. Never mind that their school, as a public institution, would be violating the First Amendment if it disapproved speakers based on the content of their speech.

And never mind that, as Morris Ratner, the provost and academic dean, advised the protesters in the few minutes when they weren't chanting and banging that not allowing a duly invited speaker to speak went against school rules. (Ironically, the white male dean spoke after the protesters wouldn't allow the more diminutive female Asian American dean of students to do so.) While Ratner was issuing his warning, I was outside conferring with the Federalist Society officers about what to do with the rest of the event. "You booked me for an hour," I told them, "so I'm fine just standing there and trying to get a word in if and when I can."

And that's exactly what happened. Right up until a few minutes before the end of the hour, when I knew that the students would have to leave to go to class, I just stood in front of the overfilled classroom and put on what I thought was a poker face—not that it mattered because the school was still enforcing a mask mandate, even on speakers. The few times that the volume of the chanting died down a bit, I tried to start talking, but then it started up again. Ratner's counsel was ignored.

Professor Little's behavior, meanwhile, contributed to my being silenced. While the disrupters were doing their thing, he rapped the table and chanted along. I could see his mask inflating in rhythm with the chants. He's even recorded on video as saying that he was "all for it," and he then signed a letter reiterating support for the disrupters because "statements of commitment to diversity and inclusion ring hollow when salient issues of racial equity are ignored or discounted in the service of prioritizing the ideal of free speech." I'd met Rory before, and he had told me that he was looking forward to engaging with me—and in a letter to the editor responding to my *Wall Street Journal* op-ed about the incident said he'd "welcome the opportunity to join [me] and offer rebuttals"—but apparently that was either disingenuous or naive.

The next day, the school's chancellor, David Faigman, wrote in a communitywide email that "[d]isrupting an event to prevent a speaker from being heard is a violation of our policies and norms, including the Code of Student Conduct and Discipline, Section 107 ('Harmful Acts and Disturbances'), which the College will—indeed, must—enforce." But it wasn't enforced and nobody was disciplined, as Faigman's further email a month later detailed: 20 pages of tightly lawyered verbiage lauding the school's DEI initiatives but declining to announce new ones.

People still ask me how it felt and whether I ever felt physically threatened—with actual violence, that is, not the "words are violence" nonsense. Well, after the four days of hell at the beginning of this process, nothing fazed me anymore. I was bemused more than anything and saddened that what had once been a highly reputed law school—it's Kamala Harris's alma mater—had fallen so far. And no, it never felt as though any of the students were about to punch or grab or bump me, though they were plenty obnoxious even without that.

Later that afternoon, I spoke at Santa Clara Law. I was warmly received by some students, met with stone faces by others. I got both friendly and hostile questions, and at the end it effectively became a general debate on affirmative action. Now, that's how you hold events where some in the audience don't like or are even offended by a speaker's message!

Back to Work

After I returned home and the Hastings contretemps had become another national news item, I got a text from a lawyer friend in Colorado. He said that he'd contributed to a letter supporting me and wanted to see if there was anything else like-minded folks could do. I told him that it was just a waiting game as we entered week six of purgatory and even if Georgetown was paying me not to work—though I was probably working harder than in normal times—it would sure be nice to go skiing. Five days later, I was in Denver speaking to the local Federalist Society chapter.

Then I did take a ski day—in Loveland, to be closer to the airport. My favorite skiing in Colorado is either Vail or Steamboat. Utah, particularly Alta, tops them both, but I had to be in New Orleans for a conference that Friday. So I raced off the slopes and, still in my sweaty ski togs, just made my flight to the Big Easy. When I landed, I was surely the only person in Louisiana wearing snow pants.

So it went the next few months. I did some legal consulting, wrote popular and academic articles, filed amicus briefs—including in the Harvard/UNC affirmative action cases that the Supreme Court would decide in June 2023—gave speeches and panel remarks, explored some idea-entrepreneurship opportunities, and otherwise kept busy so as not to think about the dragged-out "investigation." One highlight was an event at Princeton, my undergraduate alma mater, focused on threats to collegiate free speech, after which I had dinner with Professor Joshua Katz and his lovely wife, Solveig. Josh is a classicist and a genius, whose long-ago disciplinary case for an inappropriate (but consensual) relationship with a student was reopened after he bucked progressive orthodoxy in the aftermath of the George Floyd protests. He'd be stripped of his tenure and fired later that spring.

It was an emotional roller coaster. There were fun, rewarding times and plenty of both quality and quantity time with my family. But there were pits of . . . not despair, but doubt and mental exhaustion. The word is overused, but it was surreal: Was all this happening because of one tweet? Where was my career going? Sure, I had a jocular personality in public, trying to make constitutional law more accessible, but I was getting tired of being the case study and making news rather than explaining cases on news programs.

More broadly, what was happening to our country and to legal academia? Why weren't professors teaching students that they'd face bigger issues in their work than offensive speakers?

But as I mentioned in the introduction, my experience was no isolated incident—not even for that month of March! On March 10, a Yale Law School discussion bringing together Monica Miller of the American Humanist Association and Kristen Waggoner of the Alliance Defending Freedom—who agreed on little other than the importance of free speech—was interrupted by dozens of protesters who were upset about ADF's positions on LGBTQ issues. The protesters continued their disruption in the hallway outside in a way that further disrupted several classes and a faculty meeting, while Miller and Waggoner had to be escorted out of the room. It would take Dean Heather Gerken more than two weeks to respond and essentially let the disrupters off with a warning.

Then students obstructed a debate at the University of Michigan on Texas's heartbeat bill featuring its architect, former Texas solicitor general Jonathan Mitchell, with whom I overlapped in law school. They focused on the particularly clever method of holding signs at the front of the room that prevented the audience from seeing Mitchell and his presentation. (The prevalence of this method of disruption further justifies my practice of never using PowerPoint, which I joke is unconstitutional.) Somehow, that event wasn't livestreamed and didn't make national news; I learned of it only because I was due to speak at Michigan the following week.

The only thing the disrupted events had in common was that non-progressive speakers were presenting ideas that some students found objectionable. We've gotten to a place where questioning affirmative action or abortion is outside the academic Overton window, the acceptable range of policy views. We've also gotten to a place where the demand for racism—to justify allegations of "systemic racism" and racialist "antiracism"—far outstrips the supply, so outrages have to be manufactured.

At least I can report some counterexamples from my personal experience, though it's unclear whether they're green shoots or exceptions that prove the rule. My Michigan event was supposed to cover the politics of Supreme Court nominations, but in light of national and local developments was reformatted as a discussion on the importance of free speech on campus. Apparently, between the Mitchell event and mine, deans had read the leaders of student organizations the riot act, reiterating university policies on free speech and telling them, "We don't want to be Hastings or Yale." And right before my event, which also featured Northwestern law professor Andrew Koppelman, a longtime sparring partner, the dean of students (who happened to be a black woman), told the audience that I was "most welcome" and reiterated school policies on disciplinary actions against those who disrupt speaker events.

Koppelman said that my substantive legal writings on a range of constitutional issues were "a lot worse than an insulting tweet" but that paying attention to what I said would help those on the left fight their opponents. I gave as good as I got, assailing him and progressives for having upended the rule of law in favor of a constitutionally untethered pursuit of social justice. It was a fantastic event, and we ended up writing up for the *Heterodox Academy* blog our experience modeling civil engagement despite vehement disagreement over real issues.

In addition to my Michigan event, I had a thrilling and serious two-hour standing-room-only discussion at the University of Oklahoma College of Law. Dean Katheleen Guzman attended the whole thing, took copious notes, and came up to me afterward to ask what administrators should do to promote civil discourse. I suggested that just as law school deans imbue the importance of diversity and public service, they should imbue the values of free speech and civil discourse. I don't think it's that hard—unlike some of the larger issues we face in society as a whole—but there's little desire to do it or backbone to stand up to the braying mob.

Judicious Support

But more people emerged from outside the academy to advocate for free speech in the academy. Two weeks before my UC Hastings debacle, Fifth Circuit Judge James C. Ho came to Georgetown Law to give a talk on originalism. "But I hope you won't mind that I've decided to address a different topic today instead," he announced to much surprise. "I'm going to spend my time today talking about Ilya Shapiro."

Now, I should disclose that I've known Jim for about 20 years and we see each other fairly regularly. But I had no idea that he was going to do what he did.

A Taiwanese American who immigrated to the United States with his parents as a child, Jim became the first person of Asian descent to sit on the Fifth Circuit when he was appointed by Donald Trump in 2017. He's also a cochair of the Judiciary Committee of the National Asian Pacific American Bar Association, a member of the US delegation to the United Nations Committee on the Elimination of Racial Discrimination, and a former attorney in the Justice Department's Civil Rights Division. Jim's personal background featured prominently in his remarks. "I've confronted racial discrimination," he said, but "cancel culture is not just antithetical to our constitutional culture and our American culture"; it's "completely antithetical to the very legal system that each of you seeks to join."

Jim's speech, which he later annotated and published in the *Georgetown Journal of Law and Public Policy*, argued generally about the importance of freedom of speech, since it is "the foundation of our entire adversarial system of justice." Paralleling Koppelman, he explained that "[y]ou must understand your opponent's views in order to fully understand, and thus powerfully defend, your own views. And that means exposing yourself, not just to the *arguments* on the other side—but to the very *people* who most fervently believe those arguments."

Going beyond the general, he also defended my substantive point that we should be against racial preferences and for equality of opportunity, which he described as "fundamental to who we are, and to who we aspire to be, as a nation." "Ilya has said that he should have chosen different words. That ought to be enough," he said. "I have no doubt—zero doubt—that Ilya did not intend anywhere near the worst interpretation that has been applied to his remarks.

"Make no mistake," he intoned. "If there is any racial discrimination in statements like these, it's not coming from the *speaker*—it's coming from the *policy* that the speaker is criticizing." That statement was a not-so-veiled criticism of Georgetown, but he went even further to show that there was no daylight between the positions I was taking in my defense and his own views.

"Let me be clear: I stand with Ilya on the paramount importance of color blindness. And that same principle should apply whether we're talking about getting into college, getting your first job, or receiving an appointment to the highest court in the land." As evidence, he cited testimony that he had given at a House Judiciary Committee hearing on "The Importance of a Diverse Federal Judiciary," in which he had echoed my longtime criticism of race-based judicial appointments, calling it "un-American" to restrict a judgeship to members of only one race. Calling racism "a scourge" on America, he added, "the first step in fighting racial discrimination is to stop practicing it. That's all Ilya is trying to say. That's all he's ever tried to say," Jim concluded. "If Ilya Shapiro is deserving of cancellation, then you should go ahead and cancel me, too."

The speech was a national sensation. I was on a plane when he gave it, on the way to San Diego for the trip described in the last chapter, and when I landed, my phone blew up with media queries. I quickly skimmed the reporting about the speech—we didn't have a full transcript yet—and smiled. Here's what I told reporters who asked me for comment: "I'm gratified that Judge Ho supports me. He's a mensch."

I got in touch with Jim that evening to thank him. He said it had been the least he could do and asked if there was any other way he could help. I told him that more statements from federal judges couldn't hurt! Indeed, I'd had media supporters and lawyers defending me, but having a federal judge come to Georgetown to say all those powerful things was next-level support. We also joked that I should come to Dallas, where he lives, and dramatically rip up prepared remarks on originalism to instead praise Jim's jurisprudence. As it happened, I would tour Texas that spring and Jim was supposed to introduce me at an event, but flight snafus prevented his attendance.

As March gave way to April and April to May, my lawyer, Jesse Binnall, and I heard nothing about the investigation. I knew that the inquisitors had also interviewed my boss, Randy Barnett. I suspected that they'd interviewed the leader(s) of the Black Law Students Association, who had orchestrated the campaign campaign against me—to show the "harm" I had caused. So what was taking so long and what was the university paying WilmerHale, one of the poshest DC law firms, to advise it on? It was becoming ridiculous, not simply unjust.

While I was attending a conference in Southern California, my wife, who by that time we knew was pregnant, went to her first doctor's appointment for an ultrasound. I was expecting her to text me "Strong heartbeat" or "All OK" or to call if something was wrong. Instead, she texted one word: "Twins."

My eyes nearly popped out of my head as I stared at my phone. The only thing I could think to respond was "OMG." Twins don't run in our families and we hadn't used IVF, so it was totally unexpected.

The now very real expectation of our "cancellation babies" helped put things into perspective. That sobering realization was why I was doing the work, why I was standing up for what I believed, and also why simply supporting my family—which I was now confident I would be able to do regardless of what happened with Georgetown—was paramount. Not playing political games or culture wars.

In early May, I attended the Manhattan Institute's annual Alexander Hamilton Award Dinner, that year honoring Paul Gigot, the editor of the *Wall Street Journal*'s opinion page. I'd long been friends and professional colleagues with lots of folks there, notably Jim Copland, MI's head of legal policy. No, I didn't get a job offer that night—and no, I didn't orchestrate anything with a view to joining MI. But it's quite possible, given various synergies and mutual admiration, that had I not tweeted and remained at Georgetown, I'd still be an MI adjunct scholar of some sort. In any event, it was a great night in New York, where I hadn't been since before the pandemic.

I was beginning to feel antsy but cautiously optimistic. If Georgetown had wanted to fire me, it would've done so sooner. Clearly, they were waiting for the semester to end and students to leave campus. Graduation was coming up on May 22, Jesse had been having occasional contacts with Wilmer's Bruce Berman, and Randy had been having occasional contacts with Dean Treanor. We had an inkling that this would all soon be over.

CHAPTER 5

The Problem Isn't Just Ideology but Bureaucracy

So why are we seeing these trends? What's changed? Truth be told, what's different now from when I was in law school in the early 2000s isn't so much that faculties—or students—have shifted left. This is not the decades-old conservative complaint about the liberal takeover of the academy. The campus climate has changed such that everyone walks on eggshells and certain ideas can't be discussed in most settings, but the ideological ratios haven't changed all that much. Instead, it's that the radical left now drives campus culture. University officials placate, facilitate, and even foment *illiberal* mobs, with everyone else keeping their heads down so as not to be caught in the cancellation crossfire. And that's largely a story of growing bureaucracies.

The statistics on the growth of the left-skewed nonteaching staff are mind-boggling. In the 25 years ending in 2012, the number of professional university (not law school) employees who don't teach grew at about twice the rate of the number of students. In the same period, tuition at four-year public colleges more than tripled. Those trends have only accelerated, though uniform statistics for the decade-plus since then are hard to come by, as the big surveyors have stopped separating administrators and faculty or stopped collecting information entirely. The Department of Education has contributed to this obfuscation, changing method-ologies from year to year if not altogether failing to collect or disclose the relevant data.

What all this really means is that students are paying more and more every year to fund an expanding cohort of well-compensated bureaucrats, without getting anything in return. And this isn't just a budget issue. Administrators are more radical than professors, and not steeped in norms of academic freedom, all of which detracts from the educational environment. A 2018 survey found that faculty had a liberal-to-conservative ratio of about 6 to 1, with 13 percent of our nation's professors self-identifying on the right. (That number is almost certainly lower in law schools.) Students are more balanced: 42 percent of freshmen called themselves centrist, while 36 percent said they were liberal and 22 percent conservative. In contrast, two-thirds of higher-ed administrators self-identified as liberal—with 40 percent calling themselves far left—and only 5 percent said they were on the right. That makes for a liberal-to-conservative ratio of 12 to 1.[1]

Those who once were technocratic paper-pushers ensuring compliance with federal financial aid and antidiscrimination regulations—Title IX was, of course, a big deal for women's opportunities—have morphed into enforcers of racialism and radical gender ideology. As in the government, the bureaucrats' incentive is to expand their empires and grow their budgets.

The great political economist Mancur Olson detailed how the growth of bureaucracies ultimately causes the decline of nations. And that's precisely what's happened in academe, as well-paid apparatchiks with no connection to universities' teaching and research missions create and enforce codes that chill speech and eviscerate due process. Even elite law school deans cower in fear of their diversity offices and, as happened in my case, pawn off decision-making in sensitive cases to DEI offices, to which they can then defer.

Origins

The origins of university administration can be traced back to medieval Europe, when universities were typically composed of self-governing

---

1. Samuel J. Abrams, "One of the Most Liberal Groups in America," *Inside Higher Ed*, November 8, 2018.

guilds of students and teachers. The American university system took shape in the 19th century, as research universities grew out of liberal arts colleges. The first American research university was Johns Hopkins, founded in 1876. The first president of Johns Hopkins, Daniel Gilman, had done his doctoral work in Germany and realized the potential of melding the German research method of graduate study and the British seminar method of undergraduate study. Accordingly, he and his successors developed a central administration separate from faculty and students that was responsible for managing the university's overall operations. Administrative structures grew to include a president or chancellor as the chief executive officer, a provost as chief operating officer, vice presidents for specific areas such as academic affairs, research, and student affairs, and deans of the various graduate and professional schools. Eventually, the need for directors of admissions, athletics, development, and other nonacademic functions emerged.

Legal education, meanwhile, had historically been done through apprenticeship, during which students would build on their undergraduate readings (as James Madison had done at Princeton) by working with practicing lawyers to learn the trade. With the growing complexity of the legal system and the increasing demand for formal education, law schools began to appear in the early republic, beginning with Litchfield Law School in Connecticut in 1784. It wasn't until the "case method" of teaching—recall Professor Kingsfield in *The Paper Chase*—together with the reconception of law schools as university subsidiaries in the late 19th century that the need for additional administration arose. Law schools needed to manage their finances, facilities, and other operations, not just throw books and scholarly lawyers together. The first law schools were small, with power centralized in the office of the dean. Modern law school administrative structures now parallel those of the larger university of which they're a part, with a dean as the CEO, plus associate or assistant deans for academic affairs, student life, and career services, plus staff for marketing, communications, technology, and the like. There's also typically a governing body, such as a board of trustees or visitors, that's supposed to provide oversight.

In recent decades, the growth in university and law school bureaucracies has far outpaced the growth in faculties and student bodies. From

1975 to 2005, the number of professors grew by about 50 percent nation-wide, while "the number of administrators increased by 85 percent" and their attendant staff by 240 percent—with particularly pronounced growth at private schools.[2] According to Department of Education data, between 1993 and 2009, college administrative positions expanded by 60 percent, a rate of growth ten times that of tenured faculty.[3] Some schools were extreme in this regard: Arizona State University increased the number of administrators during that period by 94 percent while reducing the number of faculty by 2 percent.[4] Moreover, between 1987 and 2012, the number of administrators at private universities doubled, while their numbers in central offices of public university systems rose by a factor of 34.[5] Overall, during that period, colleges added more than half a million administrators and then even more in the decade after that. The Bureau of Labor Statistics expects their number to grow by 7 percent a year between 2021 and 2031.

Apologists for the growing educational bureaucracies explain the growth in nonteaching staff with reference to "government demands for information and an increasingly complicated regulatory environment."[6] If that were the case, you would expect to see higher administrative growth in the more tightly regulated state colleges and universities than in their private counterparts. But the reverse is true. In 1970, US private colleges employed significantly more professors (446,830) than administrators (268,952). Since then, the number of full-time professors or "full-time equivalents"—slots filled by two or more part-time faculty

2. Benjamin Ginsberg, *The Fall of the Faculty: The Rise of the All-Administrative University and Why It Matters* (New York: Oxford University Press, 2011), 28.

3. Paul F. Campos, "The Real Reason College Tuition Costs So Much," *New York Times*, April 4, 2015.

4. Jay P. Greene, "Administrative Bloat at American Universities: The Real Reason for High Costs in Higher Education," Goldwater Institute Policy Report No. 239, August 17, 2010, 1.

5. New England Center for Investigative Reporting, "New Analysis Shows Problematic Boom in Higher Ed Administrators," HuffPost, February 6, 2014 (describing a joint report with the American Institutes for Research).

6. Alan Ryan, "The Fall of the Faculty: The Rise of the All-Administrative University and Why It Matters," *Times Higher Education*, December 1, 2011.

members whose combined hours equal those of a full-timer—increased by just over 50 percent, which is comparable to the growth in student enrollment. But the number of administrators and their staffers employed by those schools increased by 85 percent and 240 percent, respectively.

Around 2010, schools started employing more administrators than full-time instructors. Through the following decade, some, especially elite places such as Harvard, Yale, Columbia, Stanford, and the Massachusetts Institute of Technology (MIT), even started having more administrators *than students*. Yale's administration rolls grew by 45 percent in 2003–21, according to *Free Press* reporting, "expanding at a rate nearly three times faster than that of the undergraduate student body." At Stanford, the number of administrators grew by 30 percent in 2017–22 alone, with the most significant growth coming in the first full pandemic year of 2020–21. Stanford now has nearly twice as many nonteaching staff as undergrads—perhaps each student should get a butler—and nearly *six times* the number of administrators as faculty. MIT likewise has six times the number of staff as faculty. The overall ratios tend to be lower at public schools, but still, administrative growth at the University of California, Los Angeles has outpaced growth in other sectors, such that there are now *four times* as many staff as faculty. Auburn, which is a public land-grant school, has maintained a low ratio of admins to undergrads (just over one staff member per student) but still has seen higher rates of growth of staff than either faculty or students.

Regardless of whether public or private schools are worse, the disproportionate increase in nonfaculty positions is also reflected in university budgets. At 198 of the leading US research universities, spending on administrative functions has been rising faster than spending on instruction and research functions. To wit, from 1993 to 2007, university expenses for administration increased by 61 percent per student, while instruction-related expenses increased by only 39 percent. That trend has only accelerated.[7] For the 2018–19 academic year—the last year before Covid-related expenses made everything look even worse—

7. Greene, "Administrative Bloat at American Universities," 9, 12.

degree-granting postsecondary institutions spent $632 billion, but less than 30 percent of that went to actual instruction. Between 2009–10 and 2018–19, instructional expenses per full-time student at four-year institutions grew by only 8 percent, while overall expenses grew by 114 percent.[8] Moreover, from 2010 to 2018, noninstructional spending—including student services (29 percent) and administration (19 percent)—grew faster than instructional spending (17 percent).[9]

Or look at Harvard, which has long regarded itself as the crown jewel of American higher education and is almost certainly the biggest global academic brand. The trend of having higher-ed institutions run by bureaucrats rather than academics accelerated in 2023 when Harvard named Claudine Gay as its next president. Even without the revelations of plagiarism that forced her resignation barely six months later, Gay had a thin scholarly record, having authored 11 insightless papers and no books. But she came from a privileged background and was elevated for advancing progressive orthodoxy while checking the right intersectional boxes. She is the apotheosis of an anti-intellectual movement that values DEI, identity, and activism over truth-seeking, merit, and education.

That trend prefers political commissars over rigorous scholars, and Harvard trumpeted Gay's status as the first African American and second woman to hold the post. Gay then made history again for serving the shortest tenure, beating out Lawrence Summers, whose time at Harvard's helm was cut short in 2006 after his "off the record" comments about the dearth of women in science and engineering were deemed politically incorrect.

Gay had previously been the dean of the Faculty of Arts and Sciences and before that a professor of government and African American studies. She had never been a superstar of the Ivy League constellation, but that's not necessarily unusual for those who go into academic administration. Indeed, her ascent can be explained by the bureaucratization of higher ed even more than by affirmative action. In 2020, *Harvard Magazine* announced that then-Dean Gay had launched "a series of initiatives to

---

8. National Center for Education Statistics, *The Condition of Education* 2013; 2021; 2023.

9. American Council of Trustees and Alumni, *The Cost of Excess: Why Colleges and Universities Must Control Runaway Spending*, August 2021.

address racial and ethnic equality—including faculty appointments and the addition of an associate dean of diversity, inclusion, and belonging" to its already robust DEI empire. Ironically, all those efforts at making students feel welcome have backfired in terms of creating a campus culture in which all feel comfortable expressing themselves; in 2023, FIRE named Harvard the worst school in the country for free speech, the only one with an "abysmal" rating.

Harvard's administrative payroll nearly doubled in this century's first two decades. In 2020, the school spent $47,706 per student on administration, which is just under the cost of undergraduate tuition (not including fees, room, and board). This bureaucratic growth accounts for almost the entire increase in the annual cost of attending Harvard, which is one of the leaders in this dubious metric alongside others in which it takes more pride.

What About Law Schools?

When looking specifically at law schools, it's particularly hard to do any sort of statistical analysis. The American Bar Association, which is the accreditor and thus main national regulator of legal education, constantly changes its reporting methods and disclosure formats. Since 2011, the ABA has not disclosed purely administrative numbers, instead reporting only "administrators who teach." After 2016, it stopped reporting on the number of administrators altogether, instead reporting only the number of faculty. We do know that from 2011 to 2015, the number of full-time faculty declined from 9,028 to 7,932, a drop of 14 percent in four years, while the number of administrators who teach grew from 1,752 to 2,032, a 16 percent increase.[10] (Part-time faculty, including adjuncts, remained flat at just over 9,000.)

Part of that story is the belated adjustment of legal education to the Great Recession, which restructured the private legal market and led schools to cut costs, and full-time professors are expensive. But regardless

---

10. Derek T. Muller, "As Full-Time Law Faculty Numbers Shrink, Law School Administrator Numbers Grow," Excess of Democracy, January 21, 2016.

of market forces, it's clear that the ratio of teachers to bureaucrats has gone in the latter direction as it has at universities writ large. The statistics for administrators appear not to be publicly available since 2016, and the ABA no longer even makes law schools self-report. Given the growth in this field generally, it's safe to assume that the problem has only gotten worse.

One example of the exponential growth of law-school administrators comes from Boston University. In 1950, the full-time administrative staff at BU Law was just six people. By 1960, it rose to nine. Then it jumped to 22 in 1970 and 30 in 1980 and doubled to 60 in 1990. Growth slowed in the 1990s, with administrative staff numbering 72 in 2000. While these numbers are a bit old, they show a bureaucratic growth rate of 1,100 percent even before the last couple of decades' explosion. Interestingly, BU's rival, Boston College, experienced a similarly amazing growth rate during that period, 788 percent. By comparison, over that same half century, the number of faculty increased by 671 percent at BU Law (just over half the growth rate of the admins) and 336 percent at BC Law (less than half that of the admins).[11] Suffice it to say that student-body growth was lower.

The DEI Angle

Having gained a sense of the overall academic bureaucrat trends, let's turn to the DEI component of administrative bloat. Diversity officers are a fairly recent phenomenon, emerging in the late 20th century out of "minority affairs" roles that began popping up in the 1970s. It wasn't until after the Supreme Court's decision in *Grutter v. Bollinger* in 2003, in which the Court affirmed the constitutionality of using race in admissions to advance diversity in education—so long as schools avoided quotas, points, or other automatic preferences—that universities fully leaned into integrating diversity officers into higher, student-facing administration. That led to the creation of a plethora of new jobs specifically focused on those issues, culminating in chief diversity officers.

---

11. Statistics in this paragraph come from Ronald A. Cass and John H. Garvey, "Law School Leviathan Explaining Administrative Growth," *University of Toledo Law Review* 35, no. 1 (Fall 2003): 37–44. Cass was dean of BU Law from 1990 until 2004. Garvey was president of the Catholic University of America from 1990 to 2022.

Some of these administrators serve as special advisers to university presidents and deans, even when their colleagues or superiors in student or faculty affairs positions don't play such a role. This means that diversity officers play a direct role in executive decision-making when administrators of ostensibly equal or higher rank, in areas ranging from research to finance, must report through the traditional hierarchy.

A 2021 survey of 65 large universities—comprising the "power five" football conferences—that represent 16 percent of all students at four-year institutions found that the average school has more than 45 people devoted to DEI, which is more than the average number of professors they have teaching history.[12] Indeed, DEI is the fastest-growing segment of the educational bureaucracy, with staffs on average four times larger than those that provide legally mandated accommodations to students with disabilities. (The study was careful to exclude people whose primary responsibility was in Title IX, equal employment opportunity, or other legal obligations to comply with federal or state civil rights laws.)

The average university had 3.4 DEI staff per 100 tenured or tenure-track faculty, though some schools were truly extreme. At the University of Michigan, 163 people had formal authority over DEI programs. (By 2023, that number had grown to 261 people—and double that when partial DEI positions are included, at a total cost of more than $30 million.[13]) At UNC Chapel Hill, there were 13.3 times as many DEI staff as those tasked with providing services to people with disabilities (second only to Michigan). When compared to faculty as a whole, Syracuse University was the worst, with 7.4 DEI staff for every 100 professors.

DEI structures tend to be similar across institutions, with units covering the entire university that create and implement assorted programs and policies. These central offices are led by people with titles such as vice president and vice provost, which principals in turn have assorted subordinates. Virginia Tech has a vice president for strategic

---

12. Jay P. Greene and James D. Paul, "Diversity University: DEI Bloat in the Academy," Heritage Foundation Backgrounder No. 3641, July 27, 2021. Many of the statistics and descriptions of DEI offices in this chapter come from this report.

13. Jennifer Kabbany, "UMich Now Has More than 500 Jobs Dedicated to DEI, Payroll Costs Exceed $30 Million," The College Fix, January 9, 2024.

affairs and diversity, who is supported by an associate vice provost of diversity education and engagement, and in turn by assistant provosts for (1) diversity and inclusion and (2) faculty diversity, respectively, plus several directors. These DEI offices are further supported by communications teams, program associates, and other administrative aides.

At larger universities, these structures are replicated on a smaller scale in colleges and departments, including, of course, law schools, as well as centers focused on providing services to people with particular racial, ethnic, or gender identities. These centers have their own bureaucratic hierarchies, going down to graduate and undergraduate interns. Of course, the total staff and faculty devoted to DEI initiatives is likely much higher than that 2021 study showed. There are likely many people on campus who don't have "DEI" or any related buzzwords in their titles yet spend a significant amount of time working on those goals.

One interesting thing to note is that in both universities as a whole and law schools specifically, an inordinate number of DEI offices have been either created or filled in the last decade, especially since the "racial reckoning" set off by the killing of George Floyd in spring 2020. Georgetown was apparently ahead of the game, creating way back in 2006 the IDEAA office I tangled with—and remarkably, the same person still leads it. I've compiled a list of newer DEI offices and officers at a cross section of prominent universities and law schools, the latest of which, at MIT, was announced in January 2024 in the fallout from the disastrous performance of that school's president, Sally Kornbluth, at a congressional hearing examining antisemitism on campus. (The two other presidents who testified, Harvard's Gay and Penn's Liz Magill, ended up resigning.)

Universities

Private

Princeton: Vice Provost for Institutional Equity and Diversity (position created in 2014)
Harvard: Chief Diversity and Inclusion Officer (position created in 2020)

Penn: Senior Vice President for Institutional Affairs/Chief Diversity Officer (position created in 2017)

Columbia: Executive Vice President for University Life (new person in 2021, with a focus on DEI)

Stanford: Vice Provost for Institutional Equity, Access, and Community/Special Advisor to the President (new person in 2021)

University of Chicago: Vice Provost for Diversity & Inclusion (new person in 2022)

Duke: Vice President for Institutional Equity/Chief Diversity Officer (new person in 2019)

Northwestern: Vice President/Associate Provost for Diversity and Inclusion/Chief Diversity Officer (new person in 2021)

Emory: Vice Provost for Diversity and Inclusion/Chief Diversity Officer/Adviser to the President (position created in 2019)

Georgetown: Vice President for DEI/Chief Diversity Officer (CDO title added 2019)

NYU: Senior Vice President for Global Inclusion, Diversity, and Strategic Innovation/Chief Diversity Officer (CDO title added in 2017)

MIT: Vice President for Equity and Inclusion (position created in 2024)

Public

University of Virginia: Vice President for DEI and Community Partnerships (office created in 2021)

University of Texas at Austin: Vice President for Campus and Community Engagement (new person in 2021; renamed from VP for *Diversity* after the Texas legislature abolished DEI offices in 2023)

UNC at Chapel Hill: Vice Provost of Equity and Inclusion/ Chief Diversity Officer (new person in 2021)

University of Michigan: Vice Provost for Equity and Inclusion/ Chief Diversity Officer (new person in 2022)

University of Florida: Chief Diversity Officer/Senior Advisor to the President (position created in 2018, new person in 2021)

UC Berkeley: Vice Chancellor for the Division of Equity & Inclusion (new person in 2021)

UCLA: Vice Chancellor for Equity, Diversity and Inclusion (new person in 2021)

Law Schools

Private

Yale: Director of DEI in the Office of Student Affairs (position vacant after the developments discussed in chapter 7)

Columbia: Assistant Dean for Social Justice Initiatives and Public Service Lawyering (recently renamed Dean of Public Interest/Public Service Law and Careers)

Harvard: Assistant Dean for Community Engagement, Equity, and Belonging (new person in 2022)

Penn: Associate Dean for Equity & Justice/Chief DEI Advisor (position created in 2019)

Cornell: Associate Dean for DEI (position created in 2022)

Stanford: Associate Dean for DEI (new person in 2021, who left in 2023; see chapter 9)

Duke: Associate Dean for DEI (position created in 2023)

Northwestern: Associate Dean of DEI (interim person appointed in 2022)

NYU School of Law: Assistant Dean for Diversity and Inclusion (new person in 2019)

Georgetown: Associate Dean for DEI (new person in 2021, one of the lawyers who defended Michigan's affirmative action in *Grutter v. Bollinger*)

Boston University: Associate Dean for Equity, Justice and Engagement (position created in 2018)

Vanderbilt: Associate Dean and Robert Belton Director of
  Diversity, Equity & Community (position created in 2020)
University of Southern California: Associate Dean for Student
  Affairs, Diversity, Inclusion and Belonging (position
  created in 2021)

Public

University of Virginia: Assistant Dean for Diversity, Equity and
  Belonging (position created in 2021)
UCLA: Assistant Dean for DEI Initiatives (new person in 2022)
Washington University in St. Louis: Assistant Dean of DEI
  (new person in 2022)
University of Florida: Assistant Dean for Inclusion (position
  created 2018)
University of Minnesota: Assistant Dean of DEI (position
  created in 2022)

One curiosity I've noticed in looking at these upper-echelon diversity officers is that before about 2018, they were made up of people of varying backgrounds and identities, including white men. Now they're almost exclusively black and mostly women.

In any event, the dramatic increase in noninstructional staff has driven tuition higher for decades, without benefiting students. That is, campus climate surveys show that students' satisfaction with their college experience generally, and with campus diversity specifically, doesn't correlate with the number of administrators, let alone the size of DEI offices.

As Jay Greene, one of the authors of that 2021 survey, has pointed out, "the real danger of hiring so many staff who don't engage in teaching or research isn't the expense but how it corrupts the core mission of higher education." Universities no longer see their role as facilitating an open search for the truth or, in the case of law schools, producing skilled lawyers and the furtherance of the rule of law. Instead, they employ an army of educrats "who either distract from that mission by providing therapeutic coddling to students or actively prevent truth-seeking by enforcing an ideological orthodoxy."[14]

The growth of administrative staff, especially of the DEI variety, subverts the traditional law school missions. Providing students with staff to organize their social lives and hold their hands while they "process" the traumas of unwelcome ideas infantilizes the students, who should be training for serious challenges in the legal workplace and public square. Instead, DEI officers enforce narrow ideological perspectives through orientations, trainings, and other programs, all to the detriment of the free intellectual inquiry that students need to become better lawyers. It also takes power away from faculty who are supposed to be instilling professional and academic norms and gives it to political commissars who have little regard for the traditional mission of legal education.

---

14. Jay P. Greene, "Administrative Bloat at Universities Raises Costs Without Helping Students," *Daily Signal*, August 24, 2021.

CHAPTER 6

How a Pyrrhic Victory Revealed That the Game Is Rigged

On April 15, 2022, FIRE put out a cheeky statement titled "Georgetown's Investigation of a Single Tweet Taking Longer than 12 Round-Trips to the Moon," invoking assorted comparisons to the 74 days I'd been in purgatory at that point. "What do the presidency of William Henry Harrison, the complete voyage of the *Mayflower*, and the gestation period of Georgetown University's mascot have in common? They're all shorter than the time it's taking Georgetown to investigate a 45-word tweet."

Twitter was also abuzz pointing out time-related perversities. Lawyer Ted Frank began noting after every Georgetown basketball loss that the team had been cursed ever since the university administration had put me under the spotlight. Already on a seven-game losing streak when I tweeted, the Hoyas did not win again the rest of the season, a total of 21 losses.

By the time exams ended in mid-May, the farcical "investigation" was approaching its four-month mark. I was starting to get plaudits all over the place for just "hanging in there" and taking the high road by not publicly attacking Georgetown's insanity and Dean Treanor's pusillanimity. It was a low bar, but I was happy to take my counsel's advice and get kudos for relative restraint.

Georgetown Law held its commencement ceremony on May 22. A week later, while I was visiting my dad in Toronto, I got a note that Treanor wanted to meet with me. It would again be over Zoom because of the continuing Covid mania—in June 2022! And so, at 1:00 p.m. on

June 2, I clicked on the link and opened the *Brady Bunch* window to reveal Treanor, Barnett, and Brooks.

It was a short meeting. Dean Treanor informed me that although both the IDEAA and HR had found that my comments had made a "significant negative impact on the Georgetown Law community," they were making no findings regarding whether I had violated university policies because I hadn't been an employee when I tweeted. Accordingly, I was being reinstated and would start work the next day, subject to certain "expectations," which Treanor presented in a letter that you can read in the appendix.

In other words, it had taken two university bureaucracies, plus untold billable Big Law hours, more than four months to determine that the policies under which I was being investigated didn't apply to me. This was an obvious attempt to split the baby, castigating me for my political incorrectness while allowing me to keep my job. I was guilty but let out of academic jail on a technicality. Long live due process—or rather, long live the public and private pressure campaigns that made the cost of firing me too high to bear even for those weaselly educrats.

I felt relieved—not fully vindicated but relieved that I could finally get to work. I celebrated the technical victory in the pages of the *Wall Street Journal*, saying that

I'm confident that even without the jurisdictional technicality, I would've prevailed. After all, Georgetown's Speech and Expression Policy provides that the "University is committed to free and open inquiry, deliberation and debate in all matters, and the untrammeled verbal and nonverbal expression of ideas." There's an exception for harassment, of course, but I wasn't harassing anyone except possibly Mr. Biden.

In any case, I look forward to teaching and engaging in a host of activities relating to constitutional education and originalism. As befitting a center for the Constitution, all students and participants in my programs can expect to be accorded the right to think and speak freely and to be treated equally. A diversity of ideas will be most welcome.

After submitting that piece, I had a happy-hour drink—a Negroni, symbolic of the trip to Sicily that I'd be taking with my family in two weeks—took my son to soccer practice, had a relaxing family dinner, and played tennis. As I concluded in my op-ed, it was "a new day."

Except it wasn't, not really. A couple of things still sat uneasily with me. The first was Treanor's public statement on June 2 about the resolution of my case, in which he framed the question as a conflict between two principles: (1) the Law Center's "dedication to speech and expression" and (2) its dedication to "building a culture of equity and inclusion." He quoted Georgetown's Speech and Expression Policy—"The freedom to debate and discuss the merits of competing ideas does not mean that individuals may say whatever they wish, wherever they wish"— noting that it doesn't supersede harassment or professional conduct policies. After running through a discussion similar to what was in his letter to me, he concluded, "I am deeply aware of the pain this incident has given rise to in our campus community," and said that while the law school is "committed to preserving and protecting the right of free and open inquiry, deliberation, and debate," it has "an equally compelling obligation to foster a campus community that is free from bias, and in which every member is treated with respect and courtesy."

Worryingly, Treanor didn't quote or discuss the part of the speech policy that says, "Deliberation or debate may not be suppressed because the ideas put forth are thought by some or even by most members of the University community to be offensive, unwise, immoral, or ill conceived." Nor did he explain how I had failed to treat any member of the community with respect. Whatever, I thought. This progressive doublespeak is what I signed up for when I decided to go into academia. If people want to protest me for imagined or manufactured slights, have at it.

But then, later that afternoon, while I was writing my *Wall Street Journal* piece, the IDEAA's investigatory report landed in my inbox. It was ten pages of turgid prose that reiterated the "significant negative impact" line and concluded with a recommendation that Treanor take "appropriate corrective measures." I skimmed it but didn't have time—

and was too mentally and emotionally exhausted—to fully digest it. Now that the ordeal was over, the legalistic details could wait.

In the sober light of morning, however, as I read the report closely, it quickly became clear that little was over except my administrative leave. The law school administration was setting me up for a fall: it appeared that the next time I said something—while speaking, writing, or teaching—that someone (anyone) claimed was offensive, I'd be back in kangaroo court.

I continued studying the IDEAA report; the HR report, which I was told was materially similar but with a focus on "unprofessional conduct," was not released to me, per university policy. In talking to Randy, my counsel, Jesse, and my wife, Kristin (a better lawyer than all of us), it became clear that my position at Georgetown was untenable. By Saturday midday, I knew that I would have to resign. It was both a terrifying and a liberating realization.

Moreover, in light of the illiberal denouement that betrayed deep injustice, it would have to be what lawyers call a "noisy withdrawal," using the spotlight I'd been given to show that all was not right at Georgetown Law even if the dean had "reinstated" me.

Deciding to quit the job that I'd fought so hard to keep was another surreal experience. The saga was over, the farce had ended, and I was out of purgatory, yet I would never be able to live the life I had been expecting to when I'd announced that I was leaving Cato, when Georgetown had celebrated my hiring. It was certainly not a hellacious period like the first days after my tweet, but it was a fast-moving, uncertain time that I would have to handle nearly perfectly to emerge into—if not quite heaven—a psychologically and professionally comfortable situation.

Over that June 4–5 weekend, I did two things: (1) put together my resignation letter and (2) found another job. The letter is possibly my best-ever lawyering, certainly outside the world of Supreme Court amicus briefs. It detailed how Dean Treanor had implicitly repealed Georgetown's vaunted free-speech policy.

First, the IDEAA report speciously found that my tweet had made a "significant negative impact," requiring "appropriate corrective measures" to address my "objectively offensive comments and to prevent the recurrence of offensive conduct based on race, gender, and sex." Although my tweet had been inartful, as I'd admitted many times, its meaning that I considered all potential candidates to be less qualified than my preferred pick is clear. Only those acting in bad faith would misconstrue what I had said to suggest otherwise.

Second, any harm or "negative impact" had been created by those seeking to get me fired. I deleted my tweet well before any student was likely to learn of it. Screen captures were then disseminated by others seeking to settle ideological scores. It was they, not I, who intentionally and knowingly caused distress to any member of the Georgetown community who later came to learn of the tweet. It is they, not I, who are morally culpable for any such resulting harm.

Third, under the reasoning of the IDEAA report, none of that analysis even mattered. As the report put it, "The University's anti-harassment policy does not require that a respondent intend to denigrate or show hostility or aversion to individuals based on a protected status. Instead, the Policy requires consideration of the 'purpose or effect' of a respondent's conduct." The mere fact that many people were offended, or claimed to be, was enough for me to have violated the relevant policies. Although there was no formal finding of a violation because I hadn't been subject to the policies when I had tweeted, so long as someone claims that a statement "denigrates" or "show[s] hostility or aversion" to a protected class, that's enough to constitute a violation of Georgetown antidiscrimination rules. Georgetown has thus adopted what constitutional law describes as an impermissible "heckler's veto."

Fourth, regardless of the "effect" of what I had tweeted, the IDEAA report found that "if [I] were to make another, similar or more serious remark as a Georgetown employee, a hostile environment based on race, gender, and sex likely would be created." On this theory, all sorts of comments that someone—anyone—could find offensive would subject me to disciplinary action.

And not only would faculty now be subject to discipline for subjective perceptions of offense, but that standard was being applied unevenly, with many left-wing faculty crazies not being "investigated" for various inflammatory statements in recent years and even months. (Not that they should've been, but it's free speech for thee and not for me.) I also gave examples of not-very-hypothetical scenarios that would subject me to renewed investigation and discipline.

You Cancel Me? I Cancel You

It was a slow-motion firing, one in which I would not participate. You can read the full letter in the appendix, but I concluded thus:

> It's all well and good to adopt free-speech policies that track the gold standard, the University of Chicago Principles of Freedom of Expression— and more broadly that same university's 1967 Kalven Report, which states that "the neutrality of the university . . . arises out of respect for free inquiry and the obligation to cherish a diversity of viewpoints"— indeed, it's essential. But it's not enough. If university administrators aren't willing to stand up to left-wing activists, Georgetown's enacted free speech and expression policy is a mere "pixel barrier."
>
> What's worse, the problem isn't limited to fearful administrators. The proliferation of IDEAA-style offices (more typically styled Diversity, Equity, and Inclusion) enforce an orthodoxy that stifles intellectual diversity, undermines equal opportunity, and excludes dissenting voices. Even a stalwart T-14 law school dean bucks these bureaucrats at his peril.
>
> Since I accepted your offer of employment, I've come to learn that Georgetown is by no means a follower in these trends. Instead, it's a leader. In contrast to the Jesuitical values that you're fond of reciting, this institution no longer stands for tolerance, respect, good faith, self-reflective learning, and generous service to others.
>
> On the GULC website it reads: "Our motto 'Law is but the means, justice is the end' sums up the core commitment of Georgetown Law." But your and IDEAA's treatment of me suggests that neither the due process of law nor justice actually prevails.
>
> I cannot again subject my family to the public attacks on my character and livelihood that you and IDEAA have now made foreseeable, indeed inevitable. As a result of the hostile work environment that you and they have created, I have no choice but to resign.

What Georgetown subjected me to, what it would've subjected me to if I'd stayed, is a heckler's veto, one that would lead to a Star Chamber. "Live not by lies," warned Aleksander Solzhenitsyn, in what has become my mantra. "Let the lie come into the world, let it even triumph. But not through me." I couldn't live that way, so I made a noisy exit that drew the nation's attention.

At the same time as I was pulling together that letter with clear-eyed resolve, I was hastening to figure out my next career steps. With two little boys and twins on the way, Kristin and I couldn't afford not to have my next gainful employment secured. It wasn't a gut-wrenching feeling like during those initial four days of hell, when I had despaired that I had blown up my entire life with one badly phrased tweet, but I couldn't dillydally. After the professional roller coaster I'd just been on, I'd need some time off before starting the next job. But I also needed the certainty of knowing where I'd end up once I'd caught my breath.

During my purgatory I'd been approached by various people and organizations offering help in that department. Just as I was gratified to see friends and allies support me publicly and privately in pushing back against cancellation, I was heartened to find that however things turned out, I'd have options.

Later in my purgatory, I began receiving queries about permanent jobs "in case Georgetown doesn't work out." I never pursued anything, thanking the interlocutor but saying that it was premature and that I'd definitely keep the opportunity in mind if and when the time came. All of that was premature because, until I processed the IDEAA report, I fully intended to stick with the job I'd been hired for. But once I decided I couldn't stick with that job, I quickly knew what I wanted to do.

I called my old friend Jim Copland at the Manhattan Institute. We'd collaborated professionally over the years but more than that simply jibed as kindred spirits in free-market public interest law and punditry. I didn't have to talk to Jim for long before he cut me off and said, "I totally get it. Let me talk to some people, and we'll get back to you." Within 48 hours of that call, less than 36 hours after I had spoken with Reihan Salam (the president) and Ilana Golant (then the executive vice president), MI put together an offer. That was all over the course of that weekend, for which

I'm eternally grateful. All of us were excited. It was a great fit—and remains so two years later.

Crucially, the employment deal came together before Monday morning, when I was planning to submit my resignation letter. So when I sent Treanor the letter, at 8:00 a.m. sharp on June 6—coincidentally the anniversary of D-Day—it was with the comfort of knowing that my professional future and, more importantly, my family were secure. Forty-five minutes later, a shorter version of the letter went live on the *Wall Street Journal* website—which piece I had finalized the night before. And we were off to the media races!

Controlling the Narrative

Over the next five days, I did more than 25 TV, radio, and podcast interviews, explaining my decision and what I'd learned about the state of American higher education and cancel culture. Most notably, the day after my resignation, I broke the news of my move to the Manhattan Institute live on Tucker Carlson's show on Fox News. "Weren't they embarrassed to be investigating you for expressing an entirely mainstream position on Twitter?" Tucker asked.

"There are a lot of cowardly administrators who refuse to stand up to the woke mob, who insist that there's no deviation from a progressive orthodoxy," I replied. "I could not stay at a place where if I'm commenting on a Supreme Court opinion or teaching a class and someone says they're uncomfortable or claims they're offended, all of a sudden I'm back in the Star Chamber."

"Yeah, that's the end of a great American institution after hundreds of years, and it's bigger than even your particular case and it says something really ominous," he concluded.

But don't take my or Tucker's word for it. Cornell law professor William Jacobson, the founder of the influential law website Legal Insurrection, was later quoted as saying that my case showed that "Diversity, Equity, and Inclusion bureaucracies are growing in size and power at almost every major university. . . . they serve as ideological commissars of a critical-race focused viewpoint." He went on to say that "the DEI focus is not on the rights of the speaker (Shapiro) but on the sensitivities of the listeners (students). This puts the power to control speech and expression in the hands of the most vocal complainers, and reverses our historical norms as to free speech."

DePauw University media studies professor Jeffrey McCall likewise lamented the state of free speech on college campuses, using the term *bureaucratic* to describe the Georgetown affair. "While Shapiro wasn't technically disciplined, the chilling effect in play here clearly would have made it difficult or even impossible for him to carry out his duties. In a sense, Georgetown has turned its back on its own free expression guidelines, supporting an atmosphere in which shrill voices stifle people with whom they disagree." And McCall would know: DePauw finished dead last in FIRE's 2021 free-speech rankings and remained in the bottom 25 in 2022 (before rising to the top 50 the following year by reforming its policies and launching free-speech initiatives). He went on to say that "universities can hardly go around shutting up any faculty member or student who says something 'inartful.' It is contrary to free expression philosophy on one level, but also quite impractical on another. . . . Georgetown, and other universities that seek to stifle robust discussion, are reducing the free expression environment of the academy to only approved dogmas or unserious topics."

I was finally in control of the media cycle, creating my own narrative! The two workweeks after I resigned were by far the most professional fun I'd had in quite some time.

I was finally a free man, free to speak my mind and liberated from the shackles of a toxic institution. A few days after my resignation, when I attended a special preopening reception at the spectacular and powerful new Victims of Communism Museum in downtown Washington, I theatrically crossed out the Georgetown affiliation on my name tag and wrote in "Free Man."

CHAPTER 7

The New Activism Is Incompatible with the Rule of Law

Alas, neither my Georgetown saga nor the disruption of my event at UC Hastings was an isolated incident or a freakish exception to law-school life these days. Repeated incidents at top law schools show how equity acolytes make it impossible for these institutions to fulfill their purpose of creating fair-minded, critically insightful lawyers and political leaders. The axioms of the new activist class fatally undermine the assumptions that make the rule of law possible, demanding that we assume that all inequities are invariably the result of malice. They refuse all compromise, stoke moral panics, and create chilling effects for moderates of goodwill. Finally, of course, they make life incredibly difficult for any student or faculty member who unwittingly steps out of line.

Georgetown Law itself had had a disturbing "scandal" less than a year before my tweet that was an eerie premonition of what I would experience. I had heard about the episode but hadn't treated it as the "Abandon all hope, ye who enter here" warning I should have.

In March 2021, two adjunct law professors, Sandra Sellers and David Batson, suddenly found themselves no longer employed by Georgetown after clips of a Zoom from the previous month were shared on social media. In the video, which was recorded after students had left the meeting and the profs thought they were having a private conversation, Sellers expressed concerns about black students' performance in their class: "I hate to say this. I end up having this, you know, angst, every semester that a lot of my lower ones are blacks. Happens almost every semester.

And it's like, oh, come on. You get some really good ones. But there are also usually some that are just plain at the bottom. It drives me crazy." Batson replied with a noncommittal "Mmhmm."

The remarks are somewhat ambiguous. What does she think is causing the disparate racial results? Admissions policies? First-year legal writing courses? Her own teaching methods? Clarifying the tangled "candid" video would have been a helpful step, but none of those questions came up before the administration had a meltdown. An assumption of bad faith was embraced so quickly that the truth didn't have a chance to come out. A student discovered the recording on the night of Sunday, March 7, reported it to administrators the next morning, and posted it on Twitter on Wednesday evening. Less than three hours later, Dean Treanor issued a statement titled "Responding to Reprehensible Statements in Our Community," saying he "found the conduct to be abhorrent," that it "has no place in our educational community," and that he had asked the IDEAA (of course) to investigate because "there is no place for bias in our grading process." The next day, Sellers attempted to resign but was instead fired. Batson was placed on leave and resigned days later. Both also issued self-flagellating letters of apology, but that wasn't enough for the woke mob.

The Black Law Students Association had urged the administration to fire Sellers, demand a public apology from Batson, improve its "subjective grading system," audit "past grading and student evaluations," and hire more black professors. More than 50 student organizations had signed on, as had nearly 800 students and 700 alumni. Georgetown Law's student government issued a statement supporting BLSA's requests. On March 15, Treanor sent a follow-up email saying that the school would continue "our work to address the many structural issues of racism reflected in this painful incident, including explicit and implicit bias, bystander responsibility, and the need for more comprehensive anti-bias training." We know all this from the breathless reporting and flame-fanning of none other than *Slate*'s Mark Joseph Stern, who also criticized Treanor for not acting quickly enough against the professors.

Neither Sellers nor Batson should've been punished under Georgetown's own protective speech policy, which I quoted in detail in chapter 3. You'd think that the questions of whether performance gaps exist between students of different racial groups and what might cause them would be one of intense interest to any educational institution. At Georgetown, alas—and Georgetown is by no means unique—these questions are to be swept under the rug and never raised because of the politically inconvenient answers one might get. After all, one might find that racial preferences in admissions cause a "mismatch" whereby members of racial minorities cluster disproportionately toward the bottom in academic achievement at selective institutions. So we see the knock-on effect of illiberal policies: treating applicants differently based on race leads to undermining other liberal principles such as due process and free speech. And everyone has to pretend that it's all about dismantling white supremacy.

As FIRE's Robert Shibley pointed out, to the minimal extent that Georgetown explained its reasoning for punishing Sellers and Batson, the concern appears to be that their comments (or lack thereof) indicated that they might have discriminated against black students in grading. But the adjuncts were *lamenting* black students' underachievement, not celebrating it. Batson expressed frustration that black students are overrepresented among those with lower grades, and Sellers seemed to agree. Most people would not, I think, jump to the conclusion that the professors' grading was biased, but a baseline axiom of the New Left is Ibram Kendi's contention that all disparate results must be due to racism. The very fact that there was a disparity proved that there must be unconscious bias at work.

If Treanor really believed that the two professors might have engaged in grading discrimination, he could've followed through on an investigation into "unconscious" bias before issuing condemnations. But he was more interested in defenestrating those who reveal inconvenient truths than defending free speech or even following his own rules.

We're Number One?

Georgetown isn't the only school where panic and retrenchment are the default responses to heterodox ideas. Yale Law School is supposed to represent the pinnacle of American legal education and indeed has been at the top of the *U.S. News & World Report* law school rankings since their inception. Without getting into an elitist food fight, it's an empirical fact that Yale produces the most law professors, Supreme Court clerks, and other legal "influencers" per capita. It's a small school—about 600 students, a third the size of Harvard and a quarter the size of Georgetown—but one that punches far above its weight in the nation's legal and political life.

I've already mentioned the March 2022 disruption, when more than 100 students shouted down a Federalist Society panel designed to show how a progressive atheist and conservative Christian could agree on certain things and promote civil discourse. Monica Miller of the American Humanist Association and Kristen Waggoner of the Alliance Defending Freedom had taken the same side in a 2021 Supreme Court case that near-unanimously upheld legal remedies for on-campus First Amendment violations. The incident stands out not just as another heckling campus mob but because of how it illustrates several truths: radicals will never accept compromise, administrators will bend over backward to try to make one anyway, and the tragic result is that many ambivalent students will be swept up into the moral panic, bullied by activists and unguided by school officials. It's a study in how a society is radicalized.

Professor Kate Stith, a former acting dean and no conservative, started to introduce Waggoner but couldn't even finish before protesters swarmed to their feet, yelling and waving signs criticizing the Alliance Defending Freedom. ADF is a nonprofit that focuses on religious liberty issues and has won several Supreme Court cases, most famously *Masterpiece Cakeshop v. Colorado Civil Rights Commission* in 2018 and, five years later, the follow-on *303 Creative v. Elenis*. It has been targeted ever since being labeled a "hate group" by the Southern Poverty Law Center.

The vehemence of the protesters' response included attempts to provoke other attendees. One protester yelled at a Federalist Society member that she would "literally fight you, bitch!" As the melee escalated, Stith invoked Yale's policies, which disallow any protest that "interferes with speakers' ability to be heard and of community members opportunity to listen." The jeering response finally pushed Stith's temper to the breaking point. She told the students to "grow up" and warned them that if they continued in this manner, "I'm going to have to ask you to leave or help you leave."

Eventually, the protesters left, but continued to sing, stomp, and shout. The noise was so loud that "it disrupted nearby classes, exams, and faculty meetings," the *Washington Free Beacon* reported. There was a danger of physical escalation, particularly because the protesters blocked the only exit and students said the crowd tried to grab them as they left. Law enforcement officers ultimately escorted these departing students, and the panelists, out of the building.

Surely, however, this protest represented only a small, intransigent group on the broader campus? Not so. In the two days after the panel, more than 400 students, representing 60 percent of the student body, signed a letter supporting the "peaceful" protesters. "The danger of police violence in this country is intensified against Black LGBTQ people, and particularly Black trans people," the letter read. "Even with all of the privilege afforded to us at YLS, the decision to allow police officers in as a response to the protest put YLS' queer student body at risk of harm." The letter also claimed that the Federalist Society had "profoundly undermined our community's values of equity and inclusivity."

Free Beacon writer Aaron Sibarium noted that, as with the Georgetown student letter condemning me, the Yale letter's long list of signatures reflected social pressure as much as genuine consensus. His reporting revealed attempts to shame anyone who didn't condemn the event. "It feels wild to me that we're at this point in history and some folks are still not immediately signing a letter like this," one student wrote to her class chat. Merely attending the event was likened to endorsing bigotry. Indeed, those coming to watch the panel found flyers denouncing their attendance. Just *hearing* the expression of wrongthink makes you a bigot.

Even Miller received an open letter as part of a broader shaming campaign. She said she was startled by the student response, not least because the case at issue was a victory for civil rights groups. "A lot of our clients are LGBT," Miller explained. "If that [lower-court ruling foreclosing lawsuits that couldn't show economic harm] stood, and LGBT rights were violated in the South, we wouldn't be able to help them." She also recognized the concerning implications for the next generation of lawyers: "If you can't talk to your opponents, you can't be an effective advocate." Several progressive groups, including the ACLU, had also filed briefs supporting ADF's client.

David Lat, a mild-mannered Yale Law alum who chronicles the legal profession at his *Original Jurisdiction* Substack (and happens to be gay), criticized Dean Gerken for neither confronting the protesters nor even issuing an immediate statement as Hastings's chancellor did in my case. Indeed, it would take Gerken more than two weeks to issue a hand-waving statement that let the disrupters off with a warning. Her message reveals abundant leadership failures, ones that are reflected in law schools across the country that don't get the same attention as Yale. "Under the University's free expression policy, student groups have every right to invite speakers to campus, and others have every right to voice opposition," she began after some throat-clearing. "Because unfettered debate is essential to our mission, we allow people to speak even when their speech is flatly inconsistent with our core values."

Okay, but recall that the panel didn't (and wasn't expected to) showcase any controversial speech, but instead covered an 8–1 Supreme Court ruling that had brought together speakers from opposite ends of the ideological spectrum. So the subject of the event at issue, and the speakers' views, far from being "flatly inconsistent with [Yale Law's] core values," supported their "commitment to free speech." Her message only grew more deceptive from there:

> In accordance with the University's free expression policy, which *includes a three-warning protocol,* those protesting exited the room after the first warning, and the event went forward. Had the protestors shut down the event, our course of action would have been straightforward—the offending students without question would have been subject to discipline. *Although the students complied with University policies inside the event,* several students engaged in rude and insulting behavior as the event began; a number made excessive noise in our hallways that interfered with several events taking place; and some refused to listen to our staff.

I've italicized the particularly curious parts. Yale's policy has since been revised, but as David Lat pointed out, at the time there was no three-strikes aspect. Instead, there were three conditions on the exercise of free speech; violation of *any* of them was all that was required, not violation of *all* of them. The policy actually read "exercise of free expression on campus is subject to three general conditions: 1) access to a university event or facility may not be blocked; 2) a university event, activity, or its regular or essential operations may not be disrupted; and 3) safety may not be compromised."

Note the shell game Gerken plays with the conditions. She takes the condition that "a university event . . . may not be disrupted" and interprets this as meaning "may not be shut down by students." The actual text says that a complete shutdown, like what happened to me at UC Hastings, is not required for there to be a violation, since the policy continues to explain that examples of "disrupting" an event include "Holding up signs in a manner that obstructs the view of those attempting to watch an event or speaker."

As recounted by Lat, the March 2022 protesters broke all of these conditions.

> The protesters disrupted not just the Fed Soc talk, "a university event," but also the "regular operations" of YLS, including multiple classes and a faculty meeting (which actually was "shut down," since it had to be moved to Zoom). The protesters interfered with both "a speaker's ability to speak," before they left Room 127, and the "attendees' ability to listen and hear," after they repaired to the hallway. Finally, the protesters blocked the main hallway of the Sterling Law Building. There is ample evidence, including audio recordings, video recordings, and eyewitness testimony, to support all of this.[1]

Gerken in effect rewrote the policy by giving protesters two free disruptions and then nullifying any violation if part of the disrupted event was allowed to proceed. And it's not as though administrators heard about the commotion only later. Ellen Cosgrove, the associate dean for student affairs, whom I've known since she was dean of students during my time at the University of Chicago Law School and who was both nice

---

1. See David Lat, "Yale Law Dean Heather Gerken Speaks Out About the March 10 Protest," *Original Jurisdiction*, March 29, 2022.

and scrupulously fair then, was present for the entire panel. Despite Yale's clear policy, Cosgrove failed to support Stith or confront any of the protesters.

Gerken halfheartedly tried to stiffen her nonpunishment decision with mild condemnation and a warning:

> This behavior was unacceptable; at a minimum it violated the norms of this Law School. This is an institution of higher learning, not a town square, and no one should interfere with others' efforts to carry on activities on campus. YLS is a professional school, and this is not how lawyers interact. We are also a community that respects our faculty and staff who have devoted their lives to helping students. Professor Kate Stith, Dean Mike Thompson, and other members of the staff should not have been treated as they were. I expect far more from our students, and I want to state unequivocally that this cannot happen again. . . .
>
> As Dean, I am deeply committed to our free speech policies and the values they safeguard. I will protect free speech without fear or favor.

That's very good as far as it goes, and I particularly enjoyed the "this is not how lawyers interact" bit, but alas, Gerken couldn't leave well enough alone. Her missive continued to complain that she'd had to say anything at all. How dare anyone ask leaders to lead?

> But I have waited to write you because it is our conversations as a community that matter most. In our statement-hungry culture, university leaders are constantly asked to be referees, encouraging our students to appeal to a higher authority rather than to engage with one another and tempting outsiders to enlist academic institutions in their own political agendas. Statements are expected instantly from institutions whose core values include deliberation and due process—values that are essential where, as here, the reporting has been so contradictory.

So she explained away the delay in responding—again unlike at UC Hastings, where Dean Faigman had taken less than 24 hours—by complaining about a "statement-hungry culture." But it wasn't a case where a mob, of whatever ideological stripe, had demanded that virtue be signaled. Nobody had asked that Dean Gerken take a partisan position, just ensure that the ground rules of debate were followed. Observers would naturally parse whatever she said for its deeper meaning, but that's because what the leader of the nation's foremost institution of legal education says about the disruption of a discussion of important constitutional values matters. Most people were looking for her "not to take sides but to articulate [Yale Law's] mission [of truth-seeking, free speech, and civil discourse] with clarity" (to further quote her latest statement). Instead, we got a master class in sophistry that skewed the facts of what had happened, misstated the applicable policies, and redirected blame for Yale's pathologies to outside agitators.

Indeed, many commentators chided Gerken for a campus culture that was spiraling out of control; the panel disruption was just the latest of several speech-related scandals from that school year alone. Most notoriously, in September 2021, administrators spent weeks pushing a student to apologize for jokingly referring to his apartment as a "trap house" in a party invitation.

We've seen what impact the new activism has on liberal teachers and conservative speakers alike, but as you might expect, the harshest effects of the moral panic fall on heterodox students who don't have the power to speak up for themselves. The backlash to the "trap house" email is a particularly startling example of how administrators are willing to use brutally exclusive tactics in pursuit of "inclusion."[2]

The student's Federalist Society membership was part of what made the email "triggering," school officials told the student. Trent Colbert, who is part Cherokee and also a member of the Native American Law Students Association (NALSA), had invited classmates to a party the two groups were hosting. "We will be christening our very own (soon to be) world-renowned NALSA Trap House . . . by throwing a Constitution Day

2. For a full description of this bizarre story, see Aaron Sibarium, "A Yale Law Student Sent a Lighthearted Email Inviting Classmates to His 'Trap House.' The School Is Now Calling Him to Account," *Washington Free Beacon*, October 13, 2021 (also providing the quotes published here).

bash in collaboration with FedSoc," Colbert wrote on the NALSA listserv. The party would thus serve "basic-bitch-American-themed snacks" such as "Popeye's chicken" and "apple pie."

The lighthearted invite was quickly shared to an online forum for all second-year students, several of whom alleged that the reference to a "trap house" suggested that this would be a blackface party. "I guess celebrating whiteness wasn't enough," the BLSA president, Marina Edwards, wrote there. "Y'all had to upgrade to cosplay/black face." She also threw in a critique of the Fed Soc cosponsorship, because the group "has historically supported anti-Black rhetoric." Nobody defended Colbert publicly, though one classmate posted an *Atlantic* article called "The New Puritans." A friend of Colbert's later said that there had been "a very 'emperor's new clothes' vibe—when someone says something is offensive, everyone else has to play along."

Trap house is apparently a term from left-wing pop culture. While it used to refer only to inner-city crack dens, it has expanded to become generic slang for a place where young people party—that's how Urban Dictionary defines it—and it was what Colbert had been lightheartedly calling the house where he was living for some time. I first heard of the phrase from the socialist podcast *Chapo Trap House*, which has received favorable treatment in a host of media outlets from the *New York Times* on down. For what it's worth, the podcast's three hosts are all white men. While it's unlikely that university administrators would have the same familiarity with slang that an internet-savvy political-nerd student would, such questions could have been resolved with an investigation. What happened instead was an inquisition. The People had been offended, so Colbert's true meaning was completely irrelevant.

Twelve hours after Colbert emailed his invite, the office of student affairs asked Colbert to come in and discuss the many complaints it had received that alleged harassment and discrimination. Colbert had the presence of mind to record the meeting—which some commentators would decry, but it ultimately saved him. (Connecticut is a "one-party consent" state for recording in-person conversations, so he didn't need anyone's permission to do so.) Associate Dean Cosgrove and DEI director Yaseen Eldik told Colbert that the word *trap* connotes blackface, hip-hop, and crack use. It was thus alarming that those "triggering associations,"

Eldik said, were combined with "the fried chicken reference," because it "is often used to undermine arguments that structural and systemic racism has contributed to racial health disparities in the U.S."

Colbert's Federalist Society membership had "triggered" his fellow students, said Eldik, who'd previously worked in the Obama White House's Office of Faith-Based and Neighborhood Partnerships. They were triggered because they "already feel like Fed Soc belongs to political affiliations that are oppressive to certain communities," he said. "That of course obviously includes the LGBTQIA community and black communities and immigrant communities."

Later that day, Cosgrove and Eldik summoned Zack Austin, the Fed Soc president, and accused him, "as a cis/het white man," of putting Colbert up to throwing a party where "people came in blackface to eat some fried chicken while dancing to trap music." Also attending that meeting was Chloe Bush, the administrator responsible for approving student-organization budgets. Subtle. Austin said that he had been pressured to apologize—for what?—and in coming weeks he would face even more hostile actions from those same administrators, including retroactive deauthorization of a retreat, deletion of board members from the chapter website, and other mistreatment, as well as gaslighting about whether anything untoward had happened.

I had to read all that several times when I first came across it. As Sibarium noted, Eldik explicitly stated that the nation's top-ranked law school now regards association with the nation's leading center-right legal organization as a legitimate ground for investigation and potential discipline. Indeed, merely holding certain positions regarding constitutional or statutory interpretation is apparently an example of "oppression." Out of everything I've learned from researching this book, that statement is perhaps the most damning and best crystallized summary of the consequences of the illiberal Left's march through academia.

The 20-minute lecture that Eldik gave Colbert sounds like a parody a right-wing polemicist would write about political correctness run amok. At one point, Yale Law's DEI director suggested that Colbert's race might save him. "As a man of color, there probably isn't as much scrutiny of you as there might be of a white person in the same position," Eldik said. "I just want to acknowledge that there's a complexity to that, too."

(One of Colbert's friends later told David Lat, "That's a frank admission of something that cuts against what we are supposed to believe about equal treatment under the law.") But at least one complaint alleged that Colbert's email "was a form of discrimination," while others alleged "harassment" based on how "psychically harmful" it had been. As in my case, if poorly chosen words or a joke that falls flat constitutes "harm" and "harassment," those concepts don't mean much anymore—and we're living in a society where there really isn't much to worry about in terms of racial discrimination.

That dynamic illustrates how DEI offices have broadened certain terms not to promote equal opportunity or a welcoming environment but to enforce progressive ideology, Sibarium noted in his reporting on the situation. He continued:

> That concept creep has been enforced by bureaucratic self-interest. Anti-discrimination officers have an incentive to address grievances in heavy-handed, public ways, a fact the audio drives home. When the student suggested letting his peers reach out to him individually to discuss their feelings about the email, Eldik responded: "I don't want to make our office look like an ineffective source of resolution."

Throughout the initial meeting and a conversation the next day, Cosgrove and Eldik suggested that Colbert needed to apologize to avoid hurting his career, such as trouble with the bar exam's "character and fitness" aspect. That review checks would-be lawyers' suitability to join the profession. State bars typically ask law schools whether they're aware of any negative information about applicants that could detract from their ability to be honorable officers of the court, regardless of whether any formal discipline was involved.

"I worry about this leaning over your reputation as a person," Eldik added. The best way to "make this go away" would be to apologize to the students who complained, led by BLSA. He conveyed the thinly veiled threat that "there's a bar you have to take. . . . So we think it's really important to give you a 360 view."

Colbert resisted, saying that at this small school, he'd prefer to have face-to-face discussions with classmates, but Eldik still drafted an apology, in accordance with his reasoning that, as he told Colbert, "you as a person want some character-driven rehabilitation." The draft apology expressed remorse for "any harm, trauma, or upset" the party invite might have caused. "I know I must learn more and grow," it concluded, "and I will actively educate myself so I can do better."

Colbert didn't issue the apology, instead telling his classmates that he was happy to talk to anybody still offended. By that point, Cosgrove and Eldik had already emailed the entire second-year class to besmirch him, writing that "an invitation was recently circulated containing pejorative and racist language. We condemn this in the strongest possible terms [and] are working on addressing this." Gerken approved the email.

Thankfully, "addressing this" didn't involve formal punishment, largely because Colbert's recordings shamed Yale. In a third meeting nearly a month after the initial "trap house" email, Cosgrove and Eldik assured Colbert that they wouldn't put anything into his file that might pose a problem for the bar. "You may have been confused," Eldik concluded.

Yale ultimately did damage control by releasing a statement saying that "no student is investigated or sanctioned for protected speech." "At no time was any disciplinary investigation launched or disciplinary action taken in this matter," it continued. "While any person may report concerns about a lawyers' character and fitness to the bar, the law school has a longstanding policy of reporting only formal disciplinary action to the Bar Association."

DEI or Bust?

Perhaps the most common justification presented for academic DEI structures and initiatives is that they exist to protect vulnerable students. The trap-house episode put Yale Law's bureaucracy in the spotlight, drawing broad criticism for chilling speech. It also belied the idea that campus DEI offices are a resource for all students that work to celebrate diverse backgrounds and make everyone feel welcome. Behind closed doors, as Sibarium noted, they're less ecumenical than their kumbaya public messaging will admit: the goal isn't to make universities more welcoming but to wield the threat of exclusion against individuals who dare affiliate with disfavored groups. Even Mark Joseph Stern saw the diversicrats as going too far here, acknowledging in his own slanted language the threat to higher education's liberal values that DEI offices represent:

> Even the slightest appearance of retaliation against conservative students for protected speech only bolsters the victimhood mentality that the Federalist Society cultivates in its members. It provides grist for the grievance-industrial complex that drives the conservative legal movement. And it allows the right to depict institutions of learning as indoctrination factories that instill students with woke groupthink. . . .
>
> Law schools should not get involved over student disputes over protected speech. Doing so does not help the speaker, or their critics, or the school itself.

Yale law professor Akhil Amar, a leading constitutional scholar (and a liberal), criticized his own school's administrators for their handling of Trap House–gate. He called them "dishonest, duplicitous, and downright deplorable," adding, perhaps with a hint of irony, that they should apologize.

The panel disruption a few months later showed that it's not just campus administrators who threaten free expression; it's often the students themselves. "If trap house illustrates the students-to-administration problem," a senior member of the Federalist Society said, "this illustrates the students-to-students problem."

The lynchpin in both was Ellen Cosgrove, the dean of students who would retire at the end of the 2021–22 school year, perhaps a bit earlier than she would've liked but no doubt with a generous exit package that had a firm nondisclosure provision. Cosgrove may have been on the outs even before the disrupted panel, as Gerken had apparently promised key stakeholders that she wouldn't be a part of the inner circle for a second term as dean. The disrupted panel was actually the third Cosgrove-related scandal; in November 2021, she, along with Gerken and Eldik, was sued for allegedly retaliating against two students who declined to make "false statements" about Amy Chua, a law professor who had crossed the administration, in a bizarre scenario that became known as Dinner Party–gate. That lawsuit, which the plaintiffs ended up dropping in September 2023, delayed Gerken's renewal as dean—and may have prompted her Trap House apologia.

Meanwhile, Eldik had his own third scandal after he suggested that the *Yale Law Journal* host a diversity trainer. This trainer, Ericka Hart, described herself as a "kinky" sex-ed teacher and according to the *Washington Free Beacon*, "told students that antisemitism is merely a form of antiblackness and suggested that the FBI artificially inflates the number of antisemitic hate crimes." Her comments "shocked members of the predominantly liberal law review [since she] labeled 'perfectionism,' 'objectivity,' 'a sense of urgency,' and 'the written word' as examples of 'white supremacy culture.'"

"Reactions to the training were almost uniformly negative," and "on a scale of 1–10, the most common score was '1.'"[3] A memo from the editors quoted one self-described "very liberal" student as saying that Hart's presentation was "almost like a conservative parody of what antiracism trainings are like." Remarkably, the training was held *the very same day* that Eldik interrogated Colbert. In summer 2022, Eldik's name disappeared from the Student Affairs website; while still employed by the law school, he became an associate director of graduate programs, which isn't a student-facing role.

Not surprisingly, FIRE lists Yale (as a whole, not just the law school) as 234th out of 248 schools in its 2024 free-speech rankings, including 185th for administrative support for free speech and 200th for students' acceptance of shouting down or violently preventing speech with which they disagree. That's even worse than the previous year, when a RealClearEducation analysis showed that Yale has drastically steered away from the free-speech and academic freedom principles it adopted in its vaunted 1974 Woodward Report. Georgetown, meanwhile, came 245th—fourth from last—after having won FIRE's "lifetime censorship award" the previous year and appeared on the "10 Worst" list in 2015, 2017, and 2019.

As we'll see in future chapters, a decade-long growth of diversity of-

---

3. See Aaron Sibarium, "Yale Law Diversity Director at Center of 'Traphouse' Controversy Got an Anti-Semite Invited to the Yale Law Journal," *Washington Free Beacon*, November 2, 2021.

fices laid the kindling that was set ablaze by the George Floyd murder in May 2020, causing all academic institutions to adopt aggressively "antiracist" policies and practices. Seeing themselves as guardians of justice and institutional reform, law schools were at the forefront of this craze and radically reoriented their missions in a social justice direction.

For example, in summer 2020, Northwestern University's Pritzker School of Law held an online training session in which administrators denounced their own alleged racism in ways reminiscent of the Chinese Cultural Revolution. "I'm Jim Speta. And I am a racist," the law school's interim dean wrote at the virtual meeting hosted by Associate Dean of Inclusion and Engagement Shannon Bartlett. Another administrator called herself a "gatekeeper of white supremacy." All followed the ritual self-denunciation with a promise "to do better."

That webinar appears to have been the first thing Northwestern Law had done to show its newfound commitment to "antiracism." One student, who wished to remain anonymous, told the *Free Beacon*'s Sibarium that the school "capitulated to a handful of angry students with Twitter accounts." Another observed, "Prof. Speta is not racist. He is a wonderful man universally loved by students. It makes me sad he was forced to say otherwise." After screenshots of the struggle session went viral, several alumni said they would no longer donate to their alma mater, while four of the eight members of the US Civil Rights Commission asked Education Secretary Betsy DeVos to investigate the law school's admissions of racism. Citing Princeton president Christopher Eisgruber's contemporaneous confession of systemic racism, they requested that DeVos "consider conducting an investigation into the Pritzker School of Law's potentially discriminatory practices."

Moving beyond thought policing to broader illiberal trends, nine student groups at Berkeley Law (known as Boalt Hall before another denaming) began the 2022–23 school year by amending their bylaws to ensure that they'll never invite speakers who support Israel or Zionism. These are groups that purport to represent a large part of the student population—including women, Asian Pacific Americans, students of African and Middle Eastern descent, and the Queer Caucus. Dean Erwin Chemerinsky, a progressive Zionist, noted that he himself would be banned, as would 90 percent of Jewish students.

The problem is that anti-Zionism is itself antisemitic. As Ken Marcus of the Brandeis Center (and former assistant secretary of education for civil rights) has observed, "using 'Zionist' as a euphemism for Jew is a confidence trick," one that was increasingly used on college campuses even before Hamas's October 7, 2023 attack. "Like other forms of Judeophobia," Marcus argued, "it is an ideology of hate, treating Israel as the 'collective Jew' and smearing the Jewish state with defamations similar to those used for centuries to vilify individual Jews. This ideology establishes a conspiratorial worldview, sometimes including replacement theory[—recall the chants at Charlottesville—]which has occasionally erupted in violence, including mass-shooting, in recent months."[4]

Since October 7, we've seen even more antisemitic speech and conduct disguised as "anti-Zionism," celebrating Hamas's "resistance," advocating the elimination of Jews worldwide—"Hitler should've finished the job"—and not letting Jewish students and faculty access "Zionist-free" parts of campuses. Zionism, the belief that Israel should exist as a homeland for the Jewish people, is part of most Jews' identity, so being against it is akin to saying "I don't hate X people, only X people who refuse to renounce their heritage."

But don't I support freedom of speech? If students want to be bigots, let them; isn't that what opposing cancel culture means? Well, yes, but discriminatory conduct isn't kosher, as it were. Although hate speech is and should be constitutionally protected—if it doesn't incite violence—and student groups shouldn't be forced to express any particular messages, they don't have the right to set blanket exclusions that reflect hate and bigotry.

We're all familiar with antidiscrimination laws that ban treating people differently based on race, sex, ethnicity, and the like. We can debate whether and how they should apply to private businesses, but these rules do apply to all educational institutions that receive federal funds. Schools, colleges, and universities aren't free to discriminate against people based on these protected categories *or to allow them to be*

---

4. See Kenneth L. Marcus, "Berkeley Establishes Jewish-Free Zones," *Jewish Journal*, September 28, 2022.

discriminated against as part of institution-supported programming (which includes recognized student groups). Because Zionism is so central to Jewish identity, discriminating against Zionists is the same as discriminating against Jews—and unlike discriminating against Republicans or environmentalists (except in certain progressive jurisdictions, like Seattle and Washington, DC, that extend civil rights protections to political views or affiliations).

Setting legalities aside, we wouldn't think that it's right for student groups to exclude members of certain ethnic backgrounds unless they promise not to speak in public or invite speakers who support their community. And that's even before getting to the "all comers" policies many universities have—including Berkeley—mandating that student groups accept all students as full members regardless of their views. This isn't just viewpoint discrimination, which is bad enough, particularly in an educational environment supposedly committed to a free exchange of ideas. That's why the Department of Education launched a civil-rights investigation of Berkeley Law in December 2022 for failing to remedy its hostile environment for Jewish students, faculty, and staff.

The real issue here is taking exclusionary action—real discrimination, not a mere assertion that someone's position on Israel (or anything) is "harmful" or denies someone's right to exist. As Marcus put it, groups that adopt anti-Zionist bylaws "are restricting their successors from cooperating with pro-Israel speakers and groups. In this way, the exclusionary bylaws operate like racially restrictive covenants, precluding minority participation into perpetuity." The Berkeley students should be ashamed of themselves, as should law school and university officials who hypocritically wring their hands about "free speech" while letting public spaces become less welcoming to Jews.

Although this chapter only discussed four law schools, these examples are emblematic of what's boiling up from below the surface of the legal academy. These are the lessons being taught to future lawyers, who will be policing the rules of our justice system—and to future public officials, who will be making decisions affecting people across America.

CHAPTER 8

The ABA Versus Truth, Justice, and the Supreme Court

We saw in chapter 1 how the legal profession, corporate America, and even the government have been bending toward illiberal concepts such as equity over equality, diversity over excellence, and political orthodoxy over the rule of law. But that's not just a story of the downstream effects of bad law-school teaching. The regulation of lawyers and of law schools—commonly known as accreditation—has also gone off the DEI rails.

Take the American Bar Association, which is supposed to be the voice of the legal profession. There was a time when the ABA was one of our leading institutions and a relatively conservative, or at least institutionalist, one. Lewis Powell Jr. eventually parlayed his presidency of the organization into a seat on the Supreme Court. Chief Justice Warren Burger started an annual State of the Judiciary address—which has since taken written form every New Year's Eve—to placate the significant portion of ABA members alienated by the Warren Court's left-wing activism. Two generations or so ago, half of the lawyers in the United States were members of the ABA. Today, that number is less than 15 percent and falling.

This decrease is often attributed to young lawyers' lack of desire to join civic organizations. Or maybe attorneys in general no longer see any gain from ABA membership because local and industry organizations—not to mention online connections—provide all the continuing legal education (CLE), networking, and client-development opportunities one could ask for. All of these factors, along with more general changes in the way law is practiced in the 21st century, are at play. But one other development is notable, particularly in the context of this book: the ABA, which had moved increasingly leftward for decades, has become a law-focused activist group. The organization's house of delegates now adopts policy positions, and its board of governors authorizes the filing of amicus briefs on a variety of controversies that go far beyond issues of particular concern to the legal profession that had previously been the group's focus. In 2019, for example, the delegates adopted a resolution on climate change that urged Congress to "provide for a just transition for the people and places most dependent on the carbon economy" and called on lawyers to engage in pro bono work to reduce greenhouse gas emissions. The organization has also taken positions on abortion and gun control, issues that are, of course, as controversial among lawyers as among the general public. The ABA long ago alienated conservatives—who now have the Federalist Society as an alternative membership organization (one that doesn't take positions or file briefs)—but in recent years it's also lost the broad middle swath of lawyers who just don't want to mix work and politics.

The National Conference of Bar Examiners, which creates and administers various components of each state's bar exam—including the interstate-portable Uniform Bar Examination, which has been adopted by 39 states and the District of Columbia—has also gotten into the act. The NCBE plans to roll out a revamped "NextGen" exam in 2026 that will test fewer areas of law in less depth. According to the group's stated goals, this watered-down exam is intended to "work toward greater equity" and "eliminate any aspects of our exams that could contribute to performance disparities," as well as "promote greater diversity and inclusion in the legal profession." Justice Jay Mitchell of the Alabama Supreme Court revealed in a *Wall Street Journal* op-ed after attending the NCBE's 2023 annual meeting that the organization is putting considerable emphasis on examinees' identity-based characteristics to try to equalize group outcomes. An ACLU representative who lectured on criminal justice issues, meanwhile, argued that states should minimize would-be lawyers' criminal convictions when determining fitness for bar admission. State bars and supreme courts, which regulate legal practice, should push back on the loss of rigor, while also insisting that the NCBE commit to neutral tests that are blind-graded.

A New Ideological Skew

To be fair, allegations of ABA bias, particularly in its evaluation of judicial nominees, go back to Richard Nixon, who called the group "a bunch of sanctimonious assholes"—though that was more for elitism, and Nixon did end up appointing Powell. Republican administrations going back to Ronald Reagan's have cried foul on the ABA's evaluations, and studies have shown that the nominees of Democratic presidents tend to be rated higher, all things being equal, justifying the decisions of George W. Bush and Donald Trump to remove the ABA from its traditional role in prescreening judicial candidates. (The Biden administration became the first Democratic administration to remove the ABA from that role, out of frustration that many of President Obama's "diverse" candidates had been rated "not qualified.") But the new slate of complaints isn't coming from political outsiders. There's a growing dissonance between the ABA and state bar associations, which admit and regulate lawyers.

The ABA's Model Rules of Professional Conduct set the standard for legal ethics nationwide. But Model Rule 8.4(g), promulgated in 2016 in the early days of our "racial reckoning," has not been well-received. Adopting this rule would make it misconduct for an attorney to "engage in conduct that the lawyer knows or reasonably should know is harassment or discrimination on the basis of race, sex, religion, national origin, ethnicity, disability, age, sexual orientation, gender identity, marital status or socioeconomic status in conduct related to the practice of law." The rule was designed to eliminate bias in the legal profession, but scholars from across the political spectrum contend that it creates a speech code for attorneys and have identified multiple constitutional defects. The ABA's formal opinion on the topic didn't even mention a binding Supreme Court precedent regarding professional speech.

Almost every state to have considered the rule rejected it. Even New York rejected the rule as proposed and instead rewrote it to resolve many First Amendment concerns. After a federal court blocked a version of the rule in Pennsylvania, the ABA filed a brief supporting the disciplining of lawyers who offend protected groups. (I filed a brief against the rule for the Manhattan Institute.) That was the organization's chance to provide research showing that the Keystone State's legal community was corrupted by racial and other prejudices. Instead, the ABA generally alleged "widespread perceptions that the legal profession is pervasively tainted by discrimination and harassment." The organization thus claimed it was trying to restore the public trust by supporting the Pennsylvania Supreme Court's mission to restore legitimacy to the state's system of justice. It provided no specific illustrations of the problem, just suggested a general crisis of public confidence.

There are other instances of the separation between the radicalized ABA and the legal profession. Florida's Supreme Court found that the ABA's diversity requirement for CLE-approved speakers (for getting "continuing legal education" credit) amounted to a discriminatory quota. The association changed its policy to ensure that Florida lawyers could still receive credit for taking ABA-approved courses. More recently, in February 2023 the ABA House of Delegates rejected a proposal to drop the LSAT requirement that had been approved the previous November by the council of the ABA's Section of Legal Education and Admissions to the Bar—though the proposal seems to be gaining in support and may still go ahead in some form in future. In April 2023, 125 deans, representing 63 percent of ABA-accredited law schools, wrote to the ABA asking it to allow schools to admit up to 25 percent of new students without a standardized test score.

This haste to change diversity-related policies seemed in part a continuation of post–George Floyd momentum and in part an attempt to get ahead of the Supreme Court's decision to upend affirmative action, to remove objective criteria so racial preferences can come in through other pretextual or subjective doorways. The ABA's next goal will presumably be to replace the bar exam with a "diploma privilege," granting a law license to anyone who graduates from an ABA-accredited law school. (Wisconsin is the only state that currently allows the diploma privilege, for graduates of in-state law schools, although New Hampshire, Oregon, and Washington in recent years changed their rules to allow admission through apprenticeship and other alternatives to the bar exam. The supreme courts of California, Minnesota, and Utah are considering similar moves.) All these measures are being championed under the auspices of equity, though it's unclear how setting up more racial minorities for professional failure—and their clients for subpar legal services—is equitable. As South Texas College of Law Houston professor Josh Blackman (with whom I occasionally coauthor articles and briefs) wrote in the *ABA Journal* in April 2023:

> An organization that purports to represent the legal profession should reflect the mainstream views of all lawyers, and not one pole of the ideological spectrum. All too often, the ABA serves as the locomotive of the legal progression, barreling through well-established barriers in the interest of progressive ends. But the ABA is better suited as a caboose: trailing behind the legal profession, codifying the best practices from the states that have reached a consensus after sufficient percolation and acceptance. As the ABA drifts further and further away from the regulation of the legal profession, and focuses more and more on achieving progressive societal goals, the organization's mandate dissolves.

Absent greater focus on its core mission and consideration of ideological diversity—adding members to relevant committees who can explain how DEI policies would affect free speech and free exercise rights, for example—it will continue to alienate the bench and bar alike. Some in the organization may now be recognizing that there's a problem; in August 2023, the Strategic Review Committee of the ABA's Section of Legal Education and Admissions proposed a new accreditation standard focused on free-expression policies, affording due process to people who claim a violation of academic freedom and condemning disruptive behavior. The new standard would still give law schools plenty of discretion to restrict speech that the First Amendment protects, however, and it wouldn't prevent "investigations" of the sort I and many others have faced for disfavored speech.

The decline in the ABA's prestige and its transformation from the voice of the legal profession to one of many lawyer-heavy progressive shops is bad enough, but at the end of the day, membership is voluntary and the group has no direct authority over lawyers. State bar associations, on the other hand, which in many states lawyers have to join and pay annual dues, are also increasingly taking political positions and engaging in activism. Accordingly, state legislatures are moving to eliminate the so-called integrated bar, thus freeing lawyers from progressive orthodoxy. The Arizona legislature, for one, passed legislation in 2023 to return the state bar association's delegated authority for attorney regulation back to the state supreme court, though Governor Katie Hobbs vetoed it. In 2021, the Fifth Circuit found that Texas's integrated bar violated the First Amendment after several lawyers complained that the association was spending their mandatory dues on promoting progressive social policies. As Josh Blackman put it: "Sooner or later, the Supreme Court will do to bar associations what it did to public-sector unions: allow dissenting members to opt out of funding choices they disagree with. Bar associations that continue to meander from their core function face the loss of mandatory dues"—and become as irrelevant as the ABA.

Accrediting Law Schools—and Taking Them Over

The corruption of the ABA has far-reaching effects. One big obstacle to any sort of innovation and disruption in the higher-education space is the rigid, government-enforced accreditation regime. Every seven years or so, accrediting agencies inspect each college and university to determine whether to renew what's effectively an operating license. Inspection teams typically include faculty members from other institutions; law school inspection teams usually also include lawyers and judges. The Department of Education recognizes the Council of the ABA Section of Legal Education and Admissions to the Bar as the only professional accrediting agency for law schools in the United States. That stamp of approval is important because it affects not only the recognition of the law schools involved—and thus student eligibility for federal loans—but also a graduate's ability to practice law. In nearly all US jurisdictions, graduation from an ABA-accredited law school is a prerequisite for being allowed to sit for the bar exam. Even states that recognize unaccredited schools within their borders—California has by far the most of this kind—will generally not recognize such schools from out of state for purposes of bar admission. That means that the ABA, despite its previously described politicization and decline, remains relevant in this area if nowhere else.

The ABA has used its accreditation monopoly to bend law schools to its ideological will. For example, in February 2022, the ABA instituted a new rule that all law schools must "provide education on bias, cross-cultural competency, and racism" through compulsory-attendance "orientation sessions, lectures, courses, or other educational experiences." Now there's a further proposal for each school to "annually assess the extent to which it has created an educational environment that is inclusive and equitable." Under this standard, law schools would risk losing accreditation for not punishing professors or students who make politically incorrect statements of the sort that got me into trouble with Georgetown. The revised standard was pulled at the last minute before the August 2022 meeting of the ABA House of Delegates, but it will no doubt return in some form.

Even before the latest DEI craze, however, the ABA's Section of Legal Education and Admissions to the Bar pressured schools to engage in racial balancing and lower academic standards in favor of diversity. In higher education generally, accreditors are often the most eager enforcers of diversity demands, making it difficult for dissenters to operate. Deans and faculty can be supportive of such enforcement for ideological reasons but also to control the competition: If one school engages in race preferences (or any kind of preference not based on merit), it hurts the academic profile of its student body and bar passage rate, both big factors in *U.S. News* rankings. But if all law schools are required to do the same, nobody will be worse off.

"In essence, the ABA enforces a 'diversity cartel' among law schools, effectively insulating schools that give large preferences from competition on issues like bar passage rate with schools that would rather give smaller preferences or none at all," writes Gail Heriot, a longtime member of the US Commission on Civil Rights. "The ABA is fully aware that the only way to comply with its standards is to give preferential treatment to students from under-represented minorities."

In its amicus brief in *Grutter v. Bollinger*, the 2003 Supreme Court case approving the use of race in admissions, the ABA wrote that "the improvement in minority participation . . . has been achieved largely by the use of race-conscious admissions policies such as those under attack here." This mutually reinforcing cartel was of dubious legality even before the Supreme Court outlawed such preferences in 2023—*Grutter* deferred to administrators in their pursuit of educational diversity, rather than green-lighting one orthodoxy—but still a regulatory conformity flourished. Indeed, the ABA hasn't hesitated to overrule the educational judgment of the law schools it regulates. In 2006, for example, Charleston School of Law unexpectedly failed to win accreditation due in part to race concerns, until the dean promised to do "whatever we have to do" and hired a new diversity director.

The case of George Mason University Law School's reaccreditation in the early 2000s is even more troubling.[1] The inspection team in 2000 "was unhappy that only 6.5 percent of entering day students and 9.5 percent of entering evening students were minorities," even as their report "conceded that GMU Law [later named after Justice Antonin Scalia] had a 'very active effort to recruit minorities.'" It noted, however, that the school was "unwilling to engage in any significant preferential affirmative action admissions program." Although faculty members differed on affirmative action generally, a strong majority opposed the overwhelming race-preferential treatment commonly practiced elsewhere. The ABA repeatedly refused to renew GMU's accreditation because of its supposed lack of diversity. Eventually the school was forced to adopt significant racial preferences, which increased the proportion of minorities in its entering class to 11 percent in 2001 and 16 percent in 2002. The ABA wasn't satisfied; slow, deliberate improvement wasn't what the accreditor had in mind. Shortly after the Supreme Court's decision in *Grutter*, an emboldened ABA summoned GMU's president and law school dean and threatened to revoke the school's accreditation. George Mason responded by further lowering admissions standards. In 2003, 17 percent of entering students were racial minorities. In 2004, it was 19 percent. That still

---

1. For the best, most painstakingly detailed account of this sordid episode, as well as a description of the Charleston Law travails described above, see Gail Heriot and Carissa Mulder, "The Sausage Factory," San Diego Legal Studies Paper No. 22-003, in *A Dubious Expediency: How Race Preferences Damage Higher Education*, ed. Gail Heriot and Maimon Schwarzschild (New York: Encounter Books, 2021).

wasn't enough, because the ABA didn't consider the admitted students to be the *right kind* of minority. "Of the 99 minority students in 2003, only 23 were African-American; of 111 minority students in 2004, the number of African Americans held at 23," the ABA grumbled. Heriot's account continued: "It didn't seem to matter that sixty-three African Americans had been offered admission or that the only way to admit more was to lower admissions standards to alarming levels. It didn't even matter that many students admitted under those circumstances would incur heavy debt, but never graduate and pass the bar."

The ABA performs reaccreditation evaluations every seven years. Incredibly, by the time GMU Law was finally reaccredited, six years had passed, which meant it was time for the ABA to start a new round of accreditation, and that new evaluation *also* raised concerns about diversity. Meanwhile, the ABA didn't care at all about the plight of the students admitted against the faculty's guidance. It was so focused on superficial appearances of social justice that it was willing to harm the ranking of an upstart law school with a commitment to open inquiry that was willing to hire star libertarian professors who were shunned elsewhere. The dean, Daniel Polsby, did care about his students, however, writing to the ABA to explain the damage its heavy-handed racialist mania had caused.

Heriot summed up the grim result:

> [W]hile GMU was under pressure to increase its racial diversity, African-American students experienced dramatically higher rates of academic failure (defined in GMU's academic rules as a GPA below 2.15). Fully 45% of African-American law students at GMU experienced academic failure as opposed to only 4% of students of other races. . . . many of these students would have stood a greater chance at success in their goal of becoming lawyers if they had attended a law school at which their entering academic credentials had been more like the median student's. But the ABA prevented that.

Dean Polsby was understandably incensed. "We have an obligation to refrain from victimizing applicants, regardless of race or color, by admitting them to an educational program in which they appear likely to fail."

More recently, the ABA has been pushing law schools to make the LSAT optional for applicants. (In many cases, this is welcome pressure, as deans began to recognize that to continue to engage in race preferences ahead of what they correctly anticipated would be the Supreme Court's elimination of them in June 2023, they would need to eliminate objective admissions criteria.) In so doing, it shows that it cares only about diversity statistics for admissions, not outcomes—even though the LSAT correlates highly with law-school achievement and bar passage. LSAT antagonists claim they oppose the test because it's not an objective measure of aptitude, but the truth is that it's too objective and gets in the way of manipulating student bodies according to race and other intersectional metrics.

It's highly unlikely that the Supreme Court would have sided with the University of Michigan in *Grutter* if the law school had argued, "We discriminate because otherwise our ideologically skewed accrediting agency would cut us off from federal aid and cut our students off from taking the bar exam." Accordingly, the Department of Education should seek other accreditation options, revoke the ABA's monopoly, and allow states to choose their own authorities. Even without that necessary step, however, Congress can eliminate accreditation standards that have essentially forced schools to adopt racial preferences. As Gail Heriot has proposed, Congress should prohibit accreditors from requiring universities to satisfy DEI objectives by limiting evaluative criteria to those spelled out in the Higher Education Act of 1965. These include the habitability of classrooms, adequacy of the campus library and other educational resources, appropriateness of program curriculum, soundness of financial management, and faculty credentials.

States should also encourage the development and recognition of alternative rating and accreditation systems—perhaps allowing schools to choose accreditors more aligned with their missions—and join interstate compacts to ensure bar reciprocity. As Harvard history professor James Hankins has written, state agencies could use FIRE free-speech rankings, among others, to grade institutions, instead of various social-justice or DEI metrics, endowment size, and other criteria that favor wealthy, progressive universities. State authorities are fully justified in directing public educational funds in ways that they consider best for producing good citizens. Indeed, they have a duty to ensure that taxpayers aren't paying for *miseducation*. They would thus be perfectly justified in withholding funding and even accreditation from schools that rank low on free speech and open inquiry. Accreditation standards should focus on academic quality, not the promotion of racial self-segregation. And state attorney general offices are better suited to protecting against civil rights violations than are education departments.

"State authorities also have a legitimate interest in seeing that state funds are not wasted by administrative bloat" of the kind we saw in chapter 5.[2] Raters and accreditors should consider the ratio of students to administrators, not just students to faculty. Both state legislatures and Congress could regulate the number of staff in public schools relative to students and faculty, while private schools might be subject to the withdrawal of state subsidies or tax privileges if bureaucratic numbers get too high. Given that nonteaching educrats are the chief agents of illiberalism, a winnowing of these nonessential personnel can't help but have positive effects. A policy that transfers education dollars from staff to students—or even from DEI bureaucracies to faculty recruitments, as the University of Florida announced in March 2024—is both good policy and good politics. Alumni would also be wise to withhold contributions until their alma mater assures them that their donations will go toward actual education. All donors, not just alumni, should demand to know how their money is spent. And at schools where alumni can vote for trustees, vigorous election campaigns should be the order of the day.

The Supreme Court Weighs In

In 2003, the Supreme Court, by a 5–4 majority, endorsed a holistic race-conscious law school admissions program (*Grutter v. Bollinger*, regarding the University of Michigan) while rejecting a mechanical system that assigned race a fixed number of points (*Gratz v. Bollinger*, regarding Michigan's undergraduate admissions). The swing vote in

---

2. James Hankins, "A Centrist Strategy for Higher Education Reform," Law & Liberty, May 30, 2023.

those affirmative-action cases, Justice Sandra Day O'Connor, suggested that "25 years from now, the use of racial preferences will no longer be necessary to further the interest approved today." Two decades after those rulings, the trend lines weren't looking good for an organic sunsetting of the evaluation of higher education applicants by the color of their skin. But then, in 2014, a civil rights organization called Students for Fair Admissions (SFFA) sued the oldest private and public universities in the country, Harvard and the University of North Carolina, respectively, presenting compelling evidence that these schools use racial preferences to a far greater extent than *Grutter* would allow. For example, at any given level of academic merit, the acceptance rate for African American applicants is many times greater than for whites and especially Asian Americans. Put another way, as Harvard's lawyer Seth Waxman—who had been solicitor general in the Clinton administration—conceded in oral argument in *Students for Fair Admissions v. President and Fellows of Harvard College*, 45 percent of current black and Hispanic students had been admitted to Harvard due to racial preferences.

At the same time, the SFFA litigation showed that the number of Asian Americans at Harvard and other elite schools has stayed relatively constant even as their proportion of qualified applicants has exploded in recent decades. That's sadly ironic, because Justice Powell, the deciding vote in the 1978 case that approved the limited use of race in admissions decisions (see chapter 10), had credited Harvard as a model admissions program without recognizing that its "holistic" approach had originated as a way to restrict the number of Jewish students in the 1920s and '30s. On the one hand, race is only one of many factors that colleges consider— and is not supposed to be determinative; on the other, if using race were outlawed, the number of Asian Americans at selective institutions would grow significantly.

Perhaps that's why a majority of justices in *SFFA v. Harvard* were skeptical of the arguments for maintaining racial preferences, or "race-conscious admissions," as the schools' advocates call them. That majority included the otherwise mercurial chief justice, John Roberts, who has been firmly opposed to government-sponsored racialism in all contexts, including the previous collegiate affirmative action case, *Fisher v. University* of Texas at Austin (Fisher II), in 2016. Most famously, he had written in a 2007 busing case, "The way to stop discrimination on the basis of race is to stop discriminating on the basis of race." So when Waxman likened the cases in which race is determinative to the times when an orchestra needs an oboe player, Roberts wryly noted, "We did not fight a Civil War about oboe players. We did fight a Civil War to eliminate racial discrimination."

Moreover, Grutter had generated no legitimate reliance interests. It could not because, as the Court had held in setting aside race preferences in government contracting (Adarand Constructors v. Peña, 1995), when precedent "undermines the fundamental principle of equal protection as a personal right," it is the principle, not precedent, that "must prevail." And because Grutter itself required that such policies "must be limited in time" and should face "sunset provisions" forcing regular "reviews to determine whether racial preferences are still necessary," the Harvard and UNC lawyers' inability to define the necessary conditions for an endpoint was telling.

What the Court authorized in Grutter was a temporary, grudging exception to America's equality ideals that, alas, metastasized into a threat blooming across the legal landscape and society as a whole. Despite Grutter's own language, the case has been taken to signal that it may be legally permissible beyond the admissions context for government actors to discriminate based on race to achieve some greater good.

But even in the educational setting, Grutter didn't achieve the benefits its proponents lauded. Instead of creating academic communities with a broad mix of perspectives and experiences or even making amends for social injustices—which the Court has never accepted as a justification for preferences—race-based admissions have entrenched wealth and privilege, as well as leading to separate housing facilities, orientation programs, and graduation ceremonies. By June 2023, it was long past time to recognize that Grutter was a deviation from equal-protection principles and had spawned pernicious race-balancing under the guise of diversity. Although the Supreme Court declined to explicitly overrule those cases, it effectively did so, ending their aberrant legal regime and thus pushing back against the racist balkanizers.

"Eliminating racial discrimination means eliminating all of it," wrote Chief Justice Roberts for the six-justice majority in *SFFA v. Harvard*. The decision's critics, most notably Harvard itself, seized on his later line that "nothing in this opinion should be construed as prohibiting universities from considering an applicant's discussion of how race affected his or her life, be it through discrimination, inspiration, or otherwise." But few bothered to quote the next line, that "despite the dissent's assertion to the contrary, universities may not simply establish through application essays or other means the regime we hold unlawful today." Higher-ed grandees will not go quietly into the colorblind night but will fight for workarounds to maintain their system of racial spoils. There will be more litigation, but it's clear that the Court has no more constitutional patience for admissions officers' social engineering or administrators' DEI posturing.

The public at large is also becoming aware of the failures of the diversity-industrial complex. Combined with the Supreme Court ruling and decisions by legislatures and university systems to roll back aspects of DEI policies—most notably diversity statements for faculty hiring (which both Harvard and MIT, among others, abandoned in the spring of 2024)—the pendulum appears to be swinging back. But it's happening in fits and starts, so individual students, professors, and staff are still very much at risk of being targeted for the sort of cancellation that I faced at Georgetown.

CHAPTER 9

The Stanford Shutdown and the Importance of Deans

On March 9, 2023, Judge Kyle Duncan of the US Court of Appeals for the Fifth Circuit was due to speak at Stanford Law School. He had been invited by the Federalist Society chapter to discuss the unsettled law surrounding Covid, guns, and social-media regulation. More technically, he was going to address how appellate courts reach decisions in areas of doctrinal flux before the Supreme Court has established clear legal rules.

It was the sort of nerdy experience with someone at the highest level of the profession that elite law schools pride themselves on providing their students. Judge Duncan could have given them a real-world perspective on how judges adapt law in changing times. These future lawyers could've talked to one of the thought leaders of his circuit and of the federal judiciary as a whole. As if that intellectual stimulation and careerist networking weren't enough, attendees were also going to get a free lunch! What more could you want?

Alas, many Stanford students weren't interested in the food offered for either mind or body. You see, Judge Duncan doesn't subscribe to contemporary academic orthodoxies. As a lawyer in private practice and then in rulings since President Trump appointed him to the bench in 2018, his work had been "problematic." Duncan had committed various apostasies against the new-age religion. As a scholar, he had written law review articles defending the traditional definition of marriage and advocating other social-conservative positions. As a lawyer, he had defended schools that wanted to maintain bathrooms segregated by biological sex. As a judge, he refused to use a convicted prisoner's preferred pronouns.

Duncan was thus deemed unfit to set foot in Stanford Law's progressive utopia. A number of left-wing student groups, as well as members of Stanford OutLaw—a self-described "social, support, and political group" that actively combats "homophobia, transphobia, heterosexism, and any discrimination based on sexual orientation or gender identity"— demanded that Duncan's speech be moved to Zoom or off-campus, if not canceled altogether. They put up posters around the law school accusing the judge of being transphobic, homophobic, and, in what must be some sort of intersectional transitive property, racist.

After the Federalist Society rejected an Outlaw/National Lawyers Guild (NLG) demand to exile Duncan, the names and photographs of Fed Soc officers began appearing on separate posters. "Meet the Federalist Society's 2022–2023 Board. YOU SHOULD BE ASHAMED," the flyers announced, with the last word scrawled in a bloodred horror-movie font.

Both the anti-Duncan and name-and-shame posters gave Stanford's administration notice that trouble might lie ahead. So on the morning of the event, the associate dean for DEI, Tirien Steinbach, who had previously been a senior lawyer with the ACLU of Northern California, sent an email to all SLS students about her office's "goals and roles in this situation." "For some members of our community," she explained, "Judge Duncan, during his time as an attorney and judge, has 'repeatedly and proudly threatened healthcare and basic rights for marginalized communities, including LGBTQ+ people, Native Americans, immigrants, prisoners, Black voters, and women, and his presence on campus represents a significant hit to their sense of belonging.'" The law school "would be taking no action to prevent the event," David Lat reported, but students were free—invited?—to protest "in compliance [with] the school's policy against disrupting speakers."

Why was Steinbach inserting herself into this event? It might be good practice for law school administrations to reiterate policies regarding speech and protest ahead of the arrival of "controversial" speakers— it's troubling that law students would need such a reminder, but such is the state of modern campuses—but why would this be the DEI dean's responsibility, rather than that of the dean of students? As I write in this book's final chapter, the head dean, the big kahuna, should be the one instilling values of free expression and civil discourse. Unlike normal university departments or other units, the highest-ranking law school administrator is selected by the school's governing board rather than the faculty or even the university president. Indeed, that's an ABA requirement, ensuring that the dean is a CEO more than the first among academic peers—and the modern dean spends much more time as a political leader and fundraiser, like the university president, than as an intellectual. Even the smallest school's dean then anoints various assistant, associate, or vice deans responsible for academics, student life, and the like.

In the last decade, we've become so accustomed to the intrusion of diversicrats into every part of academic life that at Stanford it fell to the official responsible for creating an "inclusive" environment to weigh in on a lunch talk that had nothing to do with issues of race, sex, or gender. Apparently Judge Duncan's mere presence would put the "safety" of the school's "marginalized" students at risk.

A few hours after Steinbach's email, some Fed Soc members went into the student lounge to eat breakfast and discovered protesters preparing for the event. They were asked to leave because their presence would violate the LGBTQ "safe space"—even though the chapter's president, Tim Rosenberger, was himself gay. They did leave, but noticed that the lounge had taken on a festive air, with face-painted protesters eating Mexican food and a dog decorated with the transgender flag running around.

Then it was showtime. About 100 students lined up outside the event to boo those who entered, with some trying to shame individual classmates by name. Another 50 to 70 students entered the room, compared to some 20 Fed Soc members and supporters.[1] The protesters carried signs that read "BE PRONOUN NOT PRO-BIGOT," "RESPECT TRANS RIGHTS," and, bizarrely, "DUNCAN CAN'T FIND THE CLIT." As Judge Duncan approached the door to the room, someone shouted, "I hope your daughters get raped!"

---

1. For a comprehensive account of this event, see David Lat, "Yale Law Is No Longer #1—For Free-Speech Debacles," *Original Jurisdiction*, March 10, 2023, which also collected many of the quotes I use here. FIRE also posted a transcript of Dean Steinbach's remarks on its website.

But Wait, There's More

Holding signs, even those with ugly language, isn't normally a problem if the signs don't block event attendees' view of the speaker. Similarly, so long as protesters outside or even inside an event space don't disrupt the event (or nearby classes) or others' access to it—which might be a fire code violation on top of university speech policies—there shouldn't be a problem.

But that protest didn't respect those straightforward guidelines. When Rosenberger, the Stanford Fed Soc president—who serendipitously ended up helping with this book while on a fellowship with the Manhattan Institute—began introducing the event, he was heckled. Judge Duncan then took the stage and, from the start of his attempt to give his speech, was booed and jeered continuously.

It was different from my UC Hastings shutdown, described in chapter 4, which consisted of rhythmic chanting and banging, with the occasional discernible heckle thrown in. Here the protesters simply yelled over Judge Duncan. "You couldn't get into Stanford!" "You're not welcome here, we hate you!" "Why do you hate black people?" "Leave and never come back!" "We hate Fed Soc students! Fuck them, they don't belong here, either!" "We do not respect you, and you have no right to speak here! This is our jurisdiction!"

Throughout this spectacle, Associate Dean Steinbach and four other administrators in the audience, including a designated "student-relations representative," did nothing. Before the event, Fed Soc members had discussed possible disruption with student-affairs staff, who had said they would issue warnings as needed, but only if anyone actually disrupted the presentation. At the event, despite the difficulty that Duncan was having in trying to give his remarks and the difficulty that many students had in trying to hear him, no action was taken either by the designated official or any other.

After some more back-and-forth, Judge Duncan asked for help in trying to restore—or create for the first time—order. At that point, Steinbach went up to the front and identified herself. Duncan asked to speak with her privately, but she declined, saying that she wanted all discussions to be public. After a brief exchange, punctuated by someone in the crowd screeching "Respect black women!" Steinbach did speak—pulling out prepared remarks! She said she hoped that the Fed Soc chapter knew that the event was causing "real pain" to people in the SLS community—including apparently to herself, telling Duncan that she was "pained" to have to tell him that his work had caused "real harm" to people.

"And I am also pained," she lamented, "to have to say that you are welcome here in this school to speak." She blamed Judge Duncan for not sticking with his prepared speech—he had started engaging with the protesters—and thus contributing to the disruption. "Your opinions from the bench land as absolute disenfranchisement of [students'] rights," she said, accusing Duncan of "tearing the fabric of this community."

She also said that she respected Fed Soc's right to host him but that she thought "the juice wasn't worth the squeeze" as far as "this kind of event." "Do you have something so incredibly important to say," she asked when Judge Duncan expressed puzzlement at her "juice" line, that it was worth the "division of these people?"

As reported by David Lat, Steinbach told the protesters that they were free to either stay or go but that she hoped they would give Duncan the space to speak. But the tone and tenor of her remarks, as anyone can see from the widely circulated video, suggested that she really wanted him to self-censor and leave. She also questioned the wisdom and continuing legitimacy of Stanford's free-speech policies, which she acknowledged that she had to abide by for the time being.

"This invitation was a setup," Judge Duncan interjected at one point while Steinbach harangued him, clearly frustrated that an administrator was encouraging the mob rather than calming or dispersing it so the event could proceed. It later came out that second-year law student Denni Arnold had organized the disruption. Arnold could be seen on video telling protesters to "tone down the heckling slightly so we can get to our questions" (which had the opposite effect) and later advised that "half the folks walk out in protest."

A large number of protesters eventually left, with one of them calling Duncan "scum" as she walked out. But the disruption continued; the student-relations rep tried to intervene long past the time the event went out of control, to no avail.

Not getting traction with his speech, Duncan decided to take questions. The students quieted down, but were contemptuous in what they asked. "When did you last beat your wife?" was the sort of thing that came out of the mouths of these babes. Most notoriously, one student—at a law school tied with Yale for the top spot in the *U.S. News* rankings—raised the incisive legal query, "I fuck men, I can find the prostate. Why can't you find the clit?"

At one point, Duncan said, "You are all law students. You are supposed to have reasoned debate and hear the other side, not yell at those who disagree." One student shouted back, "You don't believe that we have a right to exist, so we don't believe you have the right to our respect or to speak here!" The event ended long before its scheduled time, with Duncan giving up any attempt to speak and instead having federal marshals escort him out of the building. As he was being whisked away, protesters encircled Fed Soc members and hurled invective at them.

Apologists for the protesters might argue that the event wasn't technically "shut down," that the judge actually did get to speak a bit—and indeed, unlike either my UC Hastings appearance or Kristen Waggoner's Yale panel, the invited speaker at times antagonized his opponents. But he certainly didn't get out any of his talk about the judicial method at a time of jurisprudential flux, and it was hard to hear him. As David Lat put it, "it's a pretty sad commentary on the state of free speech in American law schools if the ability to get out a few words is the standard for acceptable events."

Afterward, Dean Steinbach claimed that the protesters stayed within the bounds of Stanford policy and that the event demonstrated "exactly what the freedom of speech was meant to look like: messy." She asserted that Judge Duncan had been the disrespectful one and that he should've kept giving his remarks if he wanted.

Duncan, for his part, called on the school to discipline the students who had disrupted his talk and to fire Steinbach for chastising him and delivering what he characterized as a "bizarre therapy session from hell." He said that the attempt to shame individual students had been the most disturbing part of the Stanford imbroglio. "Don't feel sorry for me," he told one reporter. "I'm a life-tenured federal judge. What outrages me is that these kids are being treated like dogshit by fellow students and administrators."[2]

---

2. Aaron Sibarium, "'Dogs—t': Federal Judge Decries Disruption of His Remarks by Stanford Law Students and Calls for Termination of the Stanford Dean Who Joined the Mob," *Washington Free Beacon*, March 10, 2023.

Finally, the head dean, Jenny Martinez, got involved. Late the next day, she sent a brief message to all students, lamenting that "attempts at managing the room in this instance went awry." She explained that "forms of interruption that prevent a speaker from making or completing a presentation are inconsistent with [Stanford's antidisruption] policy." "While students in the room may do things such as quietly hold signs or ask pointed questions during question-and-answer periods, they may not do so in a way that disrupts the event or prevents the speaker from delivering their remarks." The Friday afternoon email concluded that the unruly protest was "not aligned with our institutional commitment to freedom of speech" and that "the school is reviewing what transpired."

I wasn't the only one underwhelmed by that noncommittal statement, but it was still too much for student activists. In a message to its mailing list, Stanford's NLG leadership slammed Martinez for throwing "its capable and compassionate administrators . . . who interceded productively, under the bus." The chapter's board members, who had helped organize the protest, praised "every single person" who had disrupted Duncan's speech, characterizing the protesters' conduct as "Stanford Law School at its best." Meanwhile, the school's chapter of the American Constitution Society (ACS)—which styles itself as Fed Soc's counterpart on the left—objected to the administration's framing of Duncan "as a victim, when in fact he himself had made civil dialogue impossible."

Surprisingly, those sentiments did not persuade Stanford's leaders, who were obviously hearing a different message from alumni. Stanford's president, Marc Tessier-Lavigne—who would resign the following year over falsified data in his scientific papers—signaled the seriousness of the issue, joining Dean Martinez in a letter of apology to Judge Duncan. They wrote that "what happened was inconsistent with our policies on free speech, and we are very sorry about the experience you had while visiting our campus." They explained that they had been "very clear with our students that, given our commitment to free expression, if there are speakers they disagree with, they are welcome to exercise their right to protest but not to disrupt the proceedings." They also said that "staff members who should have enforced university policies failed to do so, and instead intervened in inappropriate ways that are not aligned with the university's commitment to free speech."

Speaking to Ed Whelan, a conservative lawyer and commentator who had broken the news of the disruption on Twitter, Judge Duncan expressed gratitude for the apology and added that he hoped that "a similar apology is tendered to the persons in the Stanford law school community most harmed by the mob action: the members of the Federalist Society who graciously invited me to campus." In the days after the event, Denni Arnold, the leader of the disruptive mob, and other members of Identity and Rights Affirmers for Trans Equality (IRATE) shouted at Fed Soc officers walking to class or eating meals, demanding that they resign. OutLaw created a new listserv and group text to exclude Fed Soc members, like Rosenberger, who were part of the group.

Instead of apologizing to Fed Soc, however, the SLS administration, presumably with Martinez's approval, encouraged members to "reach out" to Steinbach if they needed help dealing with the fallout from an incident that had, by that point, attracted national attention. As reported by Aaron Sibarium, Acting Associate Dean of Students Jeanne Merino, who had stood by silently as students disrupted Duncan's talk and berated those very same Fed Soc members, pointed them to "resources that you can use right now to support your safety and mental health." She also discouraged them from tweeting about the event "until this news cycle winds down," saying that "trolls are looking for a fight." In addition to Steinbach, Merino listed herself and two other administrators as possible sources of "support."

Merino's email came after Stanford endured a brutal 48 hours on social media, with numerous lawyers, including Duncan himself (and me), calling for the protesters to be punished and Steinbach fired. It raised questions about the sincerity of Stanford's apology, which Duncan ultimately accepted, though adding, "I look forward to learning what measures Stanford plans to take to restore a culture of intellectual freedom."

The following Monday, around 100 students lined the hallways to protest Martinez for apologizing to Duncan. Her classroom's whiteboard was covered in fliers defending those who had disrupted Duncan. "We, the students in your constitutional law class, are sorry for exercising our 1st Amendment rights," some fliers read. Of course, the devil is in the details with that kind of argument: a competing or later event, or nondisruptive protest in the hall or outside the school, would've been one thing, while shouting down a speaker is a heckler's veto that most definitely isn't protected speech.

Martinez said at the start of class that her inbox had been bombarded with complaints about her apology to Duncan but that they would not be relitigating that dispute. When the class adjourned, the protesters, black-clad and having donned masks reading "COUNTER-SPEECH IS FREE SPEECH," glared at Martinez as she exited the room, forming a human corridor to the building's exit. The vast majority of Martinez's class participated in the protest; the few who didn't join the protesters received the same stare-down. "It didn't feel like the inclusive, belonging atmosphere that the DEI office claims to be creating," first-year student Luke Schumacher said. Ironically, "this form of protest would have been completely fine" at the actual event, another student said.

The Letter Read 'Round the Legal World

Ten days later, on March 22, 2023, Dean Martinez issued a ten-page letter responding to the disruption. It was the best exposition of free-speech values that we've seen from a prominent university official in this contentious period. Citing Stanford's own policies, the First Amendment, and California's Leonard Law, which applies First Amendment standards to *private* schools, Martinez laid out the difference between protest and disruption. She quoted what Berkeley Law Dean Erwin Chemerinsky had written after my shutdown at UC Hastings: "Freedom of speech does not protect a right to shout down others so they cannot be heard." Moreover, she wrote, "settled First Amendment law allows many governmental restrictions on heckling to preserve the countervailing interest in free speech. . . . Even in public forums such as public streets, sidewalks, and parks . . . it is well-settled that the First Amendment allows the imposition of reasonable content-neutral time, place, and manner restrictions. And while the First Amendment bars regulation of speech on the ground that listeners might find its *content* disturbing, it permits the regulation of speech that 'substantially impairs the effective conduct of a meeting.'" Modern jurisprudence has "long recognized that some settings are 'limited public forums,' where restrictions on speech are constitutional so long as they are viewpoint-neutral and reasonable in light of the forum's function."

A classroom reserved "for a guest speaker invited by a student organization is thus a setting where the First Amendment tolerates greater limitations on speech than it would in a traditional public forum." Martinez explained that she and Stanford's president had apologized to Judge Duncan "to acknowledge that his speech was disrupted in ways that undermined his ability to deliver the remarks he wanted to give to audience members who wanted to hear them, as a result of the failure to ensure that the university's disruption policies were followed."

As strong as that first section was, the second part of Martinez's letter, in which she discussed why "our commitment to diversity and inclusion means that we *must* protect the expression of all views," is more important and controversial. There's a roiling debate over whether DEI can ever be consistent with academic freedom, and Martinez laid out her case for a grand synthesis of liberal values, both classical and modern (but not postmodern). One paragraph stands out and merits full quotation:

> I want to set expectations clearly going forward: Our commitment to
> diversity, equity, and inclusion is not going to take the form of hav
> ing the school administration announce institutional positions on a
> wide range of current social and political issues, make frequent insti
> tutional statements about current news events, or exclude or condemn
> speakers who hold views on social and political issues with whom
> some or even many in our community disagree. I believe that focus on
> these types of actions as the hallmark of an "inclusive" environment
> can lead to creating and enforcing an institutional orthodoxy that is
> not only at odds with our core commitment to academic freedom, but
> also that would create an echo chamber that ill prepares students to go
> out into and act as effective advocates in a society that disagrees about
> many important issues. Some students might feel that some points
> should not be up for argument and therefore that they should not bear
> the responsibility of arguing them (or even hearing arguments about
> them), but however appealing that position might be in some other
> context, it is incompatible with the training that must be delivered in
> a law school. Law students are entering a profession in which their
> job is to make arguments on behalf of clients whose very lives may

depend on their professional skill. Just as doctors in training must learn to face suffering and death and respond in their professional role, lawyers in training must learn to confront injustice or views they don't agree with and respond as attorneys.

All of that is great, but I'm skeptical that anyone on the illiberal left who views things through racial and gendered lenses of intersectional power dynamics will ever accept those neutral rules of the game based on objective principles of equality and dignity. As I discuss in chapter 11, radical theories of race, sex, and power maintain that existing social structures are forms of oppression. That perspective simply doesn't gel with the idea that the Federalist Society "has the same rights of free association that other student organizations at the law school have" or that it's a valid goal to "ensure the expression of a wide range of viewpoints."

Moreover, the third part of Martinez's letter, covering "next steps," shows that even clear statements of good principles aren't enough. None of the disruptive students would be disciplined in any way, including with even the mildest penalties that the law school's disciplinary code provides, such as a warning, some community service, or simply "education." That decision had been made even though the dean admitted several times that some students had clearly violated the university's policies by drowning out the judge, and even though several video recordings show who the disruptive students were and provide irrefutable evidence of the violations.

The lack of consequences for the individual disrupters and the requirement of mandatory training for *all* law students doesn't sit well with anyone who cares about reversing the illiberal takeover of higher education. The Stanford shutdown is the single worst manifestation of that trend to date—not necessarily because it involved a federal judge but because the law school officials in attendance did nothing to stop the disruption and Associate Dean Steinbach (who was later placed on leave) berated the speaker in prepared remarks.

In explaining the lack of consequences for the disrupters, Dean Martinez wrote that it was hard to "come up with a fair process for identifying and distinguishing" between students who "crossed the line into disruptive heckling" and those "engaged in constitutionally protected non-disruptive protest." If we didn't have a recording of the incident, that might make sense. But we have a video! An investigation by Stanford's Office of Community Standards, which administers student discipline, could easily do the relevant fact-finding. Some disrupters would escape punishment, but that's no excuse for letting everyone off the hook.

Martinez also wrote in her letter that administrators' failure to warn the disrupters of potential sanction, and indeed Steinbach's encouragement, had sent "conflicting signals." But that contradicts the letter's preceding statement: "Such an onsite warning might not be required in all cases, and students had been generally informed of the policy against disruptions (including by schoolwide email the morning of the event)."

Moreover, Stanford's policy is clear and doesn't require lawyerly parsing: "It is a violation of University policy for a member of the faculty, staff, or student body to: (1) Prevent or disrupt the effective carrying out of a University function or approved activity, such as lectures, meetings, interviews, ceremonies, the conduct of University business in a University office, and public events." Indeed, any student who doesn't know that it's not acceptable to shout down a judge (or any speaker) doesn't belong in college, let alone law school.

Martinez then wrote that "focusing solely on punishing those who engaged in unprotected disruptions such as noisy shouting during the lecture would leave perversely unaddressed the students whose speech was perhaps constitutionally protected but well outside the norms of civil discourse." So the dean of a major law school thinks we shouldn't punish actual rule-breakers because we can't also punish those who merely violate the more amorphous "norms of civil discourse." That makes no sense!

Why can't Stanford discipline rule-breakers—after a fair investigation and hearing, of course—while also giving mere norm-breakers a stern talking-to or remedial training? Instead, the entire law school had to endure a mandatory session on "freedom of speech and the norms of the legal profession." And that exercise turned out to be four lackluster YouTube videos, much mocked by the student body, and an unverified Google form participants had to sign upon completion of viewing.

That kind of free-speech and professional-norms training is actually a wonderful idea for incoming first-year law students, but there it came off as collective punishment of the student body—including the very Fed Soc members who had invited Judge Duncan to speak—for the misdeeds of the raucous, illiberal minority. Moreover, even Martinez's modulated actions, with a statement supporting free-speech values but no consequences for those who had showed contempt for them, were too much for activist groups. In addition to the expected denunciation of the Duncan apology by the NLG and ACS chapters, a month after the dean's letter, the school's BLSA chapter announced that it would no longer participate in recruiting efforts. The administration "has actively marginalized its Black community, most recently by scapegoating Dean Tirien Steinbach," BLSA's executive board asserted, while the apology "was intimately aligned with White supremacist practices, leaving our members ashamed of the institution we were once excited to attend."

The Stanford incident exemplifies the illiberal dynamic at the heart of this book. Of course it would be the DEI dean who commandeered the student event to start berating the speaker about the supposed "harm" his mere presence was causing. Is it any surprise that law students act in an immature and unprofessional manner if administrators validate and goad them? At least Steinbach was suspended, because, as Martinez wrote, "the administrator who responds [to a disruption] should not insert themselves into debate with their own criticism of the speaker's views and the suggestion that the speaker reconsider whether what they plan to say is worth saying, for that imposes the kind of institutional orthodoxy and coercion that the policy on Academic Freedom precludes." Martinez announced in bold type that in the future, the "role of any administrators present will be to ensure that university rules on disruption of events will be followed, and all staff will receive additional training in that regard." Four months later, she would announce that Steinbach was "leaving her role . . . for another opportunity." Martinez herself, meanwhile, would be promoted to provost of the entire university.

We'll see what happens at Stanford and elsewhere, but this sort of thing will only continue unless educational leaders (1) enforce existing policies against hecklers' vetoes by disciplining those who violate them, (2) instill a culture of free speech, toleration, and civil discourse, (3) stop indoctrinating and self-selecting for radical illiberalism via diversity statements and trainings, and (4) actively push back on the illiberal ideas that speech is violence and disagreements about public policy and legal interpretation are Manichaean battles between good and evil. But very few of them will do it of their own volition, so they will have to be forced to do so through public shaming and other external pressures, as well as state legislation (for public schools) and congressional investigation.

In commenting on his experience, Judge Duncan warned that what happens at Stanford is unlikely to stay there. "If enough of these kids get into the legal profession," he said, "the rule of law will descend into barbarism."

CHAPTER 10

Who Defines Diversity Defines the Future

As I mentioned earlier, the phrase *banality of evil* raises the specter of totalitarian bureaucrats, but that totalitarianism need not be related to a gulag or gas chamber. My experience with IDEAA was precisely that of encountering apparatchiks enforcing a ridiculous regime that expects people to bend the knee to established orthodoxy or suffer the consequences. It's not that diversicrats are sadistic purveyors of torturous persecution—neither are many civil servants in oppressive regimes—but they think that their cause is so obviously right and its enemies so immoral that compulsive means are justified.

The irony is that DEI regimes achieve only aesthetic results. They ultimately subvert intellectual diversity, tilt the playing field away from equality of opportunity, and exclude those who deviate from ideological standards. In other words, they create schools with fewer ideas, fewer opportunities, and fewer of the mavericks who so often produce outside-the-box thinking. DEI isn't just a harmless institutional add-on; the way in which each plank of its platform has been defined (and undefined) has turned its ideology into administrative acid eroding the academy. Higher education can't be about safety and diversity through conformity—placing these values highest magnifies our differences and exacerbates our conflicts—but must instead challenge students to grow both intellectually and professionally. That's why DEI makes campus life worse even for minority students, as we'll see.

Understanding how this all came about requires learning the history of how such programs developed, and how their language has become so slippery and meaningless. DEI offices that have metastasized across academia go far beyond preventing discrimination and ensuring welcoming environments. They are the realized manifestations of what those warning about political correctness decades ago feared: thought police. And that trend has only accelerated.

The rapid expansion of DEI staff empowers a destructive dogmatism while giving activists high-paying jobs. This is a full-employment program for those who prefer indoctrination to education, without improving—but more often detracting from—the campus climate. DEI offices have broadened terms such as *harassment* and *discrimination* not to promote equal opportunity or a welcoming environment but to enforce radical "progressive" ideology. Sadly, they fail on their own terms: campus climate surveys show that DEI programming increases racial tensions and decreases students'—especially black students'—sense of belonging.

As Jarrett Stepman put it in evaluating the Greene/Paul survey discussed in chapter 5, the growth of academic DEI is "in line with larger trends in American society as diversity consultants operate to inculcate woke orthodoxies in elite institutions. Legions of DEI officers populate corporate boardrooms, government agencies, and K–12 schools. There's now a vast hive-mind apparatus that keeps activists employed, dissenters cowed, and the revolution moving forward."[1]

These activists, who can now get graduate degrees in DEI administration, are, in Stepman's words, "the shock troops of a top-down social revolution being foisted on America and much of the West." We pay for the bloat and waste of our universities regardless of our station in life or perspective on the world. And we're paying not only for the "multitude of New Offices" that send "swarms of Officers to harass our people, and eat out their substance" (to quote one of the complaints in the Declaration of Independence), but for the corrosive ideas they inculcate.

---

1. Jarrett Stepman, "Bloated Diversity, Equity, and Inclusion Staffs Explode Cost of Higher Education," Daily Signal, August 2, 2021.

The Road to Hell

It all started with good intentions. The original conception of anti-discrimination was to apply colorblind standards while ensuring that historically underprivileged groups, particularly African Americans still dealing with Jim Crow and its legacy, had equal opportunities to advance themselves. The phrase *affirmative action* broke into the mainstream off the heels of President John F. Kennedy's March 6, 1961, Executive Order 10925, which, under the new Committee on Equal Employment Opportunity, required federal contractors to "take affirmative action to ensure that applicants are employed . . . without regard to their race, creed, color, or national origin." As a result of universities' close relationship with the federal government—and federal funding—and as part of the drive to end educational segregation in the aftermath of *Brown v. Board of Education*, affirmative action found its way into university admissions.

The push to implement affirmative action was catalyzed by the assassination of Martin Luther King Jr. in 1968, which sent the nation into a state of grief, with anger fueling a passionate and understandable desire for change. Black and other minority students demanded that universities make their student bodies more representative of the national population. Four weeks after MLK's death, Harvard's dean of admissions committed to admitting substantially more black students, as well as increasing "black attitudes and background" on the admissions staff. The following year, the number of black students admitted to Harvard doubled. A similar rate of growth would be seen at other Ivy League schools. In an early example of "mismatch"—harming students by admitting them to schools with more rigorous curricula than they're prepared for—only half of the black students admitted to that first post-MLK class at Columbia would complete their degree in four years.

It would be a decade before opposition to those moves came to a head. The next big moment for affirmative action, and for identity politics, was the 1978 Supreme Court decision in *Regents of the University of California v. Bakke*. That case was brought by a white applicant who had been denied admission to UC Davis School of Medicine despite having higher GPA and MCAT scores than most of the minority students who had been admitted. After the medical school's inaugural class—in 1968, as it happened—was all-white, the faculty decided to reserve 16 percent of admission spots for minority students. When Allan Bakke, who had been a marine officer in Vietnam and worked as a NASA engineer before applying to medical school, challenged that practice, it looked as though the country's history had reached an inflection point. Either higher-ed admissions would be colorblind, or universities would be free to engage in large-scale social engineering to fulfill their vision of justice.

But neither view held sway. Instead, a compromise option seemed to split the difference—a false impression, as it turned out. In *Bakke*, one justice, Lewis Powell, planted the seed of the entire diversity conceit, which is now a bigger priority in higher education than the pursuit of knowledge. Four justices would've allowed racial preferences in admissions to remedy past prejudice, while four others would've outlawed the consideration of race altogether. Powell, meanwhile, voted to invalidate UC Davis's racial quotas but to allow the use of race as one of many factors to advance what he considered to be a compelling governmental interest in educational diversity. He homed in on the use of "diversity" as a goal that would preserve a form of affirmative action without expressly permitting racial discrimination. Instead of remedying discrimination, the university would just need to promote intellectual enrichment. If an institution concluded that only through an infusion of a select number of minority students could its intellectual environment be enriched, so much the better. *Diversity*, the word, thus became divorced from what's required to create it: an indefinable balance of differences, which in a government or administrative setting means that leaders can choose according to their personal whims instead of objective criteria to reach some indeterminate goal.

As a result, diversity became the only permissible justification for universities to make amends for America's legacy of racial discrimination. According to the law clerk who worked most closely on the case, Powell's appeal to diversity was a deliberate effort to preserve racial preferences despite laws and precedents that explicitly forbade them. Lawyer Mark Mutz and medical professor Richard Gunderman have called it "an obfuscation" designed to remedy the nation's sins, "a ruse that has resulted in an almost Orwellian distortion of the meaning of diversity"—and in turn of education and broader social policy.

Proponents of racial preferences would forevermore have to argue for "diversity" rather than the need to right past wrongs or help those who were disadvantaged by racist structures—at least in court, which is perhaps less honest but didn't much change what they did in practice. A quarter century later, as we saw two chapters ago, the Supreme Court endorsed that diversity rationale as part of a holistic race-conscious admissions program while rejecting a mechanical system that assigned race a fixed number of points. That decision in the *Grutter* case gave administrators far more leeway to decide what they meant by diversity and in effect a way to do an end run around objective standards or ratios to enter a world of unchecked social engineering. And so the diversity-industrial complex moved into a new phase, with universities pursuing racial diversity much more than any other kind but cloaking their actions in legal sophistry.

In that context, it's unsurprising that activist pedagogy sprang up to defend the new ideology. DEI programming developed in parallel with affirmative action before they effectively merged. By some accounts, one in five student protests in the 1960s demanded some form of racial justice on university campuses, which resulted in the creation of more than 500 African American Studies programs, departments, and institutes by 1971.

At the same time, following trends in the corporate sector after the creation of the Equal Employment Opportunity Commission by the Civil Rights Act of 1964 and President Lyndon B. Johnson's Executive Order 11246 of September 1965, universities began to fear the costs and public-relations issues associated with EEOC complaints, fines, and training programs. They started building "diversity" programs themselves, with cost-cutting motives that became clear in the 1980s when President Reagan appointed Clarence Thomas to head up the EEOC. Diversity trainings then began to incorporate principles of social justice and awareness and "appreciation of differences." Nobody seemed satisfied with these new bureaucratic programs, however, with minorities calling them a waste of time and effort and whites accusing their purveyors of "reverse discrimination" through racial preferences and other special considerations. The need to defend against the unpopularity of the programs meant that the definition of success had to be redefined. Thus came the final piece of the DEI puzzle: equality of outcomes, or, as it later became known, "equity."

The groundwork for the full blooming of DEI was developed in three eras: the 1960s through the mid-1970s were about toleration, or the acceptance of racial minorities' integrating into workplaces, education, and neighborhoods. The mid-1970s through the mid-1990s were about multicultural awareness and recognition of minorities and their accomplishments, including dueling metaphors of melting pots and salad bowls. Finally, the mid-1990s ushered in a celebration of diversity, justified by an appeal to inclusion and with the expectation that corporate, educational, and government institutions would reflect the nation's demographics—in other words, equity. The advent of social media accelerated the desire to hold entities "accountable" to DEI metrics, while the death of George Floyd led to a precipitous rise of critical theories that pushed radical race and gender ideologies. DEI became a financially lucrative industry in both the academic and corporate spheres, with the expansion of training, messaging, and general human-resources management tinged with a diversity focus.

These DEI programs and policies are the administrative manifestation of the "critical theory" that developed in university classrooms to reveal, critique, and challenge power structures, with an understanding that certain identity groups deserve special privileges based on suffering under systems of marginalization. As education-policy researchers Jay Greene and Fredrick Hess have put it, "DEI staff operate as a political commissariat, articulating and enforcing a political orthodoxy on campus."

There's nothing hidden about that agenda; the National Association of Diversity Officers in Higher Education—that such an organization even exists is telling—describes itself as "a leading voice in the fight for social justice" and lays out a plan for "creating a framework for diversity officers to advance anti-racism strategies, particularly anti-Black racism, at their respective institutions of higher education." The group, formed in 2006, states that this effort "requires confronting systems, organizational structures, policies, practices, behaviors, and attitudes. This active process should seek to redistribute power in an effort to foster equitable outcomes."

Accordingly, in December 2021, the Council for Higher Education Accreditation (CHEA) implemented its first DEI requirement. CHEA represents 6,000 US universities and recognizes 60 accreditors. For an accreditor to receive approval, it must demonstrate that it "manifests a commitment to diversity, equity, and inclusion." This includes organizations that accredit professional and graduate schools—but not law schools, which we saw in chapter 8 are accredited by the American Bar Association.

The New Political Correctness

We'll return to those themes in the chapters that follow, but first we need to look at the development of political correctness, speech codes, and other attempts to control speech and thought—key aspects of DEI operations.

The best definition of political correctness was provided more than 30 years ago by Glenn Loury, the first black tenured professor at Harvard before a long career at Brown. Loury, now my Manhattan Institute colleague, in a televised *Firing Line* debate in 1991, identified a culture wherein "substantive issues of vital importance can no longer be discussed because the feelings of certain minority groups may be hurt." Of course, political correctness isn't simply a phenomenon where minorities object to certain topics of conversation and indeed is more often used to enforce the prevailing views of those in power. The use of the term dates back to the 1930s, when Americans used it pejoratively to describe adherence to Nazi Germany's doctrines, and even further back to the Russian Revolution and the Soviet Union, when it was used positively as a way of describing people in line with party ideologies. A similar association with progressive ideologies followed the term to the United States.

From about the mid-1980s onward, political correctness began to infect all aspects of campus life, from classrooms to Greek life, from staff parties to law school moot courts, even to the flying of the American flag. Back in 1991, a group of student protesters at the University of Cincinnati who supported the Gulf War were denounced as racist for being against Arab students. The sole black protester was spared the condemnation because the university's official stance, as enshrined in the official handbook, was that only whites could be racist. Instead, he was called a "European-influenced African." That incident, among a rising number of others, got the White House's attention, as President George H. W. Bush condemned the suppression of free speech in a commencement address at the University of Michigan.

In a 1994 *Playboy* survey of college-aged readers, 70 percent reported themselves to be politically correct, with equal numbers responding in the affirmative among both self-identified conservatives and liberals. That same year, the cult-classic film *PCU* came out, presenting an exaggerated view of contemporary college life. I remember watching it as a high schooler and laughing at the farce—not realizing that its plot elements (shutting down fraternities, replacing the school mascot, designating a building for Bisexual Asian Studies) would be quaint compared to real life in the 2020s.

Proponents of political correctness bristled at that criticism, as purveyors of DEI and apologists for cancel culture do now, arguing that it shouldn't be controversial to increase diversity, make people feel included, and stop unfair treatment based in racism, sexism, and homophobia. But then, as now, it's the means that are the problem, not the ends. Between 1986 and 1991, 137 colleges and universities adopted new speech codes, bringing the total to more than 200 institutions that punished allegedly racist or derogatory speech. Whether as a response to purported increase of racist and sexist incidents on campus or merely to avoid negative media attention, administrators became thought police. It was both a risk-minimization and an indoctrination strategy, as students protected from "dangerous" speech, the thinking went, were less likely to cause trouble.

Those speech codes were litigated even before the advent of FIRE, the Foundation for Individual Rights in Education (later Expression), with rulings going largely against the academic institutions. Some early examples:

- In 1989, a University of Michigan student who feared that in-class discussions about biological differences between sexes and races might subject him to discipline under a policy that prohibited stigmatizing speech successfully sued to strike down that policy. The federal district court found in *Doe v. University of Michigan* that the policy's terms were vague enough that enforcing them would violate due process—not to mention spark an "investigation" that might lead to remedial education about "harmful speech"—and broad enough to infringe on constitutionally protected speech.

- In a settlement of the 1990 case *Wu v. University of Connecticut*, a student who had been expelled under a speech code banning bad jokes and name-calling won a consent decree reinstating her and invalidating the policy. She had hung a sign in her dorm that joked about the shooting on sight of "preppies, bimbos, men without chest hair, racists and homos." UConn changed its policy to target "fighting words," abusive epithets that are likely to provoke a violent reaction from an ordinary person and thus aren't protected by the First Amendment.

- In the 1991 case *UWM Post v. Board of Regents*, a federal district court similarly struck down a University of Wisconsin policy that prohibited "expressive behavior" that demeaned another race, sex, or religion or created a hostile educational environment as unconstitutionally vague and overbroad. The court further held that the speech code wasn't covered by the "fighting words" exception because it punished speech that wasn't likely to provoke a violent reaction.

- In the 1995 case *Corry v. Stanford University*, a California state court similarly invalidated a Stanford speech code that prohibited harassment by "personal vilification through speech." Although private universities have more leeway to regulate students than public ones do, you'll recall from chapter 9 that California's Leonard Law affords students at private schools full First Amendment protection.

Despite those legal victories and ones that would come later, speech codes have had a chilling effect. With the constant flux of what constitutes disfavored speech, students are never sure about what could land them in hot water and the Kafkaesque nightmare they'll have to endure once a complaint is filed. On the other hand, administrators face a constant challenge of how to enforce vague policies and thus bring their own subjective biases to bear—driving an additional wedge between students and faculty, who fear being criticized for supporting "oppressive" speech and creating "unsafe" spaces. Even when formal speech codes are struck down or repealed, implicit codes enforce a rigid orthodoxy that makes everyone walk on eggshells.

As FIRE's Azhar Majeed has written, "Implicit speech codes are informal mechanisms through which administrators, on an ad hoc basis, censor and punish speech they dislike. They represent an attempt to evade the constitutional scrutiny attached to written speech codes," which at least specify what's prohibited even if they're too broad.[2] Implicit codes lack a clear set of rules and so give arbitrary power to educational officials, especially those in DEI offices, who now "investigate" the vast majority of speech complaints under "antidiscrimination" and "harassment" policies. This is also where the language of "harm" and threatening someone's "right to exist" comes in.

In 1998, University of Pennsylvania history professor Alan Charles Kors and criminal defense attorney Harvey Silverglate published *The Shadow University: The Betrayal of Liberty on America's Campuses.* That broadside by committed civil libertarians—Silverglate had served on the board of the Massachusetts ACLU—labeled speech codes, as well as multicultural "diversity education" programs, as coercive "academic thought reform." The book posited that political correctness had led to the emergence of a "shadow university," as administrators, dorm advisers, and student-life officers treated students as embodiments of abstract groups. Kors and Silverglate charged that the "political and cultural left" was the worst abuser of the principles of open, equal free speech and

---

2. Azhar Majeed, "Defying the Constitution: The Rise, Persistence, and Prevalence of Campus Speech Codes," *Georgetown Journal of Law & Public Policy* 7, no. 2 (2009): 500.

argued that a double standard prevails whereby self-appointed progressives censor voices deemed offensive to women and minorities, while these same "progressives" condone equally offensive speech directed against conservatives, religious Christians, and others. The authors documented repressive speech codes, sweeping notions of sexual harassment, and arbitrary disciplinary hearings against students and faculty that lacked due process protections. To say that their book was prescient is an understatement.

The following year, Kors and Silverglate launched FIRE to fight back against all that stuff. FIRE has been spectacularly successful in building on the early legal victories listed above, suing colleges and universities regarding speech and due process practices. The organization's efforts, including sophisticated media and public-relations strategies, have led many institutions to repeal speech codes and replace them with actual protections of free expression. But problems persist, leading the organization to rate individual universities' speech climates, including by assigning explicit speech policies a color on a traffic-light system.

Red means that a school substantially restricts protected speech; yellow means that it applies either restrictions on a narrower range of expression or vague policies that could easily be applied to restrict protected expression. In FIRE's 2023 ratings, of the nearly 500 schools evaluated, 19.3 percent received a red-light rating (13.9 percent of public schools, 37.8 percent among private), 66.7 percent received a yellow light (70.7 percent public, 53.2 percent private), and only 12.3 percent received a green light (14.9 percent public, 3.6 percent private). The rest got a "blue light," meaning a warning that it's a school that prioritizes other values over free speech. Red- and yellow-light policies at public schools would be held unconstitutional if subjected to judicial scrutiny. As for private schools, which aren't legally bound by the First Amendment—except in states that explicitly bind them, as with California's Leonard Law—they violate the contractual promises they make to community members about their commitment to free-speech values. For example, setting aside the high-profile examples of Georgetown, Yale, and Stanford, schools as different as Howard University and the University of Tulsa—both of which explicitly guarantee their students the freedom of speech—have rules that explicitly limit forms of that expression, under which controversies have arisen.

More than 100 institutions have endorsed a version of the Report of the Committee on Freedom of Expression at the University of Chicago (known as the Chicago Statement), which is the gold standard. The problem is that, as I experienced personally, so many of these speech-and-expression policies aren't worth the paper (or pixels) they're written on, falling by the wayside when seeming to conflict with the demands of DEI.

Law schools largely apply the speech codes of their parent universities and don't often have distinct policies on discrimination and harassment, event disruption, student/faculty discipline, and the like. But they do, of course, establish their own cultures and issue their own public statements to shape those cultures—as nearly all of them did in the wake of the killing of George Floyd—and they do have their own curated DEI policies. These policies, at least as applied by the diversity apparatus and in sharp contrast to Stanford Dean Martinez's letter, make clear that values such as truth-seeking and lawyer-training take a back seat to critical legal theory, with its emphasis on power dynamics. In this way of thinking, free speech isn't an absolute good but must be weighed on an intersectional scale to tear down systemically oppressive rules and structures. It's an administrative microcosm of the view that the law can't be neutral but must be read, or rewritten, in the interest of a particular type of social justice.

CHAPTER 11

Critical Theory Destroys the Law

When I was in law school in the early 2000s, critical theory, with all its Hegelian and culturally Marxist discourse, was a spent force. It was something from the 1980s and early 1990s that had run its course, with outcroppings in some academic faculties but remaining little more than a niche theory with little direct application in professional schools. But now "the crits" are back, even stronger, and not just in literature and sociology departments. In the debate over woke education, defenders of new curricula argue that critical race theory (CRT) and the like are academic ideas residing only in law schools, not grade schools. Well, regardless of what's going on in K–12 or even undergraduate teaching, Derrick Bell and Kimberlé Crenshaw have eclipsed William Blackstone and Louis Brandeis as avatars of legal education. That academic shift, when coupled with the previously described bureaucratic growth, has led many law schools to prioritize activism over inquiry, seeking social justice rather than truth.

The progenitor of CRT, critical legal studies, can be traced all the way back to a 1937 manifesto of the Institute for Social Research in Frankfurt, Germany, titled *Traditional and Critical Theory*. That school, which is at the eponymous heart of a mode of social research now known simply as the "Frankfurt School," was originally to be named the Institute for Marxism, but even the founders thought that would be too on the nose. Its mission statement, written by the school's second director, Max Horkheimer, during the height of Stalin's purges and famines, questions existing social structures and power dynamics but is sanguine about the actions committed under the political philosophy that influenced it.

Inheriting a definition of relativism from Friedrich Nietzsche, Georg William Friedrich Hegel, and Karl Marx, Horkheimer argued in a collection of essays that "he who has eyes for the meaningless injustice of the imperialist world . . . will regard the events in Russia as the progressive painful attempt to overcome this injustice." After fleeing to New York to escape the Third Reich, Horkheimer and the other Frankfurt scholars established the School of Critical Theory at Columbia University in 1935. While Horkheimer would return to Germany after the war, he left behind his students and fellow scholars, who would carry on the growth of critical theory in the United States—most notably Herbert Marcuse. With roots in sociology and literary criticism, critical theory argues that social problems stem more from political structures and cultural assumptions than from individuals and that retrograde ideology and the corrupt organizational systems it produces are the principal obstacles to human liberation.

After Horkheimer's scholars realized that critical theory was being rejected by the American working class, who believed they were able to overcome their economic origins through hard work, education, and community support instead of class revolution, a second wave of critical theorists found a new entry point of influence in the racial unrest of the 1960s. Turning their critique to social and legal systems, they strove to convince racial minorities that the system was against them and that it must be torn down and rebuilt, giving birth to critical legal studies.

Critical Legal Studies and Critical Race Theory

Critical legal studies (CLS) is a type of critical theory that developed in the United States in the 1970s. CLS adherents claim that laws enshrine biases against marginalized groups and thus preserve the status quo. The law is thus necessarily intertwined with social structures and inherently embodies racism and other biases. CLS proponents believe that the law supports the interests of those that create it, so their project is to upend the structure of modern society by using the law. CLS scholars also criticize the formalist approach to law, which they see as overly focused on analyzing the internal logic of legal doctrines, principles, and texts without considering broader social and political implications. From their perspective, the law is simply the codification of the cultural and political preferences of those in power, including the privileging of whites, men, and the wealthy over nonwhites, women, and the poor.

CLS has been closely associated with the study of race and racism in the law. CLS scholars thus look at the ways in which legal doctrine, interpretation, and practice are used to justify and maintain racial oppression. The prominent CLS theorist Duncan Kennedy encapsulated the movement in his contribution to a 2002 book of essays on progressive legal theory called *Left Originalism/Left Critique*, writing, "Critical legal studies operates at the uneasy juncture of two distinct but sometimes complementary enterprises . . . the left and modernist/post-modernist projects." He argued that leftism and CLS aim to transform existing social structures based on a critique of their injustice at the hands of a racist, capitalist patriarchy. The goal of CLS is thus to replace the system with a more socially just regime; the apparently neutral language and institutions of the law mask the relationships of power and control such that true justice can be achieved only by transforming the ways in which the law shapes and is shaped by racial hierarchies. CLS from its inception was a full-frontal assault on the edifice of jurisprudential thought, affecting the gamut of legal fields, not just constitutional law but property law, labor law, and criminal law.

In 1973, Derrick Bell, the first black tenured professor at Harvard Law School, disappointed with what he believed to be the inadequate progress made by the civil rights movement, wrote that racism was a permanent feature of American life that couldn't be remedied under existing legal structures and institutions. He believed that racial discrimination was perpetrated by the legal system itself and that these inequities then spill over into law enforcement, legislation, and the economy. Dissatisfied with Harvard's lack of support for his work, he left in 1980 to become dean at the University of Oregon. In response, students began protesting the lack of diversity on Harvard's law faculty. These protesters were dissatisfied with the limitations of CLS as such and sought to expand their studies to the area of race under the guise of equity and social justice. The *Harvard Law Review* invited Bell to write the prestigious foreword to its 1984 Supreme Court volume. Bell felt anxious about writing an academic article, so he proposed writing four *fictional* stories about race and the law. The student editors, among whom was future Supreme Court Justice Elena Kagan, agreed, allowing Bell to dispense with academic rigor and instead present his theories of racial grievance as allegorical narratives. Those establishmentarian career-builders thus helped boost Bell's status and mainstream the ideas that would become CRT.

In 1989, Kimberlé W. Crenshaw, a disciple of Bell who would become a law professor at UCLA and Columbia, organized a workshop in honor of his scholarship that established the new academic framework of critical race theory, a term she is credited with coining. Realizing that neo-Marxism would be a hard sell, she urged educators to teach the belief that racism is a fundamental part of American society that can't be corrected by the legal system, that minorities' interests are secondary in a system built by white upper-class men, and thus that any minority advancements are allowed only when they serve the systemic interest—what Bell called the "interest convergence dilemma." Crenshaw is also known for introducing and developing the study of "intersectionality," meaning how various social identities overlap and relate to systems of discrimination and oppression.

Bell ended up resigning his Oregon deanship over the university's failure to hire an Asian American woman he recommended for the law faculty. He returned to Harvard in 1986 and staged a five-day sit-in to protest the school's denial of tenure to two professors who worked on CRT. Students generally supported the sit-in but faculty were split, because some believed that the professors had been denied tenure for not meeting expectations in scholarship and teaching. By 1990, Bell was so upset at the lack of faculty diversity that he took a leave of absence, vowing not to return until HLS hired a black woman. Administrators cited a lack of qualified candidates and laid out the progress they'd made in bringing in black faculty members—of whom there were now three (including him) among the 60 tenured professors.

Although many students supported him—including a young Barack Obama, who compared him to civil rights hero Rosa Parks—Bell's protest ignited angry criticism and backlash, including from those who were sympathetic to his goals but found his means counterproductive. Opposing faculty called him "a media manipulator who unfairly attacked the school," with some women complaining that he had unfairly hijacked their issue and "deprived students of an education while he makes money on the lecture circuit." After two years, which Bell spent as a visiting professor at NYU, when Harvard had still not hired any black women, he requested an extension of his leave. The school refused, effectively ending Bell's tenure.

CRT scholars have built on Bell and Crenshaw's foundational work to conflate and even replace the traditional American belief in equality (of legal status and opportunity) with the newer idea of racial equity (equality of outcome). Racial equality, which seeks to protect individual rights regardless of race, is a term of art codified into law through the Fourteenth and Fifteenth Amendments, the Civil Rights Act of 1964, the Voting Rights Act of 1965, and subsequent legislation. CRT scholars have argued, however, that legal equality has not gone far enough and, under the pretense that the current system is one built to uphold white supremacy, have thus rejected the ideas of nondiscrimination, color-blindness, freedom of speech, meritocracy, and private property because they are tools in the systemic oppression of racial minorities. They would prefer race-conscious systems to ensure equal outcomes across races by providing groups believed to be harmed by the system additional positive rights and benefits.

In 1993, UCLA law professor Cheryl Harris published "Whiteness as Property" in the *Harvard Law Review*, arguing for suspending property rights, seizing land and wealth from the traditionally white upper class, and redistributing it along race-based lines. Fast-forward a quarter century and "Africana" studies professor Ibram X. Kendi (born Ibram Henry Rogers), in his bestselling 2019 book *How to Be an Antiracist*, argued that the opposite of racist is antiracist rather than simply nonracist and that there's no middle ground: one either confronts racial inequality or allows it to exist. "The language of color blindness—like the language of 'not racist'—is a mask to hide when someone is being racist. . . . A colorblind Constitution for a White-supremacist America." Kendi was explicitly saying that not being racist is itself being racist.

Kendi defines as racist any policy that creates disparate results between people of different skin colors; unequal outcomes based on race are always the product of racist policies, such that colorblindness is itself a form of white supremacy: "There is no such thing as a race-neutral policy. Every policy in every institution in every community in every nation is producing or sustaining either racial inequity or equity." For example, racial preferences in admissions are antiracist because they remedy past discrimination, while inaction on climate change is racist because of the disproportionately severe impact on the predominantly nonwhite Global South.

Kendi has proposed a constitutional amendment to create a Department of Antiracism. This independent body would have the unchecked power to investigate and abolish any federal, state, or local law that it unilaterally determines to have a racially inequitable impact—and would be able to censor the speech of politicians and academics. Both Kendi and Harris have advocated for the abolition of capitalism, claiming that its structure is white-supremacist. Still, Kendi charges $20,000 an hour for virtual presentations and has a merchandise line.

I've purposely not quoted any CRT critics here because its proponents provide more than enough fodder to show, and readily admit, how illiberal—against the established liberal order—this framework is. Bringing us back to the racial gloss on critical legal studies, CRT scholars Richard Delgado and Jean Stefancic, authors of the seminal *Critical Race Theory: An Introduction*, describe their movement as follows:

> The critical race theory (CRT) movement is a collection of activists and scholars interested in studying and transforming the relationship among race, racism, and power. The movement considers many of the same issues that conventional civil rights and ethnic studies discourses take up but places them in a broader perspective that includes economics, history, setting, group and self-interest, and emotions and the unconscious. Unlike traditional civil rights, which embraces incrementalism and step-by-step progress, critical race theory questions the very foundations of the liberal order, including equality theory, legal reasoning, Enlightenment rationalism, and neutral principles of constitutional law.

CRT Warps Legal Education

There's a reason I went from Harris's 1993 article to Kendi's 2019 book: in the interim, the CLS/CRT wave crested and seemed to wash away.

Baby Boomer liberals, who dominated law school faculties in the late 1990s and 2000s, frowned at both the lack of intellectual rigor of the "crits" and their preference for activism over scholarship. My law school cohort encountered CRT as a fringe theory that had faded into the academic background. And there it remained until the mid-2010s, when two developments pushed identity-focused approaches back to the fore, where they would be joined by changes to how children were raised, leading to perversions of cognitive behavioral therapy becoming embedded in higher-ed structures.

The first was the August 2014 shooting of Michael Brown in Ferguson, Missouri, and the resulting protests around the country that launched the current era of social justice activism. Although subsequent investigations debunked the "Hands up, don't shoot" narrative that blamed police for shooting an unarmed black man, fear of public retribution for ordinary law enforcement—and demands to "defund the police"—led to a police pullback. The extent of the "Ferguson effect" on crime rates, compounded by other high-profile police killings and eclipsed by the George Floyd murder six years later, is much debated, but academia took notice. For example, the Faculty Development and Instructional Design Center at Northern Illinois University published a list of strategies for how faculty can respond to national events, which included inviting counselors to talk in class and making accommodations for students emotionally affected by them. Law schools hosted panels, lectures, conferences, and seminars for months, integrating conversations about race and policing, as well as broader racial subjects, into unrelated classes.

At the same time, and as documented by Greg Lukianoff and Jonathan Haidt in their bestselling 2018 book, *The Coddling of the American Mind*, overprotection, including the advent of "trigger warnings" and "safe spaces," was having a negative effect on college students. The authors argued that many campus problems originate in three "great untruths" that have come to the fore in education: "What doesn't kill you makes you weaker"; "Always trust your feelings"; and "Life is a battle between good people and evil people." They explained how these three principles contradict both modern psychology and ancient wisdom. *Coddling* went on to discuss microaggressions, identity politics, and cancel culture (then labeled "call-out culture"). The authors despaired that "safetyism" had become a "sacred value," so there's now a system of belief in which people can't process other practical and moral concerns (which presaged responses to the Covid pandemic in the most educated parts of America). Embracing safetyism has interfered with young people's social, emotional, and intellectual development. Any ideas that challenge preconceived notions or make someone feel even slightly uncomfortable are to be banished. And layered on top of those social-emotional developments was rising political polarization such that contrasting ideological positions are "locked into a game of mutual provocation and reciprocal outrage."

An early manifestation of this dynamic came in fall 2015 to Nicholas and Erika Christakis, co-masters of one of Yale's residential colleges—professors who live on-site and are responsible for academic, intellectual, and social life. They were pilloried for their response to an email from the Intercultural Affairs Council recommending that students avoid Halloween costumes that were "culturally insensitive." After that missive rubbed many community members the wrong way, Erika sent an email drawing on her scholarship in developmental psychology and arguing that students should be free to dress themselves and questioning whether the role of administrators is to police Halloween attire. Nicholas defended his wife in an infamous public confrontation during which students berated him for making them feel unsafe. The Christakises encouraged students to engage in open dialogue and develop the ability to tolerate offense; students accused them of placing the burden of confrontation and education on racial minorities.

A few days later, 1,000 students who were immune to irony participated in a "March of Resilience" against what one protester described as an "inhospitable climate for people of color." Commentator (and Yale alum) James Kirchik chronicled in *Tablet* magazine that 200 students then descended on Yale president Peter Salovey's house with a list of demands that included requiring ethnic studies classes; adding mental health services; and, of course, that the Christakises be fired. More than 400 faculty members signed a letter expressing support for students working to undo "institutionalized inequalities that exist at our university." Two weeks after the protests, the university acceded to the demands, announcing a doubling in funding for cultural-center budgets and racial sensitivity training for administrators and faculty. The Christakises stepped down from their Silliman College posts less than a year later—Nicholas remains a Sterling Professor, Yale's highest academic rank, while Erika left teaching—and the university soon renamed their "master" positions as simply "head of college."

Similar incidents followed. In September 2016, NYU professor Michael Rectenwald created the Twitter account @antipcnyuprof and used it to criticize political correctness and social-justice activism on college campuses. After being outed by a student reporter, he was summoned by his dean and "strongly encouraged" to take a leave of absence. Then, in February 2017, responding to an email from the Faculty Diversity and Inclusion Standing Committee at Duke Divinity School urging enrollment in racial equity training—"We hope that this will be a first step in a longer process of working to ensure that DDS is an institution that is both equitable and anti-racist"—Professor Paul Griffiths argued that such training was anti-intellectual and had "illiberal roots and totalitarian tendencies." "(Re)trainings of intellectuals by bureaucrats and apparatchiks have a long and ignoble history," he noted, urging his colleagues not to waste time on the event. Griffiths was subjected to disciplinary proceedings and eventually resigned.

In March 2017, Evergreen State College biology professor Bret Weinstein wrote a letter objecting to his school's observance of a Day of Absence, during which minority students stay away from campus to highlight their contributions. An administrator had suggested that this time white students should absent themselves and instead attend an off-campus program on race issues. Weinstein wrote that the change removed the event's voluntary nature and turned it into an act of oppression in and of itself. Protests broke out on campus, disrupting one of Weinstein's classes—which he was holding in a park after police told him to avoid campus. He would later sue Evergreen State for its inability to "protect its employees from repeated provocative and corrosive verbal and written hostility based on race, as well as threats of physical violence." The college paid him and his wife $500,000 in exchange for their resignations.

All this sort of thing—the systemic cancellation of professors and disruption of guest speakers for "controversial" opinions, typically on subjects with a racial valence—is a fairly recent phenomenon, dating back no more than a decade. As Lukianoff and Haidt documented in *Coddling of the American Mind*, students are "no longer as reliably pro–free speech as [they] were before 2013–2014." Combine that trend with the bureaucratic growth in DEI offices, and you've got the perfect illiberal storm, operationalizing structural critiques of institutions in the interest of "inclusion" and to help students feel "safe." CRT has thus become both a tool and a vehicle for groups seeking to advance artificial complaints, using theoretical architecture and sophistic language to create the impression that their argument has a historical basis and possesses moral weight.

As this renewed CRT began to make its way through collegiate minds, classrooms, and social media, the students who had faced no opposition—and indeed were encouraged—in their activism in college in the late 2010s became law students. Faced with a generation of students wielding social media like a loaded gun, administrators were able to use the pandemonium of 2020 to force whatever definition of justice they desired.

In the summer of 2021, Columbia University president Lee Bollinger, who had been the president of the University of Michigan during the 2003 affirmative-action cases, said that CRT was "urgent and necessary." Starting in fall 2022, Georgetown Law has required students to take a class on the "importance of questioning the law's neutrality through its differential effects on subordinated groups." A plethora of law schools have followed, ones as diverse—pun intended—as USC, UC Irvine, Cardozo, and Boston College.

At Santa Clara University, the law school administration sent out an email claiming that the acquittal of Kyle Rittenhouse was "further evidence of the persistent racial injustice and systemic racism within our criminal justice system." UC Irvine's chief DEI officer emailed that the acquittal conveyed the message that black lives don't matter to the legal system. Professors have come forward saying that they're afraid to teach historical cases in which race, sexual violence, or the police play a role. One liberal criminal law professor at a top school has given up teaching theories of punishment altogether because of the negative reaction he received from his students to the idea of retributivism. "I got into this job because I liked to play devil's advocate," he told the *Washington Free Beacon*'s Aaron Sibarium. "I can't do that anymore. I have a family."

Nadine Strossen, the first woman to head the ACLU and a longtime professor at New York Law School, has been open about how she self-censors, assuming that every single word, facial gesture, and tone is being recorded, analyzed, and sent out across the world. She likened it to trying to teach law from inside a panopticon (a prison where inmates are constantly being observed). Harvard law professor Randall Kennedy, who in 2013 published *For Discrimination: Race, Affirmative Action and the Law*, had long been saying that the fear that law schools were becoming illiberal—shutting down unpopular voices—was overblown. At a panel in December 2020, however, he admitted to changing his mind and is now afraid that law schools have a big problem. Another Harvard law professor commented that students have told him that they have refused to participate in class because they face "social death" if they step out of ideological line. When a Boston College law professor asked his students if any of them thought that we should *not* scrap the Constitution, not a single student raised their hand.

After George Floyd and in line with a burgeoning "racial reckoning," Professor Matthew Steilen of the University of Buffalo Law School started a Twitter discussion among fellow constitutional law professors about whether to teach *Dred Scott v. Sandford* (which held that people of African descent can't be citizens and thus don't have rights) because "reading it is gratuitously insulting and demeaning" and might traumatize his students. Steilen also omitted *Plessy v. Ferguson* (which allowed segregation under the "separate but equal" doctrine) other than when discussing *Brown v. Board of Education*, which overruled it. Michigan Law's Julian Davis Mortenson takes an opposite tack, beginning his course with *Dred Scott* because it "conveys the essence of Critical Race Theory to a person encountering these ideas for the first time: this is the Supreme Court explaining how the United States has been superracist forever and endorsing the racism."[1]

---

1. Jeannie Suk Gerson, "The Importance of Teaching Dred Scott," *New Yorker*, June 8, 2021.

Yale Law School even created CRT merchandise, with the office of student affairs encouraging students to "swing by" to pick up a T-shirt that repeats the phrase "reparations & prison abolition" five times before ending with the phrase "critical race theory & yale law school." Kate Stith, the former acting Yale dean who moderated the March 2022 panel that was shouted down, commented in the media, "Law schools are in crisis. The truth doesn't matter much. The game is to signal one's virtue."

In 2020, 176 law school deans petitioned the American Bar Association to require that "every law school provide training and education around bias, cultural competence, and anti-racism." And so on February 14, 2022, the ABA, by a vote of 348–17, instituted a new rule requiring all of the law schools it accredits (around 200) to do just that. The professional-responsibility class that all law graduates have long had to take must now teach would-be lawyers that they have a duty to eliminate racism. Ten Yale law professors, including such liberal lions as Bruce Ackerman and Akhil Amar, responded with an open letter, calling it a "disturbing" attempt to "institutionalize dogma" via the process of accreditation and an attempt to circumvent law school autonomy. The new conditions would "almost certainly violate the academic freedom rights of faculty at many (probably most) schools," wrote Brian Leiter, a legal theorist at the University of Chicago whom nobody would accuse of being conservative.

And so we come full circle, with the resurrection of CRT not just through an expanding number of "crits" on faculties but the institutionalization of the ideas of Horkheimer, Bell, and Crenshaw. CRT, like its ideological predecessor CLS, turns legitimate legal inquiry into social justice advocacy and, when promulgated by official bodies, indoctrination. Instead of using the law to establish and protect individual rights and freedoms, CRT (and more broadly DEI) recasts entire categories of people as inherently victimized beyond any instances of harm, injury, or prejudice. It turns evidentiary standards upside down by asserting that a wrong has occurred ipso facto—in and of itself—in a way that would be an illegitimate nonstarter to even question, regardless of any proof or even due process. American law, however, is already rich in protections and opportunities for those who are wronged in some way. They include not only a full panoply of constitutional rights, but state and federal legislation that is constantly being expanded to provide a full tool kit to all those who may seek to advocate for their rights and interests. These tools run the gamut of public (constitutional, administrative) and private (torts, contracts) law.

To the CRT/DEI coalition, that's not good enough. Reinforcing legal rights isn't the goal, nor is equality; justice and equity are. But what exactly is justice? Normally it refers to equal treatment under the law or the prevailing of truth on behalf of those who've been injured. But that's not enough for those who believe that the very structures that are supposed to deliver these moral goods, based on neutral rules—Lady Justice is blindfolded, applying the law without fear or favor—are corrupt. And so there are demands to "burn it all down" or at least "fundamentally transform" society. It's a call to revolution.

Why has such a call, which is debated in places ranging from the proverbial college bull sessions to cable news and social media, found purchase in law schools? These are supposed to be staid institutions that teach the next generation to uphold the rule of law. Well, with the ground already softened by the loss of societal trust in institutions across the board, the Covid-19 pandemic addled minds and provided a crisis of the sort that allowed the killing of George Floyd to be used as a catalyst for spreading radical change across all of society. Not surprisingly, academic institutions, *especially* law schools, are at the forefront of this revolution.

CHAPTER 12

Covid Regulations Normalized Illogical Thinking

People who study these things point to the Ferguson protests of 2014 as the discernible moment when CRT/woke ideology broke into the mainstream. And indeed, surveys that try to measure these things point to President Obama's second term as the time when the state of "race relations," which had been on an upward trajectory for decades, since the 1992 LA riots after the acquittal of the police officers who beat Rodney King, began to decline. That timeline certainly comports with the general feeling—the changing "vibe," as the kids call it—in legal and policy circles.

The pandemic accelerated the trend toward perceiving our nation as uniquely racially intolerant, particularly as cultural influencers and idea entrepreneurs retreated to their laptops. The killing of George Floyd threw gas onto that fire, as the institutions controlled by the left—most of them—decided to radically restructure themselves overnight, centered on "antiracism." Ibram Kendi became a patron saint, along with his sidekick Robin DiAngelo of *White Fragility* fame. In academia, even the places that had been holding the classical-liberal line, including my alma mater, Princeton, fell. Everybody all of a sudden needed a vice president or associate dean for DEI. As the pandemic recedes in our collective memory, there's no indication that these illiberal trends will likewise go away.

Indeed, the pandemic was a boon to bureaucratic leviathans wishing to crawl even further into normal life. Anything could be justified as long as it was labeled a public-safety initiative. Any questioning of regulations would be labeled thought crime. In the resultant atmosphere, institutions seemed like organs of disorder and illogic, so it's little wonder that anarchic elements arose that questioned the very foundations of law and order. The nation was a tinderbox of resentment, isolation, and nonsensical rituals. All it needed was a spark to burst into chaos.

Minneapolis police officer Derek Chauvin murdered Floyd on May 25, 2020, kneeling on his neck for nine minutes while arresting him for trying to pass a counterfeit $20 bill. Protests and riots broke out around the country, described by the media as "mostly peaceful" expressions of pain and encouraged by public-health authorities that had been condemning protests of Covid-related restrictions and lockdowns. Monuments, memorials, and other civic symbols were defaced and toppled, while a section of Seattle was taken over by a lawless "autonomous zone." Essentially every corporation in every sector of American life, from Amazon and Apple to Walmart and Whataburger, issued statements condemning white supremacy and police brutality. They also made donations to black and left-leaning charities, especially Black Lives Matter—a decentralized network of racial-justice groups that emerged after the 2013 acquittal of George Zimmerman in the shooting death of Trayvon Martin—which turned out to be a major grift for its founders.

As a result of the national backlash, fueled by corporate dollars and media promotion, police were attacked verbally, politically, and physically, leading to declines in morale and resignations and a tolerance of criminal violence whose precipitous increase has been most felt by black communities. In an ominous illustration of Czech playwright and statesman Václav Havel's greengrocer—who displays a "Workers of the world, unite!" sign not as a symbol of communist enthusiasm but of his submission to the regime—business owners were pressured to place BLM signs in their windows or face boycotts, if not worse. I have a friend here in Falls Church, Virginia, whose fitness studio was slandered on social media and ultimately went out of business after she declined to put up such a sign. Charitable institutions large and small likewise scrambled to prove their social-justice bona fides; the board of our small neighborhood preschool spent an entire meeting and copious emails debating whether to issue a statement.

Not surprisingly, pretty much every university president and law school dean similarly felt the need to adopt a public CRT stance, going far beyond condemnations of police brutality to Kendi-style antiracism and messaging that warned of the hidden white supremacy in their midst. "As an academic community built on the bedrock values of diversity, inclusion, and openness, we have an obligation to ensure that the forces of these events and our feelings drive us not backward, but forward," stated Cornell president Martha Pollack in June 2020, calling for the need to take "whatever steps we can to fight against systemic racism and structural inequality." A little over a month later, she followed up with "additional actions to create a more just and equitable Cornell," which included a new required class on racism, bias, and equity; the creation of a new Anti-Racism Center "that further strengthens our research and education on systems and structures that perpetuate racism and inequality"; new programs on the history of race, racism, and colonialism; professional development opportunities "with a focus on staff of color"; and, of course, making DEI work part of performance reviews.

Pollack's statements were wholly representative of academic leaders' handwringing in the summer of 2020. The Association of American Law Schools, for its part, established the Law Deans Antiracist Clearinghouse Project to develop, curate, and disseminate antiracism resources directly to law school deans. As I mentioned earlier, nearly all law school deans petitioned the ABA to make antiracism training part of the accreditation process.

Law School Survey

The National Association for Law Placement (NALP) conducted a law-school survey over the summer of 2020 to learn more about the effect of these cultural events on law schools. The survey found that 90 percent of the law schools that answered (35 public and 53 private) had implemented new DEI efforts and initiatives after the death of George Floyd: 64 percent held a town hall, 50 percent increased DEI training for faculty and staff, 40 percent increased DEI training for students, 20 percent added an elective or mandatory course on DEI-related topics, and 4.5 percent added a DEI-related clinic. An example of the last is the trend toward offerings in "movement lawyering," an activist approach to law that the ABA defines as "building the power of the people, not the power of the law" because "support is needed as people take to the streets and hold spaces to collectively heal and as we work over the long haul to dismantle systems of oppression, including white supremacy, cis-heteropatriarchy, and capitalism in our country." In early 2023, the University of Pennsylvania Carey Law School launched an Advocacy for Racial and Civil Justice Clinic, which guides students to "read about and reflect on historical and contemporary strategies for achieving racial justice" and the "theory of movement lawyering." Penn thus joined Cornell, which has a Movement Lawyering Clinic where "law students provide legal support for social justice groups including women's liberation, Black liberation, immigrants' and LGBTQ rights, and more." And Columbia Law offered a Reading Group in Movement Lawyering in 2020. The law schools at Duke and Howard, among others, are also currently offering clinics (not just academic courses) in movement, or "social justice," lawyering.

Not wanting to be outdone, Georgetown Law reoriented its entire curriculum through the CRT lens, as documented by the *Washington Free Beacon's* Aaron Sibarium. In September 2021, the faculty implemented a new "institutional learning outcome": all students should graduate with an "ability to think critically about the law's claim to neutrality and its differential effects on subordinated groups, including those identified by race, gender, indigeneity, and class." Administrators were instructed to find professors who "advance the new institutional learning outcome" through their pedagogy already. One of these is Madhavi Sunder, who on the first day of her mandatory 1L (first-year) class teaches that American property law is "the history of dispossession and appropriation." "Possession," one lecture slide reads, "is a legal term of art for a settler capitalist society."

Of note, private schools were generally higher than public ones on all these measures of DEI adherence, which may reflect the fewer legal constraints they face in their operations but may also be a function of selection bias in terms of which schools felt free to respond to the survey. But all those survey numbers have no doubt increased since— particularly the courses and clinics, which are significant undertakings that would've been hard to develop quickly.

The NALP survey also included a question about what the law schools were doing to "support students of color." Here's a random sampling of responses that conflict with free speech, equal opportunity, and other classically liberal values: removing from common areas images and speech deemed by DEI staff to be inequitable, rejecting speakers who aren't DEI-compliant, limiting possible employers to those that can prove they are DEI-compliant, DEI-only student newsletters, clerkship programs only for students of color, compulsory "ally skills" training, restructuring of externships to prioritize DEI-championed students, training for faculty on how to make all core classes "antiracist," and writing contests on DEI topics. These are all things that were developed just between June and August 2020.

Going beyond the survey, whatever it's worth, here are some concrete actions that law schools took—again a random sample that crossed my transom while I was writing this book—official actions, not student protests or disruptions:

1. At Emory University School of Law in Atlanta, the commitment-to-DEI statement includes the goal of working within a strategic planning process to revise the school's mission and values to show "commitment to antiracism." The form that this commitment will take, considering the school's promotion of events with Kendi and Professor Dorothy Brown, author of *The Whiteness of Wealth: How the Tax System Impoverishes Black Americans—and How We Can Fix It*, is bound to come into conflict with the university's Respect for Open Expression policy. That policy has been the saving grace for students and speakers alike, but the school established a DEI subcommittee to review it. The subcommittee produced a memo with potential changes that were never made public but were confirmed by the dean to have been partially implemented.

Maybe that's why when a group of Emory law students established the Emory Free Speech Forum (EFSF) to create a place for interested students to hear, consider, and debate diverse ideas, they had a hard time gaining formal recognition as a student organization. The Student Bar Association denied the EFSF's application twice, under the pretext that the group "overlapped" with others—but also because open inquiry is "harmful." An SBA rep remarked that EFSF members were incapable of operating a free-speech group because of their perceived skin color: "I don't know how like y'all would foster like such diverse conversations because . . . like no offense . . . all of you are white." (The EFSF members are not all white.) The Foundation Against Intolerance and Racism (FAIR) sent a letter to Emory in January 2022, informing the SBA that its actions violated Title VI of the Civil Rights Act, which bars federally funded institutions from discriminating based on race. After FAIR engaged counsel, SBA notified the EFSF that it had granted its charter.

2. But apparently being "too white" is more contagious than any coronavirus. In March 2021, the co-deans of Case Western Reserve University School of Law criticized their own students for their paleness. Jessica Berg and Michael Scharf emailed that they were upset that the school had been included in "The Whitest Law Schools in America," a study prepared by a professor emerita at the University of Dayton. The report measured "diversity" at 200 law schools to identify "excess whiteness" and rank them on how "inappropriately white" they were. Although Case Western ranked 144th, making it the second-least-white law school in Ohio, Berg and Scharf, who had written in a September 2020 letter that they were "mobilized by recent incidents of racism and police brutality" to "integrat[e] racial justice into the curriculum," told students that they shouldn't be satisfied with the status quo.

3. Later that spring, the University of Washington School of Law issued social media guidelines that require students not to post anything "that could be viewed as discriminating in any way." Should students violate these guidelines, they would be referred to the university for a violation of the code of conduct. Although the guidelines are labeled as best practices to prevent bullying and racial (and other) discrimination, legal scholars commented that they're an attempt to limit speech based on some harassment exception to the First Amendment that doesn't exist. The guidelines haven't been tested but would be unlikely to survive in court.

4. The pièce de résistance that spring of 2021 was the decision of the University of Illinois Chicago to remove the name of John Marshall, the

most important chief justice in American history, from its law school. The board of trustees voted to make the change after faculty ratified the recommendation of a task force that had surveyed relevant community members and come up with principles to guide the evaluation of a potential name change. The task force concluded that Marshall is "a highly inappropriate namesake for the Law School" because of his proslavery rulings and racist views, not to mention his ownership of slaves. The school is thus now called the University of Illinois Chicago School of Law. Perhaps not surprisingly, Cleveland State University made a similar announcement in November 2022, so its law school is now known as CSU College of Law. At least these developments reduce any confusion with Atlanta's John Marshall Law School.

5. At City University of New York, DEI efforts led the law school faculty in May 2022 to *unanimously* back a student resolution that "proudly and unapologetically endorses the Palestinian-led call for BDS [Boycott, Divestment, and Sanctions] against Israel." The resolution calls for the university to stop doing everything from buying Dell computers (because Michael Dell is an "Israel Backer") to revoking free tuition for NYPD officers (because the police force has an exchange program with Israel) to serving Sabra hummus. The faculty's endorsement of the resolution flies in the face of former governor Andrew Cuomo's 2016 executive order that forbade CUNY from supporting BDS activities. One of the most concerning aspects of the faculty's endorsement is that no professor made a request for edits or qualifications, even though the resolution uses such words as *apartheid, genocide, war crimes, settler colonialism,* and, of course, *structural racism.* The resolution also called for the cancellation of any events or projects that "involve Israeli academic institutions or that otherwise promote the normalization of Israel." All of this is "problematic" because (1) CUNY is a public school, beholden to the First Amendment and thus viewpoint neutrality, and (2) how is any pro-Israel student (including most Jews) supposed to attend the school without feeling an openly hostile environment?

6. Around the same time, after an antigay slur was found on a whiteboard at the University of Idaho College of Law, the DEI office

there held a solidarity gathering in front of the campus. During that "moment of community," a lesbian law student asked the student leaders of the Christian Legal Society chapter, who were there to pray and show support, about their position on same-sex marriage. After the CLS officers told her that heterosexual marriage was the only kind the Bible affirmed, the student filed a harassment complaint and led a group of peers to denounce the group at a panel discussion. The CLS students and their faculty adviser were then all issued no-contact orders without any administrative form of due process. They in turn sued the university and several officials, in response to which the complaining student emailed the professor saying that CLS's participation in the "moment of community" had "caused me to fear for my life at the University of Idaho. I am scared to be on campus, I am scared to be in your class. I fear you." The federal judge handling the lawsuit ordered the school to rescind the no-contact orders because of the targeted nature of the regulation of the students' religious speech.

These, plus the incidents described elsewhere in this book, are by no means a comprehensive list of either administration policies or the student-mob mentalities they encourage. But students selected for activism and reinforced or even emboldened in their illiberalism by officially established cultures that emphasize identity and safety—with explicit messaging that ramped up in the 2020–21 academic year—can't help but be radicalized. And of course all of these rapid racialist developments were happening against the backdrop of a pandemic that was also raising tensions and uncertainty across personal and professional dimensions.

Pandemic-Enabled Cancel Culture

A September 2021 report by the American Council of Trustees and Alumni revealed that virtual learning environments during the Covid pandemic had led to an acceleration of academic cancel culture. To wit, "the rapid shift to online learning during the COVID-19 pandemic exacerbated the ongoing free speech crisis on college campuses, further suppressed viewpoint diversity, and encouraged more self-censorship among students." The report documented a plethora of examples of chilled speech and offered reflections by professors during that challenging time, as well as synthesizing campus climate surveys. "The lifeblood of the liberal arts is debate, dialectic, inquiry, and challenge," explained ACTA president Michael Poliakoff. "We have seen that [online education] can bless us with access to a vibrant exchange of ideas, but it also has the potential to eliminate the opportunity for growth of character and intellect."[1]

This 2021 report invoked a poll ACTA had conducted two years earlier (before the pandemic) that found self-censorship to be prevalent among college students, especially those who identify as conservative. That poll found that 61 percent of students refrained from expressing opinions "on sensitive political topics in class because of concerns the professor might disagree with them." Likewise, 85 percent reported doing so "to avoid offending other students," and 38 percent bit their tongues "because of concerns related to my college's speech policies." Nearly half (48 percent) "agree" or "strongly agree" that "pressure to conform to political correctness can negatively affect the development of close interpersonal relationships"—including more than three-quarters (78 percent) of those who called themselves strong Republicans.

ACTA's findings align with those of several other recent polls. A 2022 Knight Foundation/Ipsos survey found that the problem is worsening, with 65 percent of students agreeing "that the climate on their campus deters students from expressing themselves openly, up from 54 percent in 2016." Of note, 50 percent "are afraid of being attacked or shamed by those who disagree with them," while 44 percent agreed that "social media stifles free expression because people are afraid of being attacked or shamed by those who disagree with them." Only 32 percent answered that "the dialogue that occurs on social media is usually civil."[2]

The largest study in this area, a 2023 FIRE survey of 55,000 students on more than 150 campuses, found that only 11 percent reported

---

1. ACTA, *Building a Culture of Free Expression in the Online Classroom*, September 2021, 2.
2. Knight Foundation, *College Student Views on Free Expression and Campus Speech 2022: A Look at Key Trends in Student Speech Views Since 2016*, Knight Free Expression Research Series, January 2022, 33, 34.

feeling "very comfortable" expressing "views on a controversial political topic during an in-class discussion."[3] And of course, habits learned during Zoom school transferred into the real world. But why did the student-speech crisis get worse during the pandemic? For one, the impersonal nature of online learning decreased the social trust and good feeling that builds in a physical space—which ACTA notes is true of other social functions that have moved onto social media platforms, where anonymity and distance enable vicious behavior. It's easier to "call out," report, and mob impersonal avatars and faces on a screen than flesh-and-blood peers. For another, as described in ACTA's 2021 report, classroom recordings give an "opportunity for partisans across the political spectrum to exploit the digital records in order to further an agenda that has nothing to do with learning." Clips can be edited out of context and spread on social media. Self-censorship is a perfectly reasonable reaction when faculty and students are harassed, investigated, and punished for their speech, as in the case of Georgetown adjunct law professor Sandra Sellers, discussed in chapter 7. FIRE's data show that, unsurprisingly, race-related issues were among the hardest to discuss during the pandemic.

But it's not just freedom of speech that the pandemic affected. Universities' extreme regulations and restrictions trained the next generation to obey authority and snitch on their peers. It turns out that illiberalism isn't just about CRT and DEI, though it all contributes to an authoritarian mindset and safetyism can be physical in addition to psychological. Although 18–22 year-olds were more likely to die from seasonal flu than Covid, when students were allowed to return to campus after paying regular tuition for remote learning, they were forcibly isolated and prevented from using facilities that they'd already paid for.

Many schools forbade students to have guests in their dorm rooms. Others installed cameras in residential hallways to monitor their adherence to the rule. Most had isolation dorms where students who tested

---

3. College Pulse and FIRE, 2024 *College Free Speech Rankings: What Is the State of Free Speech on America's College Campuses?*, September 6, 2023, 13.

positive were forced to live alone for two weeks, having food slid under their door—like solitary confinement but with on-demand streaming entertainment. When leaving those dorm prisons, most students had to wear masks at all times, including outdoors and in gyms (when the gyms were open). That's right; as leftist administrators chastised anyone who questioned the ever-changing government guidelines and admonished everyone to "follow the science," they closed or strictly regimented work-out facilities even though it was clear from the beginning that being fit and healthy (and young) was the best way to protect against viral harm.

Then there were the tracking apps. At the University of Wisconsin, students were forced to take Covid tests every four days, documented on an app that students had to download to their phones to maintain access to university buildings. "They are tracking our movements," Connor Hess, a junior at UW-Madison studying chemical engineering, told Evita Duffy-Alonso, founder of the *Chicago Thinker*, an "alternative" student publication at the University of Chicago that emerged during the pandemic. Hess explained that while the university claimed to not be tracking students, the app constantly asked them to turn on location services, which used Bluetooth to monitor if students were congregating together. If students missed required tests, there would be "administrative consequences" such as being unable to use campus Wi-Fi or add/drop classes. As Duffy-Alonso chronicled, students would also be put on "disciplinary probation," which would be noted on their transcript and would affect their ability to study abroad. Similar disciplinary systems were implemented at universities across the country.

Georgetown Again

Then there's the case of law student William Spruance at our favorite institution. In August 2021, Georgetown returned to in-person instruction after 17 months of virtual learning, announcing some new policies: vaccines and masks were required and drinking water wasn't allowed in class. Mysteriously, faculty were exempt from the rules, but the dean promoted a hotline for students to report each other for violations.

Spruance soon received a notification that he had been "identified as non-compliant" for letting his mask slip beneath his nose. He met with Dean of Students Mitch Bailin—the one who had promised students a safe space to cry in during their sit-in against me—and voiced some concerns about the school policies. Bailin "had no answers to my simple questions but assured me that he 'understood my frustration,'" Spruance later wrote for the Brownstone Institute. "Then, he encouraged me to 'get involved in the conversation,' telling me there was a Student Bar Association meeting set to take place the following Wednesday."

Spruance decided he'd do exactly that. He prepared four simple and rational questions, which if he were Jewish I'd think was a nod at a Passover seder, when Jews recount their escape from Egyptian slavery:

1. What was the goal of the school's Covid policy? (Zero Covid? Flatten the curve?)
2. What was the limiting principle to that goal? (What were the trade-offs?)
3. What metrics would the community need to reach for the school to remove its mask mandate?
4. How can you explain the contradictions in your policies? For example, how could the virus be so dangerous that we could not take a sip of water but safe enough that we were required to be present? Why are faculty exempt from masking requirements?

Spruance later told me that he had been sure that he was overlooking some straightforward answer; he wasn't a scientist, and administrators were paid hundreds of thousands of dollars to come up with appropriate measures. The contrasting data seemed clear to the layman, but what did he know? He delivered his brief remarks "without a mask, standing 15 feet away from the nearest person." Spruance awaited a response, but quickly realized that the meeting wasn't about fact-finding but ratifying a fait accompli. "The speech ended in an anti-climatic [sic] silence," he wrote. "I asked the crowd what I had been missing, but there was no response. There were no answers to my questions or acknowledgements of the policies' absurd contradictions." He concluded, "It appeared to be quintessential DC: a speech with zero effect."[4]

But two days later Bailin told Spruance that he was suspended and would have to submit to a psychiatric evaluation. He would need to "voluntarily" waive his right to medical confidentiality so that the school could discuss his apostasy with state bar associations (recall the threats against Trent Colbert at Yale Law). Bailin told Spruance that to "secure permission to return to campus," he would have to attend hearings and explain himself. He would later have to provide "a statement explaining why you no longer pose a risk to the community of defying that policy or otherwise creating risks of disruption and risks to the public health."

As Spruance described it, the "disruption" was asking questions—"Which happens to be the basis of law school," or at least it used to be. Cold-calling students and the Socratic method (asking questions in a sort of argumentative dialogue to draw out ideas) were once the bread and butter of legal education but have largely gone by the wayside because these methods make students feel "uncomfortable." Indeed, students learn to invoke words like *arbitrary* and *capricious* to challenge laws and policies. Spruance naively thought his law school would welcome his calm skepticism, particularly in contrast to angry mobs. But that assumption was false, because he was questioning undebatable orthodoxy.

Public-health statistics were beside the point; the week when Spruance gave his speech, 2 of 1,002 Covid tests (less than 0.2 percent) that Georgetown Law administered came back positive. That was in a population of students who were under 30, all of whom had received school-mandated vaccinations. Banning water-drinking seemed severe. Forcing healthy young adults to get shots they didn't need *that didn't prevent viral transmission* seemed intrusive. But Spruance's intended audience wasn't receptive to either logic or humor. He was simply cast as the new antagonist in the administration's morality play.

Those in power had replaced formerly "sacrosanct educational principles" with an ideology of "power and image." They punished open

---

4. William Spruance, "What Happened at Georgetown Law with Covid?," Brownstone Institute, February 19, 2023. Much of the discussion here comes from this piece, as well as my conversations with its author.

inquiry, rewarded blind obedience. As with the DEI regime, Covid provided a pretext to implement a new system that demanded conformity and quashed dissent. Under both regimes, censors "conflate dissent with public endangerment to maintain control over speech and to slander dissidents."

As Spruance would write, "Bailin understood the system. For him, socially fashionable talking points were far more important than principles like free expression." So Spruance logged onto mandatory hearings and shrink sessions. "I will tell you when you go in. I'll let you know who we're meeting with," Bailin told him. "I want to be really, really clear. This isn't a negotiation at this point. I'm instructing you the minimum steps you can take if you wish to return to campus." One of those steps was apparently to "get out of your echo chamber."

When Spruance asked for answers to his questions, Bailin cut him off. "Our job is not to convince you of the rightness, the sensibility of the policy." That was instructive: Spruance finally understood that there was to be no dialogue, that this was a struggle session. So he let his professors know that he wouldn't be able to attend class—and soon began receiving calls from civil rights lawyers and journalists. Alumni contacted the school. Georgetown had taken too big a risk: even if the law school could've gotten away with a certain amount of enforcement of its irrational policy, the suspension and bizarre demand for psychiatric evaluation had crossed a line even in the sympathetic milieu of DC.

Spruance declined media requests for interviews, but the story was already out—and everywhere. Fourteen hours later, Bailin announced that Spruance's suspension had been lifted. Spruance's story offers a window into the power dynamic at play in these campus inquisitions and how best to respond to all kinds of illiberalism and irrationality. Mitch Bailin wasn't an educator, but a power-hungry middle manager. Spruance summed up the ending of the story:

On March 8, 2022—two years after the school left for its 17-month corona vacation—the school announced that it would lift its mask mandate. That week, 4 out of 407 Covid tests at the Law Center came back positive—a 0.98 percent positivity rate. This was twice as many cases as when I gave my speech and forty-nine times the positivity rate.

There were also far more Covid hospitalizations in DC than when I had spoken to the crowd of vaccinated young adults in September. The data hadn't changed for the better, so what prompted the policy switch?

The data hadn't changed for the better but, as Spruance noted, the politics had shifted; it became untenable for the bien-pensants in the ruling class to maintain restrictions, just in time for President Biden to give his State of the Union address in a Capitol Building that had removed its mask mandate the day before.

The oppressive Covid rules, many of which violated civil liberties without advancing public safety one iota, were an extension of the speech codes and safe spaces that had been popular on campuses before the pandemic. It's tremendously ironic; free speech was once the domain of the left, but today's progressive students ask for restrictions and regulations, and are eager to turn in those who don't comply—whether for DEI slights or Covid sins. Even the University of Chicago, a bright light in a dismal landscape, forced students to sign a nearly 2,000-word "Acknowledgement and Attestation Regarding COVID-19" on pain of having their student IDs deactivated. Educrats infantilized supposedly adult students by requiring them to agree that "the University may disclose violations of this attestation and other COVID-19-related protocols or guidance established by the University and public health authorities *to my parent(s), legal guardians(s) and other third parties.*" The *Chicago Thinker's* Evita Duffy-Campos noted, "This is what happens when universities have more administrators and lawyers than professors." As iconoclastic intellectual Camille Paglia put it in her prescient 2018 collection of essays, *Provocations*, it's the "swollen campus bureaucracy, empowered by intrusive federal regulation," that crushes freedom at universities.

The sociological effects of that early-2020s power grab are already being felt as transmogrified students enter the workforce. Recent grads are joining the growing ranks of young people terrorizing corporate executives, law firm partners, and colleagues with woke extortions. Too many Americans will have been, in the words of Duffy-Campos, "desensitized at college to oppressive rules and regulations encroaching on their personal lives," and so will be helpless in the face of illiberal intimidation.

Radical Mobs, Intolerant Faculty, and Weak Administrators

And so we have illiberal student mobs, coached by professors who increasingly see their jobs as training activists, enabled by spineless deans who allow and encourage DEI to swallow every other law school goal. Counterexamples are few and far between; they exist, but they're the exceptions that prove the rule. The University of Chicago hasn't had any real issues at its law school, for reasons we'll see later. So it's possible to nip these problems in the bud, but there's not much institutional will to do so. There was some hope that after the *mensis horribilis* of March 2022, and the waning of the pandemic, things might settle down. But it's unclear whether we've turned the corner—or, if you prefer another metaphor, we're still very much in the eye of the storm such that even during times of calm, there's a roiling mess around us.

In the summer of 2022, when Justice Clarence Thomas withdrew from the class he'd long been teaching at the George Washington University Law School, it was just one more example of the poisonous atmosphere in academia that makes it impossible to have a free exchange of ideas. GW administrators had stood up admirably to the mob demanding that he be canceled for his vote to overturn *Roe v. Wade*, citing academic-freedom guidelines that don't shield students from "ideas and opinions they find unwelcome, disagreeable, or even deeply offensive." Still, the justice presumably figured it wasn't worth the aggravation and heightened security. It's a shame that he felt the need to withdraw—and a stark contrast to the announcement that the newly retired Justice Stephen Breyer would be teaching at Harvard. It's a shameless double standard.

Then there was the disruption of a town hall meeting at the University of Florida held by the school's incoming president, Ben Sasse, in October 2022—not a law school–specific issue but indicative of the state of affairs. When Sasse formally took office in February 2023, he was met with pounding on his office door and a list of demands that included disavowing Governor Ron DeSantis's attacks on "woke higher ed." The nerdy Sasse, who had been the president of a small college in Nebraska before becoming a senator, is no fire-breathing extremist. He'd tangled with the MAGA crowd and is no favorite of Donald Trump. He has a high profile only through the force of his intellect, but if that kind of non-progressive isn't welcome in academia, none is.

The dynamic was presciently described by former Treasury Secretary Lawrence Summers, who himself had been canceled from Harvard's presidency in 2006 for discussing the generally greater variability among males in tests of cognitive abilities, leading to proportionally more men than women at both the lower and upper tails of test-score distributions. "There is a great deal of absurd political correctness [in higher education]," Summers said on Bill Kristol's podcast in January 2016. "Now, I'm somebody who believes very strongly in diversity, who resists racism in all of its many incarnations, who thinks that there is a great deal that's unjust in American society that needs to be combated, but it seems to me that there is a kind of creeping totalitarianism in terms of what kind of ideas are acceptable and are debatable on college campuses."

In that vein, let's revisit Stanford DEI Dean Steinbach's comments, which centered on whether Judge Duncan's speech justified the "harm" his visit was causing. Duncan was confused by that interjection, which was supposed to be about quieting the mob. He was there to talk about court decisions and judicial process. How could that not be worth a federal judge's presence on campus? If students didn't think his views were worth listening to, for whatever reason, they could've absented themselves. But Steinbach's message should be familiar to anyone familiar with the DEI playbook, blending cultural Marxism with therapeutic gobbledygook.

As South Texas law professor Josh Blackman wrote at the time, Stanford can't absolve itself by sacrificing Steinbach, whom it ultimately did let go. The institution itself had created the problem by creating and growing its DEI bureaucracy:

When a university empowers DEI to deem speech "harmful," DEI will deem speech "harmful." When a university empowers DEI to designate spaces as "safe," DEI will deem spaces as "safe." When a university allows DEI to treat some people as "oppressors," DEI will treat those people as "oppressors." When a university teaches students that "harmful" speech has no place on a campus, the students will take steps to prevent "harmful" speech on their campus. This protest was a direct byproduct of what students have learned for years.[5]

So let's turn Steinbach's question around: Is the DEI juice worth the squeeze? Framing the Duncan event as a clash between the values of free speech/expression and equity/inclusion—the same way Dean Treanor framed my Georgetown experience—hides the real issue here. The actual problem was revealed in the crux of Dean Jenny Martinez's letter (see chapter 9): "The university's commitment to diversity, equity, and inclusion can and should be implemented in ways that are consistent with its commitment to academic freedom and free speech."

There's an internal contradiction there. As recent NYU Law graduate Tal Fortgang wrote in an important *National Review* essay in the spring of 2023, DEI, at least as employed by its professional purveyors, "cannot be made to conform with a law school's openness to those who dissent from a very narrow progressive orthodoxy."[6] A generation of DEI-educated lawyers will act as an army of activists trained to view life as one oppression after another and far more dedicated to political machinations than the rule of law. That's because DEI, notwithstanding its facially unobjectionable name, "is predicated on contestable progressive assumptions and a thoroughly left-wing worldview that make it incompatible with the proper practice of law." To the extent such illiberal principles continue to infuse university bureaucracies, our higher-ed institutions will systemically work against anyone who is quite literally politically incorrect.

Just look at how DEI's most basic concepts are employed by DEI professionals to undermine the core liberal values of higher education. As Fortgang wrote, to focus only on the free-speech implications of Steinbach's juicy refrain is to forget that her question is often a good one:

---

5. Josh Blackman, "Is the DEI Juice Worth the Squeeze?," The Volokh Conspiracy, March 11, 2023.
6. Tal Fortgang, "Conformity, Inequity, and Exclusion," *National Review*, May 2023 (first appeared online April 13, 2023).

A stable liberal society allows and even encourages citizens to ask themselves whether exercising their right to speak freely at a given moment, in a given way, is beneficial or harmful to those around them. Sometimes a legally protected act of expression can be bad; burning an American flag, yelling one's hope for rape against a fellow citizen's family, and Sieg Heil–ing all tear at our social fabric and detract from our ability to live together peaceably.

But, Fortgang pointed out, "Steinbach deployed the metaphor before Duncan had said anything substantive and with no indication that the speech itself would involve anything objectionable." Instead, "she relied on the common DEI theory that merely platforming someone who holds certain views is intrinsically harmful."

Take Steinbach's remarks, which she had prepared as a sort of pre-buttal: "For many people in this law school who work here, who study here, and who live here, your advocacy, your opinions from the bench, land as absolute disenfranchisement of their rights. . . . For many people here, your work has caused harm."

There it is: this juice-squeezing thing isn't actually about words, but about the *people speaking the words.* Steinbach labeled Duncan and anyone who thinks like him as beyond the pale of acceptable discourse. She put a scarlet *B* (for Bigot) on him, and by extension on *any* student who agreed with *any* of his work or even respected him as a federal judge. That's worse than using her position to reject a particular message: it's drawing an official line between the kinds of speech that should be tolerated and that which shouldn't—and marking anyone who disagreed as an outcast from the community. But how can we hope to have productive discourse if the opinions and arguments of those with whom we disagree are verboten? How can we raise effective lawyers if law students are taught to think of opposing counsel—*and judges whose past rulings they don't like*—as enemies to be exiled from the professional world?

Moreover, Steinbach used the framework of free-speech advocates to advance her censorial message: "Me and many people in this administration do absolutely believe in free speech. We believe that it is necessary. . . .

We believe that the way to address speech that feels abhorrent, that feels harmful, that literally denies the humanity of people—that one way to do that is with more speech and not less." While calling for more speech to counter Duncan—to counter him as a person, not for what he was supposed to discuss that day—she denigrated those students who might "feel" differently. Steinbach's use of the now-commonplace trope that her target was "denying" someone else's "humanity" or "right to exist" is telling. It's unclear what humanity-denial even means in these contexts, but it's a conversation-stopper, because what is there to discuss with a "literal" Hitler? Yet it was an example of a DEI dean's attempt to "deploy the de-escalation techniques in which I have been trained," as Steinbach later wrote. In other words, it's the duty of someone with her job description to indoctrinate a radical ideology and label all those who disagree to be enemies of humanity.

So even as the Federalist Society must, for now, be tolerated, its members hear loud and clear that their perspectives aren't welcome at Stanford. Even as Steinbach granted Duncan the noblesse oblige "not to shut you down or censor you or censor the student group that invited you here," she made clear that she did so grudgingly to uphold speech policies that here serve to benefit an oppressor class. It was all so facetious, because in fact Steinbach was letting Duncan be shut down no less than if she or another administrator had disinvited him or told the audience that the law school couldn't let the event proceed. By not enforcing Stanford's antidisruption rules, by commandeering the speaker's time to make her own points, she was indeed censoring Duncan and censuring the students who invited him. It was ironic, given that Steinbach represented institutional authority, which she used to "punch down" on a group that's decidedly a minority within elite law schools: conservatives, and especially social conservatives.

In a sense, Steinbach employed and amplified the intersectional script, privileging those whom she deemed to have been marginalized (OutLaws and their allies) over those she deemed to be part of the tormentor class (the Federalist Society). Judge Duncan was thus the personification of institutional sexism, homophobia, transphobia, and other forbidden systems of oppression. Instead of promoting understanding among a diverse population of students such that everyone can feel understood and included, she heightened tensions.

In the end, Steinbach reinforced in the disruptive students the Critical Legal Studies lessons discussed last chapter: favoring groups according to a privilege hierarchy, pushing for equal outcomes, and dismantling any institutions that dare resist such illiberal goals. As Fortgang wrote, "this attitude could not be more inimical to the proper practice of law, which looks to precedent and existing institutions with reverence rather than incurable suspicion. The attitude thereby cultivates elites who would discard the rule of law tomorrow if it meant they could fix the injustices that are more important to them than anything else—including public etiquette at speeches and basic human decency to speakers."

There's real harm from such examples of the "praxis" (as Marxists call it) of critical theory, but it doesn't come from the words of white male "cisheteronormative" federal judges. DEI offices, far from advancing some neutral principles of access, welcome, and belonging, narrow the Overton window of acceptable discourse. Despite the insistence of non-DEI officials like Gerken, Martinez, and Treanor that DEI supports the basic principles of free speech, objective inquiry, and the development of legal and other academic traditions, it is the DEI project that marginalizes and excludes. The only way law schools will ever be reformed is if they get rid of these anti-intellectual structures that they've allowed to deform the legal-education project.

CHAPTER 13

Abolish DEI Bureaucracies to Restore Colorblind Diversity

Is the situation so hopeless that those who are interested in preserving rather than tearing down the rule of law should just abandon (most) law schools? After all, in addition to the DEI regimes and related efforts to eradicate divergent thinking, many legal faculties refuse to hire non-progressives. Georgetown has three on a faculty of about 150—the dean put out a press release when he hired me so he could brag to alumni of his significant expansion of intellectual diversity—while some places have none. The most recent survey of law school faculty, published last year, found that among the 554 professors who responded from the top 50 law schools, 77 percent identified as liberal (19 percent *very* liberal) as against 9 percent conservative.[1] A 2018 analysis of some 10,000 law professors, essentially all of them, found an 85–15 split when using a database of political donations rather than survey responses.[2] More than two-thirds of those professors rejected originalism—reading constitutional provisions according to their public meaning when enacted—as a valid interpretive method, while two-thirds support living constitutionalism, the idea that the document's meaning changes over time.

---

1. Eric Martínez and Kevin Tobia, "What Do Law Professors Believe About Law and the Legal Academy?," *Georgetown Law Journal* 112 (2023): 111–89.
2. Adam Bonica et al., "The Legal Academy's Ideological Uniformity," *Journal of Legal Studies* 47, no. 1 (2018): article 1.

What's worse than law professors' own proclivities, however, is that too many of them feel no need to present (other than to ridicule) ideas or theories with which they disagree, including originalism. Yet originalism is a powerful force, indeed the Supreme Court's dominant interpretive method, so much so that even Justices Sonia Sotomayor, Elena Kagan, and Ketanji Brown Jackson all felt obligated to pay lip service to it at their confirmation hearings. "We are all originalists now," Justice Kagan famously declared in 2010.

Moreover, the relentless emphasis on identity and "diversity" pushes the hiring of women and racial minorities, which imperative moves law schools leftward because these new hires are generally to the left of the average law professor, who's already comfortably to the left of the average American. That dynamic is particularly pronounced in the politically relevant fields of "public law"—constitutional, criminal, and administrative law, and other areas where government action is involved. At the same time, as racial preferences in admissions have replaced merit-based evaluations with identity-based grievances, those admitted with lower LSATs and GPAs have performed worse academically—and it looks bad when racial minorities, especially black students, disproportionately cluster in the lower ranks of achievement. These dynamics entrench a vicious cycle of illiberal conformity—and ideological uniformity on legal policy matters vital to the nation—that looks to become even worse as less-tolerant Zoomers (Gen Z) replace Boomers in faculty and administrative positions.

But regardless of how bad it gets, we can't give up on law schools, because they matter too much. They produce lawyers, after all, and the legal profession plays a key role in our system of government. We pride ourselves on being a "government of laws, and not of men," to quote John Adams in what now sounds like a banal aphorism but was at the founding quite literally a revolutionary idea. That means there must be transparent rules that bind everyone equally, a law enforcement regime free from arbitrariness or caprice. Legal disputes arise, of course, because people dispute the meaning of laws or how they apply in novel situations, which is why we need lawyers to advocate vigorously before neutral tribunals. These lawyers must be trained in a culture of logic and reason, understanding all sides of arguments while welcoming debate. In stark terms, if that culture of legal education declines, society declines.

To put it another way, as Northwestern law professor John McGinnis wrote in *City Journal* in the spring of 2023:

> When English departments, say, are consumed by the politics of identity, they marginalize mostly themselves. The classes they teach no longer provide students with analytic skills, and the books they assign no longer stir student souls. By contrast, law schools remain important to society, whatever their quality, because lawyers remain essential to a modern market democracy. At their best, law schools facilitate responsible advocacy and inculcate a respect in future lawyers that law isn't simply politics by another name, but instead the basis of a rule-based order needed for human flourishing. If law schools lose sight of this, society suffers.

Regardless of what's going on in law schools with regard to admissions, administration, curriculum, pedagogy, or faculty hiring, they're the places where law is taught and lawyers are trained. Like it or not, we're stuck with them. I've tried to be assiduous throughout this book in not parsing arguments within the modern political tradition, meaning that my beef here is not in the vein of debates between conservatives and liberals as a matter of law or policy. Instead, it's with those who reject the spirit of open inquiry, who argue that the foundation of our society and its legal institutions is irredeemably corrupt to the point that it must be blown up and rebuilt.

Accordingly, when I say that "we" can't give up on law schools, I don't mean people who agree with me on legal theory or judicial method, or their application in any given area of law or legal policy. It's certainly true that the "conservative legal movement," broadly defined and with many internal disagreements, ought to maintain a toehold in the legal academy, particularly at the more prestigious schools, so as to retain access to students and protect the credibility of its own legal theories. Were it not for the presence of legendary professors like Richard Epstein, Randy Barnett, Steven Calabresi, and Michael McConnell (to name just a handful of senior faculty) at elite schools, it would be easy for left-skewing legal elites to categorize all nonprogressive legal thought as fringe or unintellectual. Were it not for the network of Federalist Society chapters, there would be no place to go at most law schools to hear views that diverge from a narrow left-wing orthodoxy. But that's not my point.

After all, this book isn't about the "liberal" or even "progressive" takeover of legal education. That's a different story, one that's less interesting. For example, regardless of the ideological faculty ratio I mentioned at the outset of this chapter, which hasn't changed much in the last few decades, roughly half the federal judiciary is and will continue to be appointed by Republican presidents. Although ideological discrimination in faculty hiring continues to be a problem, conservative and libertarian students—not to mention the broader legal culture—would generally be fine if law school culture were to remain the way it was until about a decade ago. Instead, there's been an *illiberal* shift that disagrees with the rules of the game, and with the rule of law as commonly understood, which has to be fought lest today's radicalized student mob becomes tomorrow's Justice Department.

But all that doesn't mean that we should keep all our eggs in one basket and merely redouble our efforts at internal reform. As I've detailed throughout the book, most change won't happen without external pressure brought to bear by alumni, employers, media coverage, state bars, and others to whom deans and other internal actors listen and respond. Law schools don't live in nearly as much of a bubble as their purely academic counterparts do, which is why fixing them is both more important and easier than fixing the humanities or social sciences—or at least we have more tools at our disposal.

Systemic Antiracism

Many lament the decline of free speech, academic freedom, and civil discourse on college campuses while wringing their hands at what can be done about the problem. Some see cultural pathologies that simply can't be remedied through public policy. Others think that any attempt at reform would tread on academic freedom and simply replace one set of ideologues for another. Still others don't like what they see but say it's just a product of the long-ago liberal takeover of the academy.

For a long time, I was similarly pessimistic that anything could be done as a matter of public policy. But one thing will always matter to these schools: funding. A substantial majority of college students attend public institutions, and these schools are subject to state law, which means that Congress pulls a lot of strings for all higher-ed institutions. Recipients of federal education funds have to comply with a host of rules and regulations in areas ranging from civil rights to financial accounting. If legislators are determined to restore free speech and academic freedom, there's a lot they can do to stem the illiberal tide. In early 2023, I got together with my Manhattan Institute colleague Chris Rufo and the Goldwater Institute's Matt Beienburg to develop a four-part reform proposal. Here's a synopsis, without the legalese.

1. *Abolish DEI bureaucracies.* These offices are divisive ideological commissariats, promulgating and enforcing critical race theory (CRT) and related political orthodoxies as official campus policy, working actively against norms of academic freedom and truth-seeking. And as we saw in chapter 10, they make students feel less, not more, welcome or "included": larger DEI staff levels correlate to decreased student satisfaction, especially for minority students. Administrators should maintain institutional neutrality on controversial political questions extraneous to the business of educating students. Contrary to this obligation, DEI offices advance primarily political aims while fueling a bureaucratic bloat that drives student debt. Get rid of them, leaving only the lawyers and support staff tasked with ensuring compliance with federal and state civil rights laws, such as Title VI of the Civil Rights Act of 1964 and Title IX of the Education Amendments of 1972.

This reform means eliminating staff and offices that manipulate or otherwise influence the composition of the faculty or student body with reference to race, sex, color, or ethnicity, apart from ensuring colorblind and sex-neutral admissions and hiring in accordance with state and federal law. It doesn't cover academic course instruction, student or faculty research and creative works, the activities of student organizations, or guest speakers and performers.

2. *End mandatory diversity training.* This is one of the mechanisms through which DEI ideology shapes campuses. Even when DEI officials claim that their training is "voluntary," it's often required as part of incoming student orientation and annual staff antiharassment trainings, as well as for faculty who wish to perform the most basic extracurricular roles, such as serving on hiring committees. Typical training includes unscientific claims about so-called microaggressions and implicit bias, rejecting the basic American premise that everyone should be treated equally. It indoctrinates an ideology of identity-based grievance, guilt, and division. Although diversity training is supposed to make people feel more comfortable working with racial minorities, there's little evidence that it works. As even a guest *New York Times* op-ed admitted in January 2023, "the specific type of diversity training that is currently in vogue—mandatory training that blames dominant groups for D.E.I. problems—may well have a net negative effect on the outcomes managers claim to care about."[3] Universities should instead be committed to ending discrimination in all its forms, including by treating citizens as individuals, not components of racial, religious, sexual, or national classes. At public institutions, mandatory sessions consist of speech made by state employees in their official capacities, so legislatures must ensure that this speech is not discriminatory.

This reform means no more required attendance (in person or online) at programs purporting to describe or expose structures, systems, or relations of power, privilege, or subordination on the basis of race, sex, color, gender, ethnicity, gender identity, or sexual orientation. "Diversity training" doesn't include optional academic courses offered for credit or the activities of student organizations that affect only their members.

---

3. Jesse Singal, "What If Diversity Training Is Doing More Harm Than Good?," *New York Times*, January 17, 2023.

3. Stop political coercion. "Diversity statements" serve as ideological lit-mus tests to exclude students and faculty who don't adhere to CRT and other progressive beliefs. Although the Supreme Court has long held that requiring loyalty oaths in public education is unconstitutional—as are speech compulsions—universities increasingly require that prospective faculty state their belief in the importance of DEI, describe their prior efforts to promote DEI, and pledge to integrate DEI into their teaching. Applicants for many positions have been eliminated based on diversity statements alone, and many universities condition their hiring decisions on the applicant's conformity to DEI-shaped ideologies. For example, a University of California, Berkeley self-survey of the 2018–19 academic year found that 76 percent of applicants for faculty positions in the *life sciences* had been eliminated based on their diversity statements alone.

In 2021, 19 percent of postings on leading university job boards required diversity statements—40 percent for universities ranked in the *U.S. News* top 100—while half of all universities with more than 5,000 students included DEI criteria in tenure standards. That same year, a survey by the Center for the Study of Partisanship and Ideology found that over one-third of US faculty openly admit that they would discriminate based on political ideology in a professional context. The actual number is no doubt even higher; a FIRE survey found that half of all professors see diversity statements as a justifiable job re-quirement. Banning required diversity statements in job applications would defend the classroom against enforced conformity while pro-tecting arenas in which faculty applicants can exercise the freedom of mind cultivated in their own classrooms.

This means that universities could no longer solicit oral or written statements that discuss the applicant's or candidate's identity, contri-butions to DEI or social justice, or views on the differential treatment of people based on identity categories. It wouldn't prevent institutions from requiring applicants and candidates to discuss their scholarly research or creative works or certify compliance with state and federal antidiscrimination law. Universities could still consider individual applicants' perseverance in overcoming discrimination or taking on leadership roles in their communities, but they wouldn't be allowed to hire or admit them based on their adherence to any preferred ideology or other political litmus test.

A variation on diversity statements is "land acknowledgments," statements that an event or class is taking place on land once inhabited by indigenous peoples. Many universities have posted such statements, though law school–specific ones are proliferating as well. They seem like empty virtue-signaling to me—and may sow bad feelings given conflicting land claims or unrecorded land exchanges between tribes—but for purposes of this reform proposal, they simply shouldn't be required for class syllabi or student/faculty–organized events.

4. *End identity-based preferences.* The man-eating plant of DEI bureaucracy germinated from a seed planted by Justice Powell in the 1978 *Bakke* case, when his deciding vote allowed the consideration of race to advance "diversity"—which conceit has moved to the heart of the higher-education mission. The Supreme Court ended that failed experiment in 2023, finding that racial preferences in admissions are unconstitutional when used by both public schools and private ones that receive federal funds. Regardless of that ruling, however, discrimination based on race, sex, color, ethnicity, or national origin is antithetical to universities' basic missions. Explicitly ending not just admissions but hiring and contracting based on immutable characteristics—other than bona fide qualifications based on sex that are conducive to the normal operation of educational institutions—would go far to heal campus cultures by treating people as individuals and removing the stigma from minority applicants.

These rather straightforward reforms would go far to push back on some of the negative trends that have afflicted higher education—without intruding on curricula or other aspects of academic life. They would free faculty and students alike to explore intellectual ideas without fearing the thought police. And they're doable; in discussing them with state representatives, my colleagues and I found that it really took no more political capital to go big than to try to implement incremental change. It's not too late to return universities to their mission of promoting the search for truth and knowledge while maintaining academic freedom and scholarly integrity, without being transformed into factories of ideological conformity.

Happily, in 2023 alone, 38 bills of this sort were introduced in 20 states, with six gaining legislative approval and five being signed into law—in the states of Florida, North Carolina, North Dakota, Tennessee, and Texas. Florida and Texas enacted the "big ones," dismantling DEI offices at their state institutions altogether. That's not counting decisions by university trustees and presidents to end the use of diversity statements in hiring when feeling pressure from the legislature or after a change of leadership, as happened in Florida, Idaho, Missouri, North Carolina, Texas, Wisconsin, and probably more states by the time this book goes to press. (Full disclosure: In October 2023, Governor Ron DeSantis appointed me to the board of trustees of Florida Polytechnic University, which happily has not faced these sorts of issues.) There have also been plenty of executive orders regarding DEI structures and systems—notably by Arkansas Governor Sarah Huckabee Sanders and Oklahoma Governor Jevin Stitt—plus laws and orders rejecting federal funds directed to DEI, as well as restricting their use for the promulgation of CRT.

Indeed, regulations and restrictions are only one tool in the legislative shed. Educational administrators are finely attuned to their financial bottom lines, so concomitant with abolishing illiberal structures, systems, and policies is starving the beast. As Jay Greene (who coauthored the 2021 survey of DEI bureaucracy featured in chapter 5) has written, an important "strategy to curtail the nonsense and refocus universities on their core missions is to curb the excess resources that facilitate that corruption. If funds are tight, universities will have to be more attentive to what students and their families—and, for public schools, taxpayers— really want. It's unlikely that they prefer an army of ideological indoctrinators over professors and classes."

States are already reducing appropriations to public universities, although the expansion in federal subsidies and loans—which the Biden administration tried turning into gifts before the Supreme Court blocked his scheme—has swamped those fiscal gains. Ending these subsidies and reforming the student-loan behemoth would go a long way to cutting the exploding number of nonteaching staff on campus, especially the value-subtracting DEI offices.

Indeed, there have been attempts in Congress to extend free-speech protections to students at private schools—in effect, to nationalize California's Leonard Law—or at least to withhold federal grant money from schools that have speech codes. As I said in testimony to the House Education Committee's Subcommittee on Higher Education and Workforce Development in March 2023, Congress can require all recipients of higher-ed funds to certify that they will not violate constitutional standards, for example, and that they will comply with the codified sense of Congress—first passed in 1998 and updated in 2008—regarding the protection of student speech and association rights. Higher Education Act funds, those at issue in the challenge to Harvard's use of racial preferences in admissions, are already subject to all sorts of certification requirements, ranging from nondiscrimination to compliance with accounting standards. Congress can attach whatever strings it likes to pressure schools to live up to what in this case are their own stated goals.

President Trump also issued executive orders along these lines. In March 2019, he required the protection of free speech by recipients of federal education and research grants, though its operative provision— that the relevant institutions "promote free inquiry, including through compliance with all applicable Federal laws, regulations, and policies"—is vague, prompting criticism by the dean of Berkeley Law and the chancellor of UC Irvine Law that it was thus unconstitutional (but then they also wrote that "there is no crisis of free speech on campuses"). Then late in his term, in September 2020, he signed an order banning the use of federal funds for DEI or CRT training by all government contractors, which includes universities. Sadly, President Biden repealed that order, while making in his very first executive order the advancement of "racial equity" a priority for the entire federal government (see chapter 1).

These sorts of reforms are popular, whether as measured in opinion polls or in what happens when one of these illiberal practices is exposed to the sober light of day. For example, on February 7, 2023, the day after the *Wall Street Journal* published John Sailer's exposé of how Texas Tech had used job applicants' diversity statements as ideological litmus tests, the university president announced that his institution would stop its use of such statements for faculty hiring. A single investigative journalist, using publicly available information gained through the Freedom of

Information Act, was thus able to stop one of the most pernicious practices at a large university.

Stopping the Spread

Checking and reversing illiberalism in the legal profession is a more daunting proposition than reforming law schools, but in some ways, it seems more doable. On the one hand, societywide cultural change can't be checked with straightforward policy solutions, regardless of how easy or hard those reforms would be to implement. As Andrew Breitbart famously put it, politics is downstream from culture. On the other hand, legal academia is an ideological monoculture, lacking the natural give-and-take of the nation's various social, economic, and political forces. When ordinary people—not politically obsessed and very online elites—start noticing the fruits of the "woke mind virus," as some put it, the pendulum will naturally start swinging back, with a market correction that will ripple through all but the most hidebound institutions.

But lawyers, too, aren't just going to reform themselves. Like the average student or faculty member, most lawyers are too busy with their own personal and professional goals to want to engage in culture wars. Keeping your head down and following the path of least resistance is a better, less stressful survival strategy. So we need more "exogenous shocks," those originating from outside the system.

For example, after Senator Ted Cruz asked the Texas State Bar to review the "character and fitness" of bar applicants from Stanford, the state's board of law examiners announced that it was changing its bar application to add questions about whether those aspiring to be admitted to the bar have engaged in "incivility and violations of school policies." Montana Attorney General Austin Knudsen similarly requested that his state's supreme court clarify "that students' conduct in law school— including conduct at speaker events and similar occasions where a range of perspectives are presented on key issues—is relevant to an evaluation of their character and fitness for admission to the bar." Other bars are considering similar actions, with some changing their requirements in ways that could make a difference without drawing headlines. Good:

all states should scrutinize the admission of those who—as 20- and 30-somethings, not kids—openly defy the standards of the legal profession.

Employers are starting to take note, too—including judges, who annually hire freshly minted lawyers to help with their work. After the Yale disruption of March 2022, the late DC Circuit Judge Laurence Silberman emailed all of his fellow federal judges to warn against hiring clerks who could turn out to be a problem. "The latest events at Yale Law School," he concluded, "prompt me to suggest that students who are identified as those willing to disrupt any such panel discussion should be noted. All federal judges—and all federal judges are presumably committed to free speech—should carefully consider whether any student so identified should be disqualified from potential clerkships."

That fall, Fifth Circuit Judge James Ho picked up the gauntlet, announcing in a speech that starting with the following year's entering class—current students would be unaffected—he wouldn't hire anyone from Yale because of the law school's hostility to the freedom of speech and indeed its enabling of mobs who shout down speakers and even the hiring of deans who punish those who deviate from ever-left-shifting progressive orthodoxy. Eleventh Circuit Judge Lisa Branch quickly joined Ho's boycott, saying that her colleague has raised "legitimate concerns about the lack of free speech on law school campuses." A dozen other judges answered the call to arms, though they declined to announce themselves publicly, while others offered rhetorical support. Still others adopted Ho's policy or were already practicing it, without being counted officially.

At the time, I wrote and commented in the media in support of Judge Ho's move; he and I have frequently discussed what can be done about the troubling developments that are the subject of this book. But others who are sympathetic to the goal of rolling back the illiberal tide disagreed with this tactic, and those criticisms deserve consideration because that only makes my call for exogenous shocks stronger.

Criticism 1: It hurts only students, and pro-free-speech students at that. Although Ho's policy is prospective, why punish even future matriculants who are "on notice"? They're just collateral damage in the culture wars. Why engage in collective punishment for the sins of the administration and other students? The thing is, it's not as though academic superstars have no other options. Harvard's Federalist Society chapter almost immediately began recruiting would-be Yalies—and I'd hope that other schools do the same, perhaps offering scholarship incentives to compete for these in-demand, principled students. Those who attend Yale regardless send the signal that they care more about its supposed "prestige" advantage *over other elite schools* than they do about truth, justice, and the American way. It makes them less sympathetic victims. Moreover, students are already being hurt by the cancel culture Yale foments. All Yale has to do to end the boycott is stop undermining the civil discourse that it purports to value.

Criticism 2: It won't change anything. What if Yale ignores the boycott or doubles down? Well, then Judge Ho's attempt to change the school's culture, and by proxy all of legal academia, will have failed—but that's not an argument for not trying. Indeed, less than two weeks later, Dean Heather Gerken felt compelled to issue a statement that detailed what Yale has done "to reaffirm our enduring commitment to the free and unfettered exchange of ideas." Time will tell whether these measures are more than window dressing, but this step could be evidence that Ho's gambit is already working. Imagine what would happen if more than 15 judges (out of 870 Article III judgeships) publicly joined in. If any Supreme Court justice did so, especially one of the four who graduated from Yale Law, it would be game over.

Criticism 3: It's not appropriate for a federal judge. Judges shouldn't use public threats to achieve political goals, especially when too many people see judges as politicians in robes. But if those with life tenure can't take a stand against injustices that directly affect their applicant pool and the future of the legal profession, who can? Would it have been inappropriate for judges during the Jim Crow era to boycott law schools that racially discriminated? And remember that Ho isn't even trying to impose an external political agenda—such as, say, hiring more conservative faculty—but a principle of neutrality and free speech that Yale itself says it supports.

Criticism 4: It's just attention-seeking. Judge Ho is known for his sharp pen and has made national waves before. Isn't this just shameless self-promotion? Well, the maneuver certainly kept Ho in the news and may put judges who publicly join the boycott onto future Supreme Court short lists. But can anyone seriously argue that Ho—who's written fervently in defense of free speech regardless of viewpoint—isn't sincerely concerned about the state of the academy and wants to use the tools at his disposal to change it? Judges often write provocative opinions in the hope of shifting legal culture, and this is just an example of that trend. It would be even more effective if presidential contenders were to announce that they wouldn't hire from Yale.

   Criticism 5: It's hypocritical, embracing cancel culture. Conservatives often criticize "the ends justify the means" reasoning and attack progressive jurists for being purely results-oriented. Isn't canceling an entire law school unprincipled speech-suppression? That argument rings hollow. As William F. Buckley Jr. said, it's hardly fair to denounce both those who push old ladies into the path of a bus and those who push them out of the way of the bus for pushing old ladies around. Judge Ho isn't trying to shut down anyone's speech but rather to facilitate a free exchange of ideas. "I don't want to cancel Yale," he said. "I want Yale to stop cancelling people like me."

   After the Stanford shutdown of his Fifth Circuit colleague Kyle Duncan, Ho extended his boycott to that school, which happens to be his undergraduate alma mater. He criticized Dean Martinez for not accompanying the "good words" in her letter with concrete actions. "Look, I get that no one wants to be vindictive. I believe in redemption and grace. But we're not talking about good faith mistakes here," he explained. "Do these future leaders really not have fair notice that they shouldn't ridicule a judge's sex life? I'm all for second chances. But I'm not a schmuck."

   So spare me the sanctimony. Both campus and law-firm/business climates have only gotten worse in recent years, but are those who believe in civil discourse supposed to just take it? Do those who agree with Judge Ho's diagnosis but disagree with his prescription have any better ideas? As Ho himself put it in his Yale-boycott speech, "Any school that refuses to stand up against cancel culture—and instead caters to it and even engages in it—is not a school that is interested in educational diversity. And it's not a school I want to have anything to do with."

   Of course, these problems aren't limited to one or two schools. But, as Ho noted, Yale and Stanford hold themselves out as the very best law schools. "Yet they're the worst when it comes to legal cancellation." And what happens at these elite schools affects both the profession and the country.

Judge Ho didn't stop at making that critique. In spring 2023, when he announced the expansion of his boycott in a speech to an annual meeting of the *Texas Review of Law and Politics*—which had named him its "jurist of the year," an honor that comes with the commissioning of a snazzy bobblehead—he pointed out, "The real problem in the academy is not disruption—but discrimination. . . . Against students, faculty, and anyone else who dares to voice a view that may be mainstream across America—but contrary to the views of cultural elites." Until we take real action to solve the real problem, he said, "all we're doing is giving speeches."

In May 2024, Judges Ho, Branch, and 11 colleagues launched a further boycott of Columbia University over its handling of that spring's anti-Israel protests and encampments. Columbia "has become ground zero for the explosion of student disruptions, anti-semitism, and hatred for diverse viewpoints on campuses across the Nation," the judges wrote to university president Minouche Shafik and law school dean Gillian Lester. They would thus refrain from hiring Columbia graduates (beginning with those who matriculate in fall 2024) until the university undertakes three reforms: (1) disciplining students and faculty who "participated in campus disruptions and violated established rules concerning the use of university facilities and public spaces and threats against fellow members of the university community"; (2) "Neutrality and nondiscrimination" in protecting free speech and enforcing conduct policies; and (3) "Viewpoint diversity on the faculty and across the administration—including the admissions office." The judicial missive ends with a cheeky reference to Justice William Brennan's refusal to hire clerks from Harvard after faculty criticized the Supreme Court. "The objective of our boycott is different—it is not to hamper academic freedom, but to restore it at Columbia University."

So it's up to employers and alumni, stakeholders and donors, to stand up for fairness and merit, good faith and decency. Withholding contributions gets deans' attention, as does getting together alumni on a coordinated letter or email campaign. For that matter, law firms and corporate legal departments should consider whether someone who shouts,

"We hope your daughters get raped!" merits employment. Is that juice, such as it is, worth the squeeze? No one's required to hire students who aren't taught to live under the rule of law. Legal education is in crisis—a microcosm of societal issues, but also a critical venue for them, given that lawyers become policymakers. Heterodox problems require novel solutions.

CHAPTER 14

A Culture of Free Speech and Intellectual Diversity Doesn't Happen by Itself

This isn't rocket science. University officials—in the context of law schools, deans—know how to set campus culture. Whether it's DEI, public service and pro bono (unpaid) legal work, environmental consciousness, or any number of ideals, they instill values in their students all the time. It wouldn't be that hard to do with commitments to free speech, academic freedom, intellectual diversity, civil discourse, and generally returning to the traditional higher-ed mission of truth-seeking and knowledge-creation. Compared to societywide problems, fixing campus cultures seems like a straightforward management issue.

Indeed, the University of Chicago, which was always a league leader for "the life of the mind," has avoided any sort of cancel-culture issues even in the last five years of campus upheaval and DEI metastasis. Former president Robert Zimmer was a rarity among his peers in standing up to all sorts of moral panics, most notably in defending geophysics professor Dorian Abbot's right to criticize his department's DEI efforts and the university's affirmative action programs. As Zimmer put it in November 2020, "Faculty are free to agree or disagree with any policy or approach of the university, its departments, schools or divisions without being subject to discipline, reprimand or other form of punishment." The mob calling for Abbot to be disciplined dispersed, his classes remained oversubscribed, and life went on.

UChicago's law school, which is where I got my JD, has similarly avoided speaker shutdowns and the like, because it actually enforces its free-speech policies. For example, in April 2019, when a student facilitated the disruptive protest of an event regarding Israel, he was effectively expelled. Five nonstudent protesters drowned out law professor Eugene Kontorovich, who was visiting from George Mason University's Antonin Scalia Law School to discuss First Amendment issues surrounding the Boycott, Divestment, and Sanctions movement. After the disrupters ignored a request by Dean of Students Charles Todd to leave, police were called and escorted them out. "This chanting did violate the University's policies," Todd emailed the student body. "It is the right of any speaker invited to our campus to be heard and for all who choose to be present to hear the speaker. Moreover, it is the right of members of the audience to ask tough questions of those speakers. The heckler's veto is contrary to our principles. Protests that prevent a speaker from being heard limit the freedoms of other students to listen, engage, and learn." The law student who organized the protest thought he had found a loophole in the antidisruption rule by bringing in outsiders rather than organizing students; the administration didn't buy it and expelled him with the right to apply for reinstatement, which he never did.

The UChicago administration did the right thing in throwing the protesters off campus, and there haven't been any such incidents at the law school since.

The Chicago Way

Creating such an environment requires an intentional effort, which is to say: leadership. UChicago Law School Dean Thomas Miles gave a presentation to alumni returning for their reunions in May 2023 that explained the simple formula. First, he set out the "community priorities," which consisted of: (1) imparting the law school's core values (things such as academic rigor, free inquiry, intellectual curiosity, and dialogue), (2) fostering a climate in which students build community and class affinity, (3) encouraging professionalism and respectful communication, (4) fostering inclusivity and a sense of belonging, and (5) promoting wellness and cultivating resilience. Miles had a separate slide regarding the freedom of expression, in which he discussed introducing all students to the Chicago Principles (on which more shortly) and John Boyer's seminal work *Academic Freedom and the Modern University*. Miles noted that he and the faculty work hard to "educate our community" and instill core values, including with orientation exercises and the practice of model discourse, as at roundtables where professors debate controversial issues, named after the esteemed liberal philosopher Martha Nussbaum. And he announced that the next academic year, there would be a universitywide Forum on Free Expression (later renamed the Forum for Free Inquiry and Expression), to be led by a law professor.

It's also notable that this culture was one where *diversity* meant what it said. Dean Miles also had a slide on diversity and inclusion, but there were no postmodern buzzwords there; even the word *equity* was notably absent. He referenced "hearing one another" workshops—more civil dialogue opportunities—plus a partnership with the Council on Legal Education Opportunity, an interdisciplinary speakers series, and assorted grants and fellowships. There's also a preorientation program for students who are the first in their family to attend college, come from underrepresented backgrounds, or may find the transition to law school financially, socially, or academically challenging. In other words, the University of Chicago Law School's approach is to actually bring people of diverse backgrounds together and help them feel welcome and prepared to succeed—while emphasizing that academic freedom and free expression are the lodestars for doing so. As I said, it's not rocket science.

Although UChicago has the most comprehensive structure in place for developing, instilling, and maintaining classical academic values, it's not the only place that has modeled positive responses to attempts at cancellation or postmodern ideologization. Recall from the introduction that Cornell's law dean refused to punish William Jacobson for his Black Lives Matter apostasies in 2020, and Dean Peñalver's concluding message is instructive: "As an administrator, I do not share my views on a faculty member's speech lightly, but it is important to make clear that the Law School's commitment to academic freedom does not constitute endorsement or approval of individual faculty speech. But to take disciplinary action against him for the views he has expressed would fatally pit our values against one another in ways that would corrode our ability to operate as an academic institution." While Cornell's then-president, Martha Pollack, was no Bob Zimmer—as we saw in chapter 12, she at least paid lip service to DEI tropes, and ended up retiring in June 2024 after a rocky tenure—she did in April 2023 reject a student assembly demand that would've required faculty to give trigger warnings about "traumatic" classroom content, saying that such a rule would infringe on academic freedom and inhibit student learning. Indeed, research suggests that trigger warnings often have the opposite of their intended effect by reducing students' confidence and courage in tackling tough subjects.

UChicago also hasn't cornered the market on preventing disruption. In September 2021, Eighth Circuit Judge David Stras spoke at Duke Law School on "What My Grandparents' Experiences in the Holocaust Taught Me about the First Amendment," a topic he's discussed frequently, including at an event I hosted for the Cato Institute. This time, in the middle of Stras's remarks, when he started discussing a Minnesota law that would've compelled a videographer to produce a video for a same-sex wedding, two dozen students stood up and one began to read from prepared remarks: "I am a queer Jewish law student. Lawyers, politicians, and others who advocate for LGBT antidiscrimination laws are not comparable to Nazis. Suggesting otherwise as you have is abhorrent and although we came to listen to you speak we are not going to sit here and listen to blatant homophobia. Thank you for coming today." Judge Stras replied, "Thank you for speaking out." That was apparently the end of it—though I wonder if Duke administrators were prepared (or are prepared now) for a Stanford-style disruption.

Speaking of elite-school comparisons, Harvard is also doing better than its smaller rival in New Haven, at least if we focus on the law school. Elena Kagan's transformative deanship from 2003 to 2009 set the tone. Kagan's consensus-building leadership style defused the school's previous discord and also changed what had been a harsh environment into one that was more student-friendly and ideologically diverse, including by hiring conservative faculty. "I love the Federalist Society," she said at a 2005 banquet when Harvard's chapter hosted the national student symposium, even though "you are not my people." That dynamic has continued through the leadership of John Manning, a conservative who clerked for Robert Bork and Antonin Scalia and was brought in during Kagan's tenure. (In 2024, he left the deanship to become the university's provost.) Although Harvard Law is almost as big as Georgetown Law, with complex faculty politics and a large administrative staff, it has avoided the sorts of scandals that have plagued the Hoya Lawyas.

For example, when students demanded that the law school take down an Instagram profile of the Federalist Society president in the wake of the leak of the draft opinion in *Dobbs*—calling it "tone-deaf" and "transphobic"—administrators refused and disabled comments. And when about 75 students walked out on a post-*Dobbs* panel hosted by the school's pro-life group, the assistant dean for community engagement, equity, and belonging stood up and read a statement about the law school's free-speech policy—and then the event continued. That was it: Tirien Steinbach, take note. The law school has mostly staved off ideological mania despite the larger university's being at the bottom of FIRE's rankings. Still, in January 2024, as part of a lawsuit against the university for failing to protect Jewish students from "severe and pervasive" harassment, the plaintiffs made several serious complaints about the law school specifically—including some that predate the Israel-Hamas war. *Harvard Law Review* editor Ibrahim Bharmal (also a teaching fellow) gained media notoriety—but no official discipline— for being part of a mob that swarmed around and blocked an Israeli student, but the refusal of law school administrators to do anything about protesters' invasions of the student center and other disruptions of educational activities is even more damning institutionally.

Harvard law professor Mark Ramseyer lamented in December 2023 that "Harvard is a vastly less tolerant place than it was when I arrived in 1998" and that the faculty "let it happen." "The canceling, the punishments, the DEI bureaucracy, the DEI statements, the endless list that we could all recite—all this happened on our watch. We saw it happen, but we did nothing. We were too busy. We were scared to speak up. We—we on the faculty—let Harvard become what it is. The Harvard that we have is the result of our own collective moral failure."

Of course, the Harvard faculty isn't unique in that failure. There appears to be no research on the rate of deans' standing up to the mob— the airplane that doesn't crash doesn't make national news!—but even more than the refusal to cave to illiberal demands or handle potential disruptions, instilling a healthy culture at the outset reduces the number of instances when university leaders' mettle even needs to be tested. As I told the dean of the University of Oklahoma's law school after a standing-room-only event on civil discourse in April 2022, the way to inculcate liberal values is to inculcate liberal values. (I'd have a similar experience with the law dean at the University of Maine in September 2023.) Don't wait for the Federalist Society to put on debates, and don't host panels that are completely one-sided. You have to make people uncomfortable to promote learning—and to teach students that having their deepest beliefs challenged isn't "harmful" but is the reason they're there in the first place. Freedom is, as famed Princeton professor Robby George (a one-man counter to the left-wing skew there) has written, "a culture, not merely a set of rules, and a culture must be nurtured. Free speech, free inquiry, tolerance for opposing views, meeting such views with argument, logic, and fact, and abstaining from ad-hominem attacks, character assassination, doxing, and other unethical behavior must be highlighted in the orientation materials for all new students and employees."[1]

Many law schools have still not taken very basic steps to protect free speech and intellectual diversity. There are still some with restrictive speech codes and others with exceptions that swallow the rule. But, as the repeated incidents documented in this book demonstrate, and as Greg Lukianoff has observed, "it's not enough to adopt a policy that protects free speech and academic freedom"; law school administrators must constantly "remind their communities of these values." Deans must establish an institutional culture of social tolerance and mutual respect such that controversial, unpopular, and politically incorrect speech doesn't face calls for punishment, let alone formal investigation. As UChicago has done and as Stanford is implementing in a remedial fashion, law schools must emphasize free speech, academic freedom, and truth-seeking in their orientation programs—because their students' colleges will undoubtedly have failed to do so. Finally, to address the

---

1. Robert P. George, "How Universities Can Restore Academic Freedom and Free Speech," *Deseret News*, November 27, 2022.

problem, we must understand the problem, so all law schools must collect solid data by regularly surveying their students and faculty; don't wait for FIRE and others to do it for you.

Now let's revisit what the two institutions that had national speech controversies during my Georgetown saga have done. In October 2022, UC Law SF adopted a new events policy to address controversial speech, potential disruption, and other protest-related issues. A cornerstone of the policy establishes the difference between peaceful protest and outright cancellation of speakers. It distinguishes between "organizing a counter event in a different room, holding a rally in an external space, passing resolutions, issuing pre- or post-event statements, carrying signs, distributing flyers . . . and using social media to express counterviews" and "preventing a person from speaking or being heard via such means as heckling, making noise, standing in the area of a room reserved for the speaker, blocking the speaker or event organizers from accessing AV equipment, blocking the views of attendees attempting to view the speaker," and, for virtual or streamed events, "using or implementing technology features, such as the mute button and the camera button." In other words, can the speaker still speak? Can the audience listen to the speech? The policy also calls for students, administrators, and campus security personnel to work together to preserve both public order and expressive freedom and to develop counterstrategies if there has been notice of opposition or potential disruption. Notably, administrators can't cancel student events "based on . . . the views of the speaker(s)" and "students engaged in disruptive behavior are subject to discipline" under the code of conduct.

That's all well and good—I probably couldn't craft a better policy—but I'm not sure that it covers behavior that was otherwise allowed, or that students could be reasonably unclear about whether shouting down a speaker was acceptable. After all, the day after I was shouted down there, Dean Faigman emailed the law school community that "silencing a speaker is fundamentally contrary to the values of this school as an institution of higher learning; it is contrary to the pedagogical mission of training students for a profession in which they will prevail through the power of analysis and argument." Students didn't need further clarification to know the difference between permissible protest and impermissible disruption.

Yale Law School similarly updated its disciplinary code to include as a major violation "substantially interfering with student-sponsored or student group-sponsored events or functions in a manner that is purposeful, knowing, or *reckless*." The new policy incorporates by reference the university's updated "guidance regarding free expression and peaceable assembly," which in turn gives "examples of conduct that disrupts or interferes with university events." Then, on October 12, 2022, Dean Heather Gerken issued a message to alumni on free speech, which clarified not only antidisruption policy but also, curiously, a new policy against "surreptitious recordings." Gerken claimed that this anti-recording policy "mirrors policies that the University of Chicago and other peer institutions have put in place to encourage the free expression of ideas," but the move drew criticism from observers ranging from Judge Jim Ho to Scalia Law professor David Bernstein to the left-wing Above the Law website. "But then why not mirror the University of Chicago's speech policy itself?" wrote Ho in a letter to Gerken, and "its actual practice of robust enforcement when students violate the policy." And indeed, UChicago's policy prohibits the recording only of classes and public events, not of disciplinary meetings of the kind that shone light on the "Trap House" scandal (see chapter 7). Curiously, between the time of writing this book and when it went to press, Yale Law's "surreptitious recordings" policy disappeared from its website.

Gerken also announced that YLS had redesigned its 1L (first-year) orientation to "center around discussions of free expression and the importance of respectful engagement." Apparently, nearly all faculty members discussed these values on the first day of class. Interestingly, she also got rid of a student listserv (The Wall) that had enabled flame wars and other mob actions. Sadly, replacing the digital Wall with a physical bulletin board didn't recreate previous generations' experiences; enterprising students quickly created The Window, which operates on an opt-in basis without official monitoring. The final point in Gerken's message noted the appointment of a new dean of students, one "who is focused on ensuring students learn to resolve disagreements among themselves whenever possible rather than reflexively looking to the institution to serve as a referee." That last bit made me chuckle, because it sounds like a behavioral guide for grade schoolers rather than students at the most prestigious law school in the land.

So is Yale turning the corner? There's reason to be cautiously optimistic, in part due to the new policies and attempts at creating a healthier culture, in part because some of the most acrimonious activists graduated, to be replaced with new students who by anecdotal accounts seem to be more interested in learning about the law than deconstructing it. Even Kristen Waggoner returned to YLS in January 2023 without incident—except that members of the press were excluded—even as her topic, the *303 Creative* websites-for-gay-weddings case, was more controversial. Although there was no on-site protest, critics of Waggoner and ADF were able to make their views heard at a panel hosted by the OutLaws earlier in the week—which was attended by several Fed Soc members, just as the Waggoner event was attended by several OutLaws. And in 2024, Yale Law hired two nonprogressive faculty members, one junior (Garrett West, who clerked for Justice Samuel Alito) and one senior (Princeton's Keith Whittington, who founded the Academic Freedom Alliance). So far, so good, but the price of liberty is eternal vigilance—and alumni are telling Judge Ho not to let up on his boycott quite yet.

The experiences of UChicago, UC Hastings/Law SF, and Yale, as well as my experience at Michigan (see chapter 4) are in any case instructive regarding what to do regarding the problem of disruptive protests. First, have a clear policy. Second, make students aware of the policy. Third, if you learn of a potential disruption, take steps to guide would-be disrupters toward forms of protest that will comply with the rules, such as leafleting or "tabling" outside an event, hosting a counter-event, or wearing T-shirts or holding nonobstructive signs. Fourth, for particularly controversial events, an administrator or senior faculty member should orally restate the policy at the outset, so all attendees, including any nonstudents who wouldn't have received earlier communications, are clear on what won't be tolerated. Fifth, if there's still a disruption, enforce the policy through a gradual escalation: making a request to stop, instructing the protesters to leave, and then having campus security remove the disrupters. Students violating the policy should be disciplined, while outsiders could be charged with trespassing or disturbing the peace.

Take the further example of an attempted disruption of a talk by the Israeli politician Michal Cotler-Wunsh at NYU Law on April 20, 2023. Right after the disruption began, a staff member stood up, defended Cotler-Wunsh's right to speak, and explained how heckler's vetoes violated NYU policy. The disrupters left the room, the speaker continued her presentation, and the event otherwise took place as scheduled. The intervention was reinforced by an official statement by the university spokesman the next day that "we reject efforts to interfere with a speaker's right to communicate and an audience's right to hear a speaker."

The goal isn't to punish—nobody wants to be spiteful—but to prevent and stop disruption and to enable discourse. Rules aren't rules if they don't have consequences, and students who blatantly violate rules don't belong in the legal profession. (If they want to engage in civil disobedience, so be it, but that involves a willingness to accept consequences that shine a light on an unjust rule.) Suffice it to say that administrators who promote intolerance don't belong in legal education. Even before setting and enforcing rules, however, there's the question of how to establish a culture of open discourse that would obviate the need to mete out discipline.

The Chicago Trifecta

As a matter of policy, the best way any institution of higher education can push back against the illiberal tide is by adopting what's become known as the "Chicago Trifecta": the Kalven Report, which requires institutional neutrality on political and social controversies; the Shils Report, which makes academic achievement and merit (not viewpoint or ideology) the sole basis for hiring and promotions; and the Chicago Principles of Free Speech. During the tumult of the 1960s, University of Chicago president George Beadle appointed law professor Harry Kalven to chair a committee that would develop a statement on the university's role in political and social action. The committee reported in November 1967, in what became known as the Kalven Report, that while a university plays a large role in developing social and political values, it cannot take collective action on controversial issues without threatening free inquiry. The university is a community that doesn't take a majority vote but sponsors critics from all sides. Fundamentally, its core purpose is to promote the pursuit of knowledge:

> The mission of the university is the discovery, improvement, and dissemination of knowledge. Its domain of inquiry and scrutiny includes all aspects and all values of society. A university faithful to its mission will provide enduring challenges to social values, policies, practices, and institutions. By design and by effect, it is the institution which creates discontent with the existing social arrangements and proposes new ones. In brief, a good university, like Socrates, will be upsetting. . . .
>
> The neutrality of the university as an institution arises then not from a lack of courage nor out of indifference and insensitivity. It arises out of respect for free inquiry and the obligation to cherish a diversity of viewpoints. And this neutrality as an institution has its complement in the fullest freedom for its faculty and students as individuals to participate in political action and social protest. It finds its complement, too, in the obligation of the university to provide a forum for the most searching and candid discussion of public issues.

A few years later, President Edward Levi, who would serve as attorney general in the Ford administration, established the Committee on the Criteria of Academic Appointments. Its chairman was the distinguished sociology professor Edward Shils, who steered the committee to complete its work by July 1970. The Shils Report concluded that candidates for appointment and promotion must be evaluated on their performance or potential in the areas of research, teaching, contribution to the intellectual community, and service—ignoring elements like the financial backing they might bring in. Moreover, there was to be "no consideration of sex, ethnic or national characteristics, or political or religious beliefs or affiliations in any decision regarding appointment, promotion, or reappointment at any level of the academic staff." Toward the end, in a section on contribution to the intellectual community, the report noted that "disruptive activities cannot claim the protection of academic freedom, which is the freedom of the individual to investigate, publish, and teach in accordance with his intellectual convictions. Indeed, the only connection between disruptive actions within the University and academic freedom is that the disruptive actions interfere with the very action which academic freedom is intended to protect."

Finally, the Chicago Principles of Free Speech, also known as the Chicago Statement, came out of the Committee on Freedom of Expression that President Zimmer created in July 2014 in response to "recent events nationwide that have tested institutional commitments to free and open discourse." The Chicago Principles guarantee all members of the university community "the broadest possible latitude to speak, write, listen, challenge, and learn." Believing that intellectual conflict in higher education to be a natural and desirable occurrence, the university declared that it's improper to attempt to shield individuals from ideas that offend them. The Principles go even further by condemning the use of concerns about civility as a justification for suppressing free speech. There are exceptions: "The University may restrict expression that violates the law, that falsely defames a specific individual, that constitutes a genuine threat or harassment, that unjustifiably invades substantial privacy or confidentiality interests, or that is otherwise directly incompatible with the functioning of the University." Administrators may also "reasonably regulate the time, place, and manner of expression to ensure that it does not disrupt the ordinary activities of the University." But these are narrow exceptions—"And it is vitally important that these exceptions never be used in a manner that is inconsistent with the University's commitment to a completely free and open discussion of ideas."

The Principles first garnered national attention in 2016, when Dean of Students John Ellison wrote a letter to the incoming undergraduate class of 2020, affirming the Chicago Statement and condemning the use of trigger warnings and safe spaces. More than 100 universities have adopted the Chicago Principles, including such large statewide systems as the universities of North Carolina, Texas, and Wisconsin. Still, adopting the Principles and actively upholding them aren't the same thing. Indeed, adopting them seems to be a necessary but not sufficient condition for a campus culture that welcomes free expression and a spirit of open inquiry. Enforcement is very much an issue; Georgetown and Columbia have endorsed the Principles, for example, but their values are very much in doubt among both students and faculty.

A 2021 survey by the Knight Foundation found that only 47 percent of college students thought that free-speech rights were secure (down from 73 percent just five years earlier), while 65 percent felt that their school's campus climate stifled expression (up from 54 percent). Only 59 percent believed that it's more important for colleges to allow students to be exposed to all types of speech (down from 78 percent) and only 60 percent opposed restricting the expression of "upsetting" or "offensive" political views (down from 74 percent). Similarly, in 2022, FIRE found that only 61 percent of faculty agreed that "a university professor should be free to express any of their ideas or convictions on any subject," only 52 percent said speech should be restricted only "where words are certain to incite physical violence," and only 55 percent said that students' shouting down a speaker is never acceptable. More than half of faculty reported being worried about losing their jobs if someone misunderstands something they've said or done or posts something from their past online—and this is of course much higher among conservative faculty. Granted, neither of these surveys looked at law schools, and faculty in the arts, humanities, education were much worse than those in STEM and business, but it's readily apparent that the same concerning results and worrying trend lines afflict legal education.

Still, the Chicago Trifecta has been at the heart of a national push to have universities recommit themselves to supporting an environment of academic freedom, free speech, and free expression. For example, the Stanford Academic Freedom Declaration, launched in the fall of 2022, is an open letter that calls on universities and professors to adopt the Chicago Trifecta. As of June 2023, it had garnered about 1,700 signatures. It also advises faculty to create and join nonpartisan associations aimed at defending these values both on campus and nationally, groups like the Academic Freedom Alliance, Heterodox Academy, American College of Trustees and Alumni, National Association of Scholars, and Foundation Against Intolerance and Racism (on whose board I briefly served in 2023).

As the Stanford Declaration explains:

The loss of academic freedom results in part from a leadership crisis. While many university leaders issue statements that support open debate, they nonetheless oversee and expand politicized bureaucracies that harass, intimidate, and punish those who express views deemed to be incorrect[,] and enforce ideological conformity in hiring. A boilerplate defense of free speech does little good if at the same time administrators conduct investigations in secret, without due process, and based on anonymous complaints; if administrators publicly ostracize the victim to all potential future employers. Boards of trustees, alumni organizations, donors, government agencies, and other institutional stakeholders likewise fail to uphold the principles of academic freedom.

Universities and professional organizations are moving headlong into institutional political and ideological activism. Departments and other university units make public statements of political views, thus effectively branding as heretics—and even bigots—members who may question those causes.

Cancellation victims and others who make national news are the tip of the iceberg. As we see from survey results, self-censorship pervades academia, detracting from any intellectual mission, to say the least. Knowledge is never developed and many "old school" professors leave academia entirely—such as the famed First Amendment scholar Eugene Volokh's move from UCLA School of Law to the Hoover Institution and the early retirement of five right-of-center law professors from the University of San Diego (which used to be a bastion of originalism). Universities are at best failing to resist these illiberal forces and at worst encouraging them. As the Stanford Declaration states: "Free speech, they say, so long as the speech does not offend or exclude; free speech, so long as it does not challenge institutionally approved narratives and conceptions of social justice; free speech, but only within narrow credentialed boundaries. These restrictions are counterproductive, sometimes even to their goal of advancing a particular ideology. People infer from censorship a desire to protect lies from being exposed." Without even having to resort to analogies to the totalitarian regimes of the 20th century, look at the historically low level of institutional trust America now faces. Bad ideas can be defeated only by argument and persuasion, not by suppression. Justice and freedom cannot exist without each other.

Other Reforms

Fundamentally, the mission of the university is, as Robby George puts it, "the pursuit of truth and the advancement and dissemination of knowledge." Free speech and academic freedom are essential to that mission. But people resist intellectual progress that threatens the status quo, so bad ideas can be weeded out only by unfettered critical analysis. Universities, and especially law schools, should commit to all students, faculty, and staff that they won't punish free expression.

But it goes both ways. As the *Washington Examiner*'s Quin Hillyer has suggested for colleges, law schools should require all applicants to sign a no-exceptions contract guaranteeing respect for free expression. Any student, at any time, who takes physical or verbal action resulting in a denial of speech rights—as defined in policies like those discussed above—should be suspended, while a second offense should result in expulsion. If a prospective student won't sign such a contract, his application should be invalid. These rules should be nonnegotiable such that law schools return to being safe spaces for unfettered intellectual inquiry and exchange. Those who don't respect these terms don't belong in law school, much less in a court of law.

For that matter, while much of this book has been concerned with deans of student affairs and DEI, admissions deans should be evaluated for admitting students with the character to respect norms of free speech and open inquiry. It's all well and good to screen for academic achievement via GPA and reasoning skills via LSAT—which, along with racial diversity, have long been the primary metrics for law school applicants—but admissions offices, particularly at higher-ranked schools, have been too focused on admitting activists instead of advocates, social-justice warriors instead of scholars. Anecdotal evidence suggests that some schools screen for or otherwise attract the sorts of people who would undermine the rule of law instead of upholding it. It would significantly change law-school cultures if admissions officers valued life experiences or a desire to be a workaday lawyer more than, or at least as much as, a "change the world," chip-on-your-shoulder messianic fervor.

Moreover, commitments to the freedom of speech, as well as to open inquiry and ideological neutrality, ought to be part of law school rankings. It shouldn't be left to FIRE or the Knight Foundation, neither of which focuses on law schools, to conduct student surveys. *U.S. News & World Report* rejiggered its rankings in response to school decisions not to provide information—in part to hide objective academic measures and thus reinforce diversity regimes ahead of the Supreme Court ruling that outlawed racial preferences—so why not add a free-speech-protection criterion, as suggested by Randolph May of the Free State Foundation? And why not include it in the checklist that the ABA looks at when renewing law school accreditations? Both of these institutions and their competitors ought to look even more broadly at campus cultures, because to be truly inclusive, educational institutions must provide students the freedom to engage the law—and even to play devil's advocate. That'll also make them better lawyers, including for progressive causes.

As the previous sections discussed, and as the Stanford Declaration underlines, healthy campus cultures are better transmitted "by social norms than by extensive rules enforced by non-academic bureaucrats. If community members or groups petition school leaders for the sanction or punishment of a faculty member or a student for expressing their point of view, university leaders should . . . respond with a statement affirming that the University is a place to discuss and debate all views," and that punishing "incorrect" views goes against community standards.

Progressive activist and CNN commentator Van Jones has also told students interested in advancing social justice not to avoid or condemn ideas they don't like, including at a 2017 event at the University of Chicago:

> There are two ideas about safe spaces: One is a very good idea and one is a terrible idea. The idea of being physically safe on a campus . . . I am perfectly fine with that. . . .
>
> But there's another view that is now, I think, ascendent, which I

think is just a horrible view, which is that "I need to be safe ideologically. I need to be safe emotionally. I just need to feel good all the time, and if someone says something that I don't like, that's a problem for everybody else including the administration."

I think that is a terrible idea for the following reasons: I don't want you to be safe, ideologically. I don't want you to be safe, emotionally. I want you to be strong. . . .

I want you to be offended every single day on this campus. I want you to be deeply aggrieved and offended and upset, and then to learn how to speak back. Because that's what we need from you in these communities.

As FIRE's Robert Shibley wrote in response to Georgetown's defenestration of the two adjunct law professors (discussed in chapter 7), "Colleges and universities are among the very few institutions in the world that have the luxury—and the responsibility—to think about the results of the decisions they make not on timescales determined by quarterly profits or social media firestorms, but in terms of decades and centuries." Georgetown University celebrated its 235th birthday in 2024; in all likelihood, it'll still be around in another 235 years. "University decision-makers are insulated from much of the pressure that accompanies other jobs precisely so they can make principled decisions that will bear examination in the decades and centuries to come."

But they're not going to do it themselves, because the incentive structures they face are misaligned. It's much easier to go along with current fads and grease the squeaky wheels. That's why we need external pressure, including through government action, to eliminate the root of the problem.

Conclusion

I never intended to become a poster boy for cancel culture. Nor do I intend to let those four months of Georgetown farce define my life or career. But I'm using this chance to expose the institutional rot in academia and trace it to the illiberal winds blowing across America.

I wouldn't wish what I went through on anyone, except maybe the trolls who enflamed those first four days of hell. Two years later, I still marvel at the perfect storm I walked into. As William Spruance, a Georgetown alum who had his own contretemps (see chapter 12), wrote, "It was an unholy trilogy that attacked Shapiro. There were the remarkably stupid who lacked the basic skills to understand his statement; there were grifters who saw an opportunity for self-advancement; and there were the invertebrates who saw appeasement as an easy alternative to integrity."

The central commonality of all of Georgetown's recent problems is the unprincipled and weak leadership of Dean Bill Treanor. Although a successful fundraiser and gifted scholar—though with a tin ear for current affairs—Treanor has proven himself again and again to be just the kind of "invertebrate" whose lack of integrity plagues law schools across the country. After my situation exploded, Luke Bunting, a Georgetown student leader, told *National Review* that he "puts a lot of the blame on the dean" for the volatile environment. "His email poured gasoline on the fire. And now, his silence—not coming out forcefully and saying, 'We support the free speech of faculty outside of the school,' like they've done previously with liberal professors who've said offensive things. Letting this hang out there has just made things worse. It's almost been a kind of de facto endorsement of the group calling for his ouster."

You can judge for yourself, but Treanor didn't bathe himself in glory in managing my contretemps. Although he continues to be paid a million-dollar salary in his cushy job—nice work if you can get it—his career seems to have stalled. When I spoke at Fordham Law in fall 2022, the scuttlebutt was that Treanor, who was dean there before moving to DC, had lost out on that university's presidency over the way he had handled my case. If true, that's well-deserved karma.

As for me, two and a half years later I'm enjoying my new job as director of constitutional studies at the wonderful Manhattan Institute. MI, as it's known, describes itself as "a think tank whose mission is to develop and disseminate new ideas that foster greater economic choice and individual responsibility," one that "works to keep America and its great cities prosperous, safe, and free." That sounds pretty good to me—and is a better fit than Georgetown would've been. I've been delighted to join old friends and make new ones at an institution I've long admired.

Although MI has long had legal scholars doing excellent work in areas ranging from criminal justice to civil litigation and the administrative state, it never had a constitutional focus as such. So this is a natural fit and a mutually beneficial relationship. Both in that day job and beyond, I've remained in the arena, trying to influence the climate of ideas in areas ranging from the First Amendment and federalism to civil rights and deregulation. I published a dozen op-eds during my four-month purgatory, and I've maintained that prodigious output of commentary. And I'm still watching the Supreme Court, particularly with the updated paperback edition of my last book, *Supreme Disorder*, having come out just as I joined MI.

With my newfound "lived experience," I've continued, and will continue, to comment on culture and politics. I care deeply about this country and believe it's man's last, best hope for freedom in this world. That means constitutionalism, it means (classical) liberal values, and it means gratitude for the tremendous opportunities we enjoy here—and why so many people still want to come here and live the American dream. I'm generally long on America—to quote Brett Kavanaugh at his confirmation hearings, I live on the "sunrise side of the mountain"—but I'm pessimistic about academia, if slightly less so than in the summer of 2022. Perhaps we've passed "peak woke" in society writ large, as normal people, concerned with their families and livelihoods rather than performative virtue-signaling, call out progressive fascists. The pandemic showed a lot of parents the faddish theories their kids were being taught, and they didn't like them. But we may have passed the point of no return on the illiberal takeover of higher education. The backlash to antisemitism that exploded on campuses nationwide after Hamas's October 7, 2023, attack on Israel is another inflection point and may provide an opportunity for reform, but we're still in the eye of that storm, so it's too soon to tell.

In that urtext of law schools in popular culture, *The Paper Chase*, the demanding Professor Kingsfield, who enforces a logician's ear for argument, nonetheless scolds a student that "nobody inhibits you from expressing yourself." Half a century later, too many law schools flip that script. Through a combination of agenda-driven administrators, radical faculty, and weak leadership, a culture of conformity has arisen that's merciless in its enforcement of radical ideological norms. If educrats continue their hegemonic growth and overreach into every facet of law school life, graduating lawyers will be ignorant, ahistorical activists who possess limited analytical and reasoning skills. Deans say they want students to feel "safe" to engage with new ideas, but it's that very safetyism that prevents open discourse and rigorous legal training.

In June 2023, as I was completing the first draft of this book, the journalist Bret Stephens gave a wonderfully apt Class Day speech at the University of Chicago that deserves excerpting:

> Institutions and their leaders invariably say they support independent thinking and free speech—but only when that support is easy and costs them nothing, not when it's hard and requires them to take a stand. They want provocative thinking—provided it isn't too pointed and only offends the people who don't count in their social network. They want to foster a culture of argument and intellectual challenge—so long as nobody ever says the wrong thing and feelings don't get hurt.
>
> But this doesn't always have to be the case. Institutions *can*, in fact, practice what they preach. They *can* declare principles, set a tone, announce norms—and then live up to their principles through regular practice. They *can* explain to every incoming class of students or new

employees that they champion independent thinking and free expression in both word *and* deed. They *can* prove that they won't cave to outrage mobs and other forms of public pressure, either by canceling invited speakers or by never inviting controversial speakers in the first place.

There's a way this is done. It's called leadership. . . .

Bob [Zimmer, the former university president] created an institutional culture that, as Salman Rushdie once said, serves as a safe space *for* thought, not a safe space *from* thought.

As observers like my MI colleague Chris Rufo and Cornell law professor William Jacobson have described, these dangerous times we're living in parallel the Chinese Cultural Revolution. Students denounced professors (and their own peers) for wrongthink, insisting on absolute ideological purity. Some are made public examples of, *pour encourager les autres* (to use an exampie from pre-revolutionary France), to scare the others away from voicing dissenting views. As Nate Cohn, the *New York Times'* chief political analyst, astutely analyzed in a March 2023 column called "What's 'Woke' and Why It Matters," this pernicious dynamic is a product of the "successor ideology" that emerged in the aftermath of Barack Obama's reelection in 2012.

At the time, liberalism seemed utterly triumphant. Yet for young progressives, "hope" and "change" had given way to the realization that Mr. Obama's presidency hadn't cured income inequality, racial inequality or climate change. These dynamics opened a space for a new left, as young progressives started to reach for more ambitious politics, just as the triumph of the Obama coalition gave progressives the confidence to embrace ideas that would have been unimaginable in the Bush era.

A decade later, this new left is everywhere. On economic issues, there has been the Bernie Sanders campaign and calls for Medicare for all; democratic socialism; and the Green New Deal. On race, there has been the Black Lives Matter movement; kneeling in protest during the national anthem; and defund the police. On gender and sex, there has been the Me Too movement and the sharing of preferred pronouns and more.

On class and economics, it's easy to delineate the new left. Mr. Sanders helpfully embraced the democratic socialism label to distinguish himself from those who would incrementally smooth out the rough edges of capitalism. It's harder to distinguish the new left from Obama-era liberals on race, gender and sexuality. There is no widely shared ideological term like democratic socialism to make it easy.

And yet the differences between Obama-era liberals and the new left on race, sexuality and gender are extremely significant, with big consequences for American politics.

Cohn identified the differences between this New Left and the old one as: (1) speaking with righteousness, urgency, and moral absolutism, as opposed to searching for compromise and commonality; (2) being very conscious of identity, elevating "marginalized voices" and race-based policies, such that the personal is political; (3) seeing society as a web of overlapping power structures, constituted by language and norms as much as by law and policy, with academic jargon entering the mainstream and the equation of hurt feelings with the physical harms of traditional oppression, such that everything might have to change to end systemic racism; (4) viewing racism, sexism, and other "intersectional" hierarchies as deeply embedded, leading to a pessimistic view of America that can't be redeemed by Obama-era (let alone Boomer) liberalism; and (5) prioritizing the pursuit of a more equitable society over Enlightenment-era values, such that "equal rights are a veneer that conceal and justify structural inequality." That's not a full diagnosis of the complex social phenomena afflicting our society, but it covers much of how the "woke" or postmodern social justice movement operates and what it hopes to achieve.

And we see repeatedly the real harm it has done to legal education; I was relieved when the 2022–23 academic year ended so I didn't have to keep adding new material on the latest illiberal outrage to the initial manuscript of this book that I was then completing. But that didn't fully save me; in late June 2023, Boston University School of Law offered its law students "wellness resources" to help them "navigate these times" of Supreme Court rulings they may not like. The highest-profile decisions—on affirmative action, student loans, and the right of a graphic designer not to make websites for same-sex weddings—were supported by a majority of ordinary citizens and certainly shouldn't cause distress in reasonable people.

It's reminiscent of what happened after Donald Trump's election in 2016. GW law professor John Banzhaf, known for consumer-focused legal activism and not exactly an ultra-MAGA groupie, colorfully described how law schools are "wussifying" their students: "To help students cope with the 'trauma' of having backed the losing candidate in the presidential election, law school professors are cancelling classes, postponing exams, providing grief counseling, etc." He went on to describe how "law schools are treating their students not just as fragile 'snowflakes' but as emotionally distraught young children in need of cuddling[;] the Michigan Law School scheduled a session with the law school's 'embedded psychologist' where these ultra sensitive souls would use play dough or Legos and blow bubbles to help regain their ability to continue studying." As this book goes to press, we're on the verge of another presidential election. Although campuses, including law schools, will be calmer if Kamala Harris wins than if Trump completes a Grover Cleveland–esque return to the White House, the underlying problems revealed in the last few years aren't going anywhere.

Even beyond their ideological perversions, law schools are raising a generation of lawyers unable to stand up to tough judges and opposing counsel to protect the freedom, financial welfare, and sometimes even the lives of their clients. It's a worrying development, to say the least. To show that this creation of "wimpy lawyers" is an aberration, Banzhaf invokes a long line of American attorneys, "from the fictional Atticus Finch (who stood up to racist pressures) to real life lawyers including Andrew Hamilton (who defied a judge to establish freedom of the press), and John Adams (defending soldiers in the Boston Massacre)." We've depended on legal professionals to advocate for the rule of law and defend constitutional rights in the face of public pressure.

Alas, illiberalism has infected American law schools. As Paul du Quenoy has written with respect to the related crisis in medical education, these trends exploit "the utter lack of principle that now seems prerequisite for a career in higher education administration. . . . Like virtually all fields of study, [legal] education is now subject to deconstruction for its supposed 'systemic racism' and the inherent sin of 'whiteness.' In many schools, aspiring [lawyers and law professors] must declare their allegiance to and receive instruction in DEI principles on par with [legal] knowledge, just as students of any subject in the Soviet Union also had to master the tenets of Marxism-Leninism."[1]

Law schools are thus further diverted from their necessarily circumscribed mission, which is to organize and transmit knowledge in a focused set of core legal subjects, along with writing and rhetorical skills. When they say that free speech, due process, equal treatment, and other liberal values can mesh harmoniously with DEI—one of the main points of Jenny Martinez's letter discussed in chapter 9—they engage in wishful thinking. Instead, we should remember the words of the indomitable former president of the University of Chicago Hanna Holborn Gray (one of the first women to lead a major university): "Education should not be intended to make people comfortable, it is meant to make them think. Universities should be expected to provide the conditions within which hard thought, and therefore strong disagreement, independent judgment, and the questioning of stubborn assumptions, can flourish in an environment of the greatest freedom." Anyone concerned about the quality of our nation's legal and political institutions must stand up and speak out. DEI will disappear only when its postmodernist identitarian leftism returns to the ideological fringes.

Look, there's nothing wrong with diversity, equity, or inclusion—as words, values, or goals. It's good to bring together students and faculty with diverse backgrounds and views, to prevent groupthink, promote a market of ideas, and advance a productive search for knowledge. Equity is a centuries-old concept in Anglo-American law that boils down to fairness and justice, and indeed we ought to treat everyone fairly. Who can object to people feeling welcome and included at their place of study, to better engage in their educational mission? The problem arises when DEI dogma perverts those basic words to mean the opposite of their

1. Paul du Quenoy, "Med School Departures from Rankings System Is Symptom of Bad Medicine," *Newsweek*, January 28, 2023. Paul, who now heads up the Palm Beach Freedom Institute, had his own experience with illiberalism and cancel culture while on faculty at the American University of Beirut.

dictionary definitions, to stifle intellectual diversity, undermine equal opportunity, and exclude dissenting voices. DEI as practiced stands for discrimination, exclusion, and indoctrination.

Whatever good faith the diversity-industrial complex brings to bear, it ends up bludgeoning people into mouthing platitudes they don't believe and excluding them if they resist. It is at the root of the illiberal takeover of legal education, so we must excise it root and branch from our institutions. We must instead embrace real diversity and celebrate the power of debate, dialogue, and disagreement. We must allow ideas to flow freely so our law schools and lawyers can realize their true potential. Nothing less than the health of our democracy is at stake.

Dean Treanor's Letter Reinstating Me

(The italicized block-quoted comments are mine.)

June 2, 2022

Dear Mr. Shapiro,

The Office of Institutional Diversity, Equity, and Affirmative Action ("IDEAA") and the Department of Human Resources ("HR") have concluded their reviews of whether communications posted to social media by you violated University policies. IDEAA and HR both found that your comments had a significant negative impact on the Georgetown Law community, including current and prospective students, alumni, staff, and faculty.

> *What does a "significant negative impact" mean? Just that many people didn't like my tweets and some were even offended? I'm sure lots of people don't like what any professor says or writes on a daily basis. I wasn't even disparaging Georgetown or any of its students ("current or prospective"), alumni, staff, or faculty. This is the crux of the matter.*

Because you were a third party and not an employee at the time you posted the comments on Twitter, IDEAA made no determination as to whether your actions violated IDEAA policies on Equal Opportunity and Non-Discrimination in Employment and Education, and the Policy Statement on Harassment (Relating to Protected Categories). However, IDEAA has significant concerns about the way in which you expressed yourself, in that it "could have the effect of limiting Black women students' access to courses taught by [you] and undermine Georgetown Law's commitment to maintain inclusive learning and working environments." Consistent with IDEAA's Grievance Procedures to Investigate Allegations of Discrimination and Harassment, IDEAA referred this matter to me with recommendations for measures to address the impact of your comments and to prevent the recurrence of offensive conduct based on race, gender, and sex.

> *How could I possibly be discriminating against any student, whatever their race or sex, when I hadn't directed my comments at them? And the idea that the decision by a student not to take my class, for whatever reason, constitutes my limiting access to educational opportunities is laughable. If I hadn't been hired, nobody would've had an opportunity to take my class. Indeed, it could be argued that if I were a secret racist misogynist who wanted to discriminate against some of my students, my comments did those students a service by signaling that they should avoid me.*

Similarly, because you were not an employee at the time of the tweets, HR did not make a finding as to whether you violated HR Policy #401 on Professional Conduct. However, HR also has serious concerns that your pre-employment conduct could negatively impact your ability to perform your responsibilities at work. HR also provided me with recommendations given the impact of your comments on the Law Center community.

> *As I mentioned in chapter 6, I wasn't given the HR report. To the extent there was anything there that differed from or added to the IDEAA report with regard to my ability to do my job, it's unclear what that would be given that I still possessed all the talents, credentials, contacts, and other qualities for which I was hired. If anything, it's this investigation and its negative findings that threw a shadow on my ability to operate in the Georgetown community, along with the chill on my future speech.*

I want to remind you of some of Georgetown's core values. Georgetown is committed to providing a safe and inclusive environment for all members of our community to work and study, free from harassment and discrimination, and takes violations of its policies on Equal Opportunity and Non-Discrimination in Employment and Education, and the Policy Statement on Harassment (Relating to Protected Categories) seriously. Georgetown also expects its employees "to behave in a professional, business-like manner at work, on University premises, and whenever representing the University. Employees are accountable for behavior outside of work that has a negative impact on the individual's ability to perform his/her responsibilities at work," as provided in HR Policy #401 on Professional Conduct. Georgetown is also committed to free and open inquiry, as set forth in the University's Speech and Expression Policy.

> *I said from the outset that I phrased my tweet poorly. We all make mistakes, and many of us make missteps on social media, but there's no need to make national news when a simple email saying, "Ilya, please be more careful on Twitter," would've sufficed. Indeed, Randy Barnett had already conveyed that message to me, so there was really no need for Dean Treanor to get involved beyond pointing to the university's speech policy and saying that Georgetown doesn't police its faculty's extramural speech.*

After considering recommendations from IDEAA and HR as to appropriate actions, I want to set the following expectations:

1. As a member of Law Center staff and the Executive Director of the Georgetown Center for the Constitution, you are, in partnership with the Faculty Director, responsible for strategic planning, Center program and events development, fundraising, teaching, scholarship, and external relations, including promoting the Center's mission, teaching, scholarship, and advocacy. In this role you are responsible for designing, managing and

communicating effectively about Center initiatives, programs and events, and working with multiple diverse stakeholders. Given the multi-faceted nature of your role and the expectation that you will interact with many different constituencies as you direct the Center, including students, alumni, faculty, staff, and donors, communicating carefully and thoughtfully is critical to developing good relationships with stakeholders, and hence to success as the Executive Director for the Center. I expect you will communicate in a professional manner in your role.

Again, on day one I said that I should've phrased my tweet better, which is why I deleted it, which should've been the end of the story.

2. I appreciate that you told University investigators that you would seek Georgetown PR guidance on how to best advance communications in your role at the Center. Going forward, we encourage you to work closely with your supervisor to ensure that your communications and social media interactions related to your role at Georgetown are professional and comply with our University policies. The Law Center communications team is also available to you as a resource.

Randy had no interest in micromanaging my statements, and had conveyed that to Treanor, but he and I would of course be working together closely in running the Center.

3. Any course that you might teach will be subject to the standard Office of Academic Affairs review process.

There's an open question as to whether, in teaching a seminar on economic liberty under the Constitution or a class on Supreme Court amicus strategy—which is what I had planned for my first year—I would be required to include woke or otherwise politically correct aspects to get past this "standard" review.

4. I ask that you make yourself available to meet with student leaders concerned about your ability to treat students fairly.

   This sounded ominous and some later likened it to a "struggle session," but I'd have always been open to meeting with students about anything. Moreover, I doubt that anyone would've made such a request; nobody had taken me up on my open offer to meet during the "purgatory" period when I was on leave.

5. You will participate this summer in a training program which will be required of senior staff, including Center Directors, which will include programming on implicit bias, cultural competence, and non-discrimination.

   Sorry, former colleagues, for causing you to be subjected to programs that are useless at best. These diversity trainings tend to make unscientific claims about so-called microaggressions and implicit bias—and reject the basic American premise that everyone should be treated equally.

6. You are expected to comply with University policies relating to non-discrimination, anti-harassment, and non-retaliation, as well as professional conduct, and will, like any other employee, be subject to disciplinary action for any violations.

   Well, I've never discriminated against anyone nor planned to, so nothing to worry about here.

7. Today will be your last day on administrative leave with pay, and you will begin your duties tomorrow.

   Hurray! My long national nightmare was over—except it wasn't.

In closing, I remind you of this language in your offer letter: "I invite you, as a new Georgetown University employee, to learn more about the rich traditions embodied in the Mission of the University: our belief that diversity promotes understanding, our intellectual openness, our international character and our commitment to the principles of lifelong self-reflective learning, responsible community membership, the common good and generous service to others." It is my expectation that you will embrace these principles.

> *I remain as committed to those principles as I was on the day you hired me, but I invite you to self-reflect and learn from this experience to actually commit yourself and the law school to intellectual openness, responsible community membership, and generosity of spirit—as well as to its policies on free speech and academic freedom.*

Sincerely,
William M. Treanor
Dean and Executive Vice President
Paul Regis Dean Leadership Chair

IDEAA Confidential Report

(The italicized block-quoted comments are mine.)

Office of Institutional Diversity, Equity, and Affirmative Action
CONFIDENTIAL REPORT OF ADMINISTRATIVE REVIEW

<u>Investigators</u>
Bisi L. Okubadejo
Associate Vice President for Equal Opportunity,
Affirmative Action, and Compliance

Kay Bhagat-Smith
Senior Civil Rights Investigator and Compliance Manager

Date of Report: June 2, 2022

I. Introduction

IDEAA has the authority to investigate allegations of discrimination or harassment that may have an impact on the Georgetown community. On February 1, 2022, pursuant to a request from the Dean of the Georgetown University Law Center (Dean), the Office of Institutional Diversity, Equity, and Affirmative Action (IDEAA) opened an administrative review of certain alleged conduct by Ilya Shapiro (Respondent), Executive Director of the Georgetown Center for the Constitution (Center).

> *Already we have a legal flaw: I wasn't yet the executive director—which became the deciding factor in my reinstatement.*

In particular, IDEAA considered whether the Respondent engaged in conduct in violation of the University's policies on Equal Opportunity and Non-Discrimination in Employment and Education, and the Policy Statement on Harassment (Relating to Protected Categories), which are located at https://ideaa.georgetown.edu/policies/, when on January 26, 2022, at or around 10:36 p.m., the Respondent posted a series of tweets on social media, that questioned President Biden's announced decision to nominate a Black woman for the open seat on the United States Supreme Court. These tweets included the text below.

> Objectively best pick for Biden is Sri Srinivasan, who is solid prog & v smart. Even has identity politics benefit of being first Asian (Indian) American. But alas doesn't fit into latest intersectionality hierarchy so we'll get lesser black woman. Thank heaven for small favors?

During the review, IDEAA reviewed relevant documentation, including the Respondent's job responsibilities; letters signed by more than 1,000 students, alumni, and others who were offended by the Respondent's tweet; the Respondent's subsequent apologies; and the Dean's response to the Georgetown Law community. IDEAA also interviewed the Respondent, his supervisor (the Faculty Director), and an Associate Dean who received feedback, including complaints and concerns, from Law Center faculty, staff, students, alumni, and prospective students.

Curiously, in setting the stage for the investigation, there's no mention of the Speech and Expression Policy. There was also apparently no need to mention the letters supporting me and the feedback various university officials, not least Dean Treanor, received regarding the need to protect the freedom of speech and promote intellectual diversity.

After carefully considering the available information, IDEAA found that the Respondent's comments had a significant negative impact on the Georgetown Law community, which includes current and prospective students, alumni, staff, and faculty. IDEAA respects Georgetown

University's commitment to the free and open discussion of ideas and does not seek to infringe speech that does not violate the University's non-discrimination or anti-harassment policy. However, IDEAA has significant concerns about the Respondent's comments, particularly as they could have the effect of limiting Black women students' access to courses taught by the Respondent and undermine Georgetown Law's commitment to maintain inclusive learning and working environments. The Respondent's comments also may discourage Black women and their allies from seeking internships and employment at the Center.

> *Here's that "significant negative impact" language again. What does this mean? People's feelings were hurt? Donations dried up? Admitted students decided not to attend? How can a tweet posted publicly, not even speech directed at a particular person, even constitute "harassment" or "discrimination"?*

As the Respondent was a third party and not an employee at the time that he posted the comments on Twitter, IDEAA makes no determination as to whether his actions violate IDEAA policy. Instead, consistent with IDEAA's *Grievance Procedures to Investigate Allegations of Discrimination and Harassment*, IDEAA refers this matter to the Dean with a recommendation of appropriate corrective measures to address the impact of the Respondent's objectively offensive comments and to prevent the recurrence of offensive conduct based on race, gender, and sex.

> *A lot to "unpack" here, as academics say. Isn't a finding of "significant negative impact" a determination, particularly as that finding includes the conclusion that I've limited educational opportunities to black women specifically? Separately, if I wasn't an employee and IDEAA had no jurisdiction over me regarding this incident, how could it make any recommendations to the dean? Finally, if some people found my comments offensive and others didn't, how are my comments "objectively" offensive? Some people criticized me for saying that Judge Srinivasan was the "objectively" best pick, because even if he's highly qualified, there's no single objective metric of what*

makes "the best" Supreme Court nominee; it's a parlor game. Fair enough, but then my comments should get the benefit of that doubt as well.

A more detailed description of IDEAA's review is discussed below.

II. Summary of Review

A. Responses to the Respondent's Tweet

IDEAA reviewed responses from students, alumni, faculty, and staff to the Respondent's tweet; the Respondent's subsequent written statements; and the Dean's communication to the community.

In response to the Respondent's tweet, a faculty member tweeted, "[Respondent], as one of your future[1] Georgetown colleague[s], I am curious: is your phrase 'lesser Black woman' meant to describe a particular Black woman or do you intend 'lesser Black woman' to encompass the general set of Black women under consideration for the seat?" In response to this tweet, on January 27, 2022, at 9:36 a.m., the Respondent tweeted, "I apologize. I meant no offense, but it was an inartful tweet. I have taken it down."

> *For the record, because this continues to be confused, let me definitively state that I was not referring to Ketanji Brown Jackson or anyone else in particular, but rather to my opinion that the entire universe of people, which of course includes all black women and every other demographic subset of the human race, was "lesser"—meaning less qualified—than Judge Srinivasan in the context of a Democratic president making a Supreme Court nomination.*

On January 27, 2022, at 1:15 p.m., the Dean emailed the Georgetown Law community to address the Respondent's tweets, stating:

---

1. On January 21, 2022, Georgetown Law publicly announced that the Respondent was scheduled to start his new role as Executive Director of the Center on February 1, 2022.

Ilya Shapiro, who was recently hired to direct one of Georgetown Law's research institutes, posted a series of tweets on Twitter that he has since deleted. The tweets' suggestion that the best Supreme Court nominee could not be a Black woman and their use of demeaning language are appalling. The tweets are at odds with everything we stand for at Georgetown Law and are damaging to the culture of equity and inclusion that Georgetown Law is building every day.

On January 28, 2022, the Law Center's Black Law Students Association (BLSA) wrote an open letter "on behalf of the Georgetown Law Center student body" to the Georgetown Law administration that was signed by more than 1,000 students and student groups, including the American Constitutional Society, Georgetown Law Journal, and the Georgetown National Security Law Society. The BLSA letter "demand[ed] the revocation of [the Respondent's] employment contract and to condemn his racist tweets." The BLSA letter further clarified that, "[o]ur concern and frustration is not rooted in [the Respondent's] opinion that someone else is more qualified for the position. Instead, our anger stems from [the Respondent's] suggestion that *any* Black woman, regardless of their qualifications, would be a 'lesser' choice for the Court" (emphasis in original). The letter characterized the Respondent's tweet as "offensive, racist, sexist, misogynistic, inflammatory, deplorable, insensitive, and unprofessional." Finally, the letter referenced the "hurt felt today by the Black community, and in particular Black women."

> *As I wrote in the introduction, it's ridiculous to read my tweet as saying that no black woman could ever be qualified for the Supreme Court. Dean Treanor's statement to that effect ignited the situation and BLSA then fanned the flames. (Incidentally, there are two grammatical errors in this paragraph alone; I'm not picking those kinds of nits in these annotations.)*

On January 31, 2022, the Dean again emailed the members of the Georgetown Law Center community, under the subject "Update on Ilya Shapiro." In his email, the Dean stated,

Over the past several days, I have heard the pain and outrage of so many at Georgetown Law, and particularly from our Black female students, staff, alumni, and faculty. . . . I am writing to inform you that I have placed [the Respondent] on administrative leave, pending an investigation. . . . Racial stereotypes about individual capabilities and qualifications remain a pernicious force in our society and our profession. I am keenly aware that our law school is not exempt.

On February 1, 2022, Georgetown Law students organized a "sit-in" "to call for the immediate termination of [the Respondent]." In the days that followed, other Georgetown groups publicly expressed their reactions to the Respondent's tweet. For example, a letter to Georgetown's President and the Dean, dated February 10, 2022, on behalf of more than 50 Georgetown Law Black alumni, stated that, "[the Respondent] has every right to believe what he wants, but his statements . . . reflect unfair racial bias. His own statements suggest he lacks the objectivity and integrity to evaluate fairly the contributions of racially diverse students, colleagues, scholars, and staff."

I discuss these developments in chapter 3 so will not belabor them here, other than to note that the chronology here is incomplete in that it fails to describe letters and press statements from students and alumni that supported me, not to mention the letters signed by outside academics.

B. Respondent's Job Description

As the Executive Director of the Georgetown Center for the Constitution, the Respondent is responsible for promoting the Center's mission, teaching, scholarship, and advocacy. His role is to design and manage Center initiatives, programs, and events, and achieve programmatic success while working with multiple stakeholders. In addition, it is expected that he will assist the Faculty Director in developing new fundraising initiatives. The Respondent's Job Description includes the following responsibilities:

- Promote the Center's reach and influence in popular media.
- Teach a for-credit course to Georgetown JD students.
- Provide career advice to JD and L.L.M. students.
- Represent the Center in speaking engagements.
- Attend strategic planning meetings and/or serve on University and Law Center–wide committees/task forces to represent the Center and build awareness around strategic initiatives.
- Stand in for the Faculty Director at Center programs.

This is probably the most objective—there's that word again—part of the report. No notes.

C. *Summary of Interviews*

IDEAA[2] met with the Respondent, the Faculty Director, and the Associate Dean. Below is a summary of the information that these individuals provided to IDEAA.

Respondent

In a written statement and in a discussion with IDEAA and HR, the Respondent acknowledged that on January 26 at 10:36 p.m., he posted the tweet at issue. He later characterized his tweet as "poorly phrased" and "inartful," and explained that he "meant no offense."

The Respondent told IDEAA and HR that it would be "unfair" and in "bad faith" to read his comments in a "derogatory or misogynistic manner." He acknowledged to IDEAA and HR that "people have commented

---

2. As the Department of Human Resources (HR) is conducting an investigation into the Respondent's conduct, HR personnel participated in the meetings with the Respondent and the Faculty Director.

that they were offended," by the tweet. According to the Respondent, in hindsight, he intended in the tweet to convey that he was "upset" that President Biden limited his candidates for a Supreme Court justice selection to Black women. The Respondent explained that, upon reflection, he meant to convey that Sri Srinivasan was the most qualified and that "everybody is lesser" than Srinivasan. In his written statement, the Respondent explained, "once I settled on my pick [for Srinivasan], everyone else, regardless of race, gender or any other factor, became a less qualified or 'lesser' choice." He claimed that he was not referring to a specific Black woman; but he said that he was aware of the pool of Black women contenders and they are all not as qualified as Srinivasan. The Respondent stated, "[t]o any unbiased reader, this was the plain meaning of my admittedly inartful tweet."

> *Indeed. I said all that in the Zoom with the inquisitors and maintain it to this day.*

The Respondent attributed the "inartful[ness]" of his tweets to being in a "festive and feisty mood," because he was traveling and celebrating a friend's job-change. The Respondent clarified that he typically does not tweet before bed when he is at home, but that he has tweeted "before bed" when he is "on the road." According to the Respondent, prior to posting his tweet, he was "scrolling" through his cell phone and felt "upset" that selecting a justice based on race was not the "right way" to select a Supreme Court justice. Only after he awoke the next morning and found that individuals were offended by his tweet did the Respondent apologize and remove his tweet. He recalled thinking that there was a "mob against [him]," which did not advance his argument and did "not mak[e] [him] look good." The Respondent also recalls thinking: "I need to get ahead of this."

> *Am I the only one amused that they felt the need to highlight my comments about tweeting "before bed" and "on the road"? One slight correction: it's not the fact that people were offended that prompted me to delete my tweet—people are offended on social media all the*

time!—but that I recognized the cancellation mob for what it was and wanted to save my job.

The Respondent acknowledged that his tweet was sent in both his personal and professional capacities, as separating his personal self from his professional self is an "eternal dilemma" or a "metaphysical question," particularly in his role as an "expert and communicator" regarding the Supreme Court. In his written statement, the Respondent stated, "[t]o say that I am an expert on judicial nominations and Supreme Court politics is, frankly, a bit of an understatement, which is probably why Georgetown's Center for the Constitution hired me in the first place. . . . I say this to provide insight as to why I was opining about the Supreme Court vacancy in the first place." He also volunteered that he lists his professional role in his Twitter biography.

> *We're all advised to put in our social-media profiles that "opinions are my own," "RTs are not endorsements," and other legalistic disclaimers. That's good practice legally speaking, but to the lay observer, it doesn't much matter. Nor does it matter whether you're posting "after hours" or "outside the office." The internet consumer doesn't differentiate. Now, you may be wondering why I "volunteered" that I have my professional affiliation in my Twitter bio and otherwise discussed my "expertise." It was to establish that I wasn't going on what lawyers call "frolic and detour"; it would've arguably appeared worse if I were to have posted an "inartful" tweet on some subject I know nothing about, making an underlying point I couldn't back up.*

In reflecting on his new role at the Law Center, the Respondent explained that he plans to take the Center to the next level by "building its brand," engaging with students, faculty, and practitioners, and turning the Center into a "crown jewel." He stated that he will be working directly with students: teaching law students in a class every semester,[3]

---

3. IDEAA notes that the Respondent's job description, outlined above, describes the Respondent teaching one course.

supervising and mentoring students, providing career advice to students, and eventually hiring students for fellowships and other opportunities. Also, the Respondent stated that he will be representing the Center and promoting the Center through popular media, which may include social media. The Respondent informed IDEAA and HR that he was uncertain whether he expected to promote the Center via Twitter.

Yes, I had grand plans for the Center. Sigh . . .

When provided an opportunity to respond to IDEAA regarding the number of current students, faculty, staff, and alumni who publicly expressed their offense at and concerns with his tweet, the Respondent stated that "all I can do is say my tweet didn't mean any of the offensive or negative things that have been attributed to it or me." In his written statement, he explained that "students can select professors who fit their ideological presuppositions. This is something that happens naturally and is not cause for concern." He explained that he will not use the phrase "lesser Black woman" again and "will swear" that he will not engage on Twitter in the same way again. The Respondent pointed out that there was "large support" for him that showed "disgust" at the Law Center for conducting an investigation into his conduct.

The Respondent acknowledged that his tweet was a "failure in communication." He argued, however, that conducting an investigation into his conduct was giving in to the "heckler's veto" and could have a chilling effect on speech. Though the Respondent acknowledged that some individuals interpret his political views as racist, he denied being accused of making similar comments or statements in the past that were interpreted as showing a bias based on race, gender, and/or sex.

1. The inquisitors had never heard the phrase "heckler's veto," which is astonishing.
2. To be precise on the issue of previous accusations, I told them that I wasn't accused of race/gender/sex-related bias any more than any

*nonprogressive is when discussing certain sensitive or controversial
topics.*

Faculty Director

The Faculty Director informed IDEAA and HR that he has had a "close
professional" relationship with the Respondent for fifteen years, and initially started discussing the Georgetown position with him in October
2021. The Faculty Director characterized the January 26 tweet at issue
as "recklessly framed," and "obviously fraught in a racist manner."[4] He also
informed IDEAA and HR that "[he doesn't] like repeating" those three
words (*i.e.*, "lesser Black woman") even in a confidential meeting about
them. He acknowledged that "a person who was racist could use" that
phrasing. However, the Faculty Director explained that, despite the plain
language of his tweet, the Respondent "didn't have the intent" to be
racist instead he "fail[ed] to communicate" what he was trying to say; the
Faculty Director further noted, "[f]or someone whose job it is to communicate, he needs to do a better job."

> *Fair enough, Randy, assuming "fraught in a racist manner" means
> igniting controversy over issues relating to race. (Perhaps racial is
> a better word than racist in that sense.) And yes, a racist could
> certainly use those words, though I'd argue it's awkward phrasing
> even for a racist. Compare, for example, "lesser X" with "every X is
> a lesser human."*

Despite the Faculty Director's characterization of the Respondent's
tweet as "obviously fraught in a racist manner," he did not have concerns
about the Respondent performing his role at the Center. The Faculty

---

4. Later in the discussion with IDEAA and HR, the Faculty Director stated that the
Respondent's words were "ambiguous," and indicated that there were two possible
meanings. He explained that if one considers the "context of the words" "lesser Black
woman," the Respondent's "intention was clear and not racist," particularly given that
the Respondent later "clarified" his intent and deleted the tweet.

Director acknowledged that the Respondent's tweet will "affect his relationship" with colleagues and students "who are very angry at what he
said and consider what he said to be damaging." However, the Faculty
Director pointed out that the Respondent provided "a very prompt apology," but "we can't make people accept apologies; that's really on them."
The Faculty Director opined that following this incident, the Respondent
might be a "better person" who will "handle social media more carefully
and cautiously." The Faculty Director also informed IDEAA and HR
that students are not compelled to take the Respondent's courses and
suggested that "only people who have either forgiven him for this one
particular trespass or are unaware of it" will take his course.

> *So had I stayed, would Randy have been complicit in denying educa-
> tional access to students who didn't take my classes? Would the Law
> Center itself have been opening itself up to liability under Title VI of
> the Education Act for denying equal educational opportunities? The
> logic here creates quite the slippery slope.*

Associate Dean

The Associate Dean informed IDEAA that students were "very concerned"
about taking a class where the Respondent would grade them because
he appears to view Black students as "lesser" and "not qualified." The
Associate Dean and the Dean conducted a town hall with students
who participated in the sit-in, during which students expressed their
concerns about the Respondent. The Associate Dean also recounted
meeting with conservative and libertarian students who feared the Law
Center was engaging in "cancel culture." The Associate Dean also recalled meeting with Christian students who pointed out that as a Jesuit
institution, the Law Center should show mercy and allow "room for
people to mess up."

> *This is Mitch Bailin, the dean of students who had the Covid-related
> run-in with William Spruance I detailed in chapter 12. I'm sure
> this is a decent summary of the student comments that he fielded.
> The last point is interesting. The Christian students didn't parse my*

words or argue over speech protections, but instead focused on the concept of grace. This recognition that we're all imperfect humans now plays a larger role in my worldview—and it doesn't have to come from a religious background, but rather simple kindness.

In addition to receiving concerns from the students, the Associate Dean relayed that "a lot of faculty" expressed "deep concern" about the Respondent's comments. They expressed "outrage" about how his tweet "harms our environment" and "sends the wrong message to our students" with regard to the Law Center's efforts to promote equity and inclusion.

Had I stayed, what would these faculty members' response have been to my legal arguments and activism against DEI structures and the critical theory on which they're based? I discuss this point about how I'd inevitably have again run afoul of the IDEAA, just by expressing heterodox policy views, in my resignation letter (which you can read in the next appendix).

Also, some staff members informed the Associate Dean that they will not participate in any program or activity with the Center and that they did not want to work with the Respondent. Staff members expressed hurt at the Respondent's tweet and stated how "disruptive" it would be if he were physically present on the Law Center's campus.

It's a free country. I imagine most of these staff members already didn't want to work with the Center. I do wonder, though, what's so "disruptive" about seeing someone you don't like on campus. It's not like my "bad tweet" betrayed a propensity to barge into people's offices or run around harassing them.

Finally, the Associate Dean reported to IDEAA that external stakeholders, including alumni and prospective students, have expressed concerns about the Respondent's comments. Some alumni are "very upset," and have called for the Respondent to be "fired right away," whereas other alumni have spoken out against "cancel culture." Some Law Center admittees have expressed concern about whether Georgetown is a place where they would be welcome as a result of the Respondent's comments.

> *Whatever any prospective student thinks of me, could anyone plausibly think that either the good-faith or bad-faith interpretation of my tweet was held by a significant part of the Georgetown faculty and staff?*

III. Applicable Policies

The University's *Policies on Equal Opportunity and Non-Discrimination in Employment and Education* prohibit unlawful harassment based on race, gender, and sex. According to the University's *Policy Statement on Harassment (Relating to Protected Categories)*, harassment is,

> verbal or physical conduct that denigrates or shows hostility or aversion to an individual because of [race, gender, and/or sex] when such conduct has the purpose or effect of: unreasonably interfering with an individual or third party's academic or work performance; creating an intimidating, hostile, or offensive educational or work environment; or otherwise adversely affecting an individual or third party's academic or employment opportunities.

Examples of harassment under the University's *Policy Statement on Harassment* include "stereotyping" and "offensive jokes and comments." The University's *Policy Statement on Harassment* clarifies that harassment includes "conduct carried out through the internet, email, social media, or other electronic means." Also, the University's *Policy Statement on Harassment* applies to "any" allegation of harassment "regardless of where the alleged conduct occurred."

> *This is all well and good, but doesn't harassment, including through digital means, have to be directed at someone? I never said anything about anyone at Georgetown. How do I create a hostile educational or work environment by disparaging potential Biden nominees— none of whom were members of the Georgetown community—if that's what I did?*

The crux of determining whether conduct based on race, sex, and/or gender constitutes harassment is whether it is "severe or pervasive." A single incident can create a hostile environment if it is sufficiently serious. The University's *Policy Statement on Harassment* instructs that determining whether conduct based on race, gender, and/or sex is severe or pervasive requires consideration of factors such as the "nature, scope, frequency, and duration of the conduct and number of persons involved. Simple teasing, offhand comments, or isolated incidents that are not severe or pervasive do not create a hostile or offensive environment." University policy cautions that harassment is "especially serious" when it occurs between supervisors and subordinates; "harassment unfairly exploits the power inherent in a faculty member's or supervisor's position."

Again, this policy contemplates someone harassing a coworker or fellow student. And regardless, if a tweeted "hot take" isn't an "offhand comment," I'm not sure what is in the social-media context.

In determining the severity of the conduct, the University's *Policy Statement on Harassment* clarifies that the conduct must be intimidating, hostile, or offensive and must interfere with a person's ability to participate in employment or educational programs from both a subjective and an objective standard (*i.e.*, from the perspectives of the specific individuals affected by the conduct and from an objective or reasonable person's perspective).[5] The University's *Policy Statement on Harassment* further instructs that "the injured party's perception of the offensiveness of the alleged conduct, standing alone, is not sufficient by itself to constitute harassment."

So the fact that someone's offended, or feigns offense, isn't enough to create a hostile environment.

The University's *Speech and Expression Policy* states that Georgetown "is committed to free and open inquiry, deliberation and debate in all

---

5. An objective standard considers the perspective of a reasonable person in the impacted individual's position, considering all the circumstances.

matters, and the untrammeled verbal and nonverbal expression of ideas." The *Speech and Expression Policy* underscores that it is Georgetown's policy to provide its community with "the broadest possible latitude to speak, write, listen, challenge, and learn." The *Speech and Expression Policy* also makes clear that it "is not the proper role of a University to insulate individuals from ideas and opinions they find unwelcome, disagreeable or even deeply offensive." However, the *Speech and Expression Policy* clarifies that its provision of free speech is not unfettered. The *Speech and Expression Policy* cautions that "[t]he freedom to debate and discuss the merits of competing ideas does not mean that individuals may say whatever they wish, whenever they want." Instead, Georgetown prohibits speech and expression that "violates the University's Harassment Policy," among other exceptions.

> *I agree with this exception: (actual) harassment and intimidation aren't protected by either the First Amendment or Georgetown's First Amendment–adjacent policy.*

IV. Discussion

IDEAA found that the Respondent's publicly posted words of "lesser Black woman"[6] denigrated individuals based on race, gender, and sex. His plain words not only explicitly identified the race, sex, and gender of a group of individuals (*i.e.*, Black women) but also categorized Black women as "lesser." Though the Respondent did not himself describe his comments as offensive or acknowledge that his comments could reasonably be interpreted to denigrate individuals, he promptly removed the tweet and apologized after others expressed their criticism or concern about how the Respondent expressed himself. The University's anti-harassment policy does not require that a respondent intend to denigrate or show hostility or aversion to individuals based on a protected status.

---

6. Pursuant to the University's *Speech and Expression Policy*, IDEAA did not base any of its findings on the viewpoint that the Respondent expressed with respect to President Biden's intention to nominate a Black woman to the Supreme Court. Instead, IDEAA's review focused on the Respondent's use of the term: "lesser Black woman," which implicates the University's *Policy Statement on Harassment*.

Instead, the Policy requires consideration of the "purpose or effect" of a respondent's conduct.

Here, the actual impact of the Respondent's conduct has been profound. More than 1,000 students and student organizations signed a letter "to condemn his racist tweet" and to give voice to the "hurt felt today by the Black community, and in particular Black women." Through various means, including public-facing letters from alumni groups, a sit-in by Georgetown law students, a town hall, meetings with Law Center leadership, emails, and a public-facing Georgetown website, many faculty, staff, alumni, and prospective students expressed their outrage, concern, and hurt. The evidence establishes that the Respondent's conduct adversely affected the Law Center's environment.

> *So intent doesn't matter—you can unintentionally harass or discriminate against someone, I guess—but people expressing offense is enough to establish harm. That contradicts the policy described just a few paragraphs ago.*

Whether the Respondent's publicly posted words objectively created a hostile environment depends on whether they were "severe or pervasive." IDEAA considered the context of the Respondent's words and his role as the leader of a Georgetown Center. By posting his words on a social media platform, the Respondent's words had the potential to reach millions of individuals, including each member of the Georgetown Law community. As a self-described "expert" in "judicial nominations and Supreme Court politics" and as a "communicator," the Respondent acknowledged that his tweet was posted in both his personal and professional capacities. In fact, he told IDEAA, his expertise in Supreme Court politics "is probably why Georgetown's Center for the Constitution hired me in the first place," thereby linking his tweet directly to his role at Georgetown.

> *So I guess it was a mistake to talk about my expertise and how it's hard to separate personal and professional capacities? I bet if I had said that I was tweeting only in my personal capacity, they would've written that I was disingenuous because I was obviously aware of the professional and intellectual impact my pronouncements had in this*

legal-policy field. Separately, if I had fewer Twitter followers (I had about 30,000 at the time), would my offense have been less serious?

As the Executive Director of the Center, the Respondent holds a significant position, where he is expected to collaborate with academic and administrative teams, along with other Centers and Institutes, across the Law Center and hire, supervise, mentor, teach, and grade students and fellows. The Respondent's comment categorized Black women as "lesser" contenders for one of the most prestigious positions within the legal profession. It is future legal professionals of all backgrounds and identities that the Respondent is charged with shaping—as he hires, supervises, mentors, teaches, and grades law students and fellows. In response to concerns about the Respondent's ability to grade all students fairly, both the Respondent and the Faculty Director pointed out that students are not compelled to take his courses. In fact, the Respondent explained that "students can select professors who fit their ideological presuppositions," and the Faculty Director stated that "only people who have either forgiven him for this one particular trespass or are unaware of it" will take his courses. These explanations suggest that the Respondent's courses—including a course on amicus brief writing, which likely would otherwise appeal broadly to students and which the Respondent expects to teach—may be less available to law students impacted by the Respondent's tweets than to those who were not.

There it is again, this point about educational access or opportunity.

IDEAA also considered that the Respondent's conduct occurred on one occasion, was not directed at a particular individual, and preceded his employment at Georgetown.

And? These things didn't matter or mitigate in any way the severity of the "harm" I had caused? This reads like something's missing here.

As detailed in this report, Respondent's conduct had a significant negative impact on the Georgetown community. However, as the Respondent was a third party and not an employee at the time he posted the comments on Twitter, consistent with IDEAA's *Grievance Procedures to Investigate Allegations of Discrimination and Harassment*, IDEAA refers this matter to the Dean to consider and implement appropriate corrective measures to address the impact of the Respondent's objectively offensive comment. It is important to note that, given the Respondent's role in the Law Center, if he were to make another, similar or more serious remark as a Georgetown employee, a hostile environment based on race, gender, and sex likely would be created.

> *Aha! This final paragraph reads as a disjunction, like it was added in haste at the last moment. It seems that IDEAA (and HR) were getting ready to recommend my dismissal but in the end were overruled, perhaps by Georgetown's general counsel to minimize risk of my suing or possibly by other higher-ups concerned about the reputational harm to the university from firing me, likely on the advice of outside counsel.*

V. Recommendations
IDEAA has shared with the Dean recommendations to consider to address the impact of the Respondent's tweets.

> *You saw my response to those recommendations in the previous appendix.*

VI. Notice of Right to Appeal
The Respondent may request an appeal within 14 business days of IDEAA's notification of the results. To obtain an appeal, the appellant must demonstrate: (1) a material failure to follow IDEAA's *Grievance Procedures to Investigate Allegations of Discrimination and Harassment* during the investigation; and/or that (2) significant evidence was not considered, which would have altered the outcome of the review.

> *Well, to coin a phrase, thank heaven for small favors. In any event, an appeal would've obviously been pointless.*

APPENDIX C

My Resignation Letter

Ilya Shapiro
Executive Director & Senior Lecturer
Center for the Constitution
Georgetown University Law Center

William M. Treanor
Dean & Executive Vice President
Paul Regis Dean Leadership Chair
Georgetown University Law Center

Via email
June 6, 2022

Dear Dean Treanor,

After full consideration of the report of the Office of Institutional Diversity, Equity, and Affirmative Action ("IDEAA Report"), and upon consultation with counsel, family, and trusted advisers, it has become apparent that my remaining at Georgetown has become untenable. Although I celebrated my "technical victory" in the *Wall Street Journal*, further analysis shows that you've made it impossible for me to fulfill the duties of my appointed post.

You cleared me on a jurisdictional technicality, but the IDEAA Report—and your own statements to the Law Center community—implicitly repealed Georgetown's vaunted Speech and Expression Policy and set me up for discipline the next time I transgress progressive orthodoxy.

You told me when we met last week that you want me to be successful in my new role and that you will "have my back." But instead, you've painted a target on my back such that I could never do the job I was hired for, advancing the mission of the Center for the Constitution.

First, the IDEAA Report speciously found that my tweet criticizing President Biden for selecting Supreme Court justices by race and sex had a "significant negative impact," requiring "appropriate corrective measures" to address my "objectively offensive comments and to prevent the recurrence of offensive conduct based on race, gender, and sex." It found that my comments "could have the effect of limiting Black women students' access to courses taught by [me]" and "discourage Black women and their allies from seeking internships and employment at the Center." You reiterated these concerns in your June 2 statement to the Georgetown Law community, further noting the "harmful" nature of my tweets and the "pain" they have caused.

Contrary to your June 2 statement, no reasonable person acting in good faith could construe what I tweeted to be "objectively offensive." It's a complete miscomprehension to read what I said to suggest that "the best Supreme Court nominee could not be a Black woman," as you did in your very first statement back on January 27, or that I considered all black women to be "lesser than" everyone else. Although my tweet was inartful, as I've readily admitted many times, its meaning that I considered one possible candidate to be best and thus all others to be *less qualified* is clear. Only those acting in bad faith to get me fired because of my political beliefs would misconstrue what I said to suggest otherwise.

Second, any harm done by my tweet was done by those seeking that Georgetown fire me. I deleted my tweet well before any student was likely to learn of it. Screen captures of the tweet were then disseminated by others seeking to harm me because of my political views. It was they, not I, who intentionally and knowingly caused any harm to any student who later came to learn of and read their screen captures of the tweet. It is they, not I, who are morally culpable for any such resulting harm.

Third, under the reasoning of the IDEAA Report, none of this objective textual analysis even matters. As the report put it, "The University's anti-harassment policy does not require that a respondent intend to denigrate or show hostility or aversion to individuals based on a protected status. Instead, the Policy requires consideration of the 'purpose or effect' of a respondent's conduct." According to this theory, the mere fact that many people were offended, or claimed to be, is enough for me to have violated the policies under which I was being investigated. Although there was no formal finding of a violation because of the procedural fact that I wasn't an employee when I tweeted and so not subject to those policies, so long as some unstated number of students, faculty, or staff claim that a statement "denigrates" or "show[s] hostility or aversion" to a protected class, that's enough to constitute a violation of Georgetown antidiscrimination rules. The falsity of such a claim is immaterial to being found guilty. Georgetown has adopted what First Amendment jurisprudence describes as an impermissible "heckler's veto."

Fourth, regardless even of the "effect" of what I tweeted on January 26, the IDEAA Report found that "if [I] were to make another, similar or more serious remark as a Georgetown employee, a hostile environment based on race, gender, and sex *likely would be* created" (emphasis added). On this theory, all sorts of comments that someone—anyone—could find offensive would subject me to disciplinary action. This would be a huge Sword of Damocles over my head as I try to engage in my educational mission. Consider the following quite realistic hypotheticals:

- Later this month, I laud Supreme Court decisions that overrule *Roe v. Wade* and protect the right to carry arms. A campus activist claims that my comments "deny women's humanity" and makes her feel "unsafe" and "directly threatened with physical violence."
- In August, when I'm meeting with students concerned about my ability to treat everyone fairly, as you've asked me to do, one attendee, upon hearing my defense of free speech and equality of opportunity, files a complaint because I am "disingenuous" and the "embodiment of white supremacy."
- In October, when the Court hears arguments in the Harvard/UNC affirmative action cases, I express the opinion that the Fourteenth Amendment prohibits racial preferences in college admissions. Hundreds of Georgetown community members sign a letter asserting that my comments "are antithetical to the work that we do here every day to build inclusion, belonging, and respect for diversity" (quoting your statements of January 31 and June 2).
- Later this fall, in a class I'm teaching, a student feels uncomfortable with his assigned position in a mock oral argument in *303*

Creative LLC v. Elenis, a case on next term's docket that considers whether a designer can be compelled to create a website for a same-sex wedding. "To argue that someone can deny service to members of the LGBTQIA+ community is to treat our brothers and sisters as second-class citizens and I will not participate in Shapiro's denigrating charade," he writes on the student listserv.

Each of these purported offenses would subject me to investigation and discipline under the logic of the IDEAA Report. Nobody can work that way. Ironically, it is you and IDEAA who have created an unacceptably hostile work environment for me on account of my political views and affiliations.

Fundamentally, what you've done, what you've allowed IDEAA to do, is to repeal the Speech and Expression Policy that you claim to hold so dear. The IDEAA Report states that "IDEAA respects Georgetown university's commitment to the free and open discussion of ideas and does not seek to infringe speech that does not violate the University's non-discrimination or anti-harassment policy. *However . . .*" (emphasis added). The freedom to speak unless someone finds what you say offensive or infringing some nebulous conception of equity is no freedom at all.

What's worse, your treatment of me—starting with the launch of a sham investigation that apparently could've been resolved by looking at a calendar—shows how the University applies even these self-contradicting free speech "principles" in an inconsistent manner, depending on where on the ideological spectrum an "offense" arises. Contrast my situation with these recent examples:

- In 2018, Georgetown protected this tweet from Professor Carol Christine Fair during Justice Kavanaugh's confirmation process: "Look at this chorus of entitled white men justifying a serial rapist's arrogated entitlement. All of them deserve miserable deaths while feminists laugh as they take their last gasps. Bonus: we castrate their corpses and feed them to swine? Yes." When Prof. Fair advocated mass murder and castration based on race and gender, Georgetown did not initiate an investigation, but instead invoked Georgetown's free-expression policy.

- In 2020, Georgetown took no action when law professor Heidi Feldblum [sic—should be Feldman] tweeted "law professors and law school deans" should "not support applications from our students to clerk for" judges appointed by President Donald Trump. "To work for such a judge," Prof. Feld[man] continued, "indelibly marks a lawyer as lacking in the character and judgment necessary for the practice of law." These comments have the potential to threaten the careers of all of our conservative and libertarian students, or indeed anyone who clerks for duly confirmed Article III judges.

- In April of this year—well after my own tweet—Prof. Feld[man] tweeted, "we have only one political party in this country, the Democrats. The other group is a combination of a cult and an insurrection-supporting crime syndicate." She went on to reference Ron DeSantis, Ted Cruz, and Mitch McConnell and say, "The only ethically and politically responsible stance to take toward the Republican 'party' is to consistently point out that it is no longer a legitimate participant in U.S. constitutional democracy." As you know, unlike me, Prof. Feld[man] teaches 1Ls in mandatory courses. On the IDEAA theory, this pattern of remarks certainly created a hostile educational environment for our Republican students, who are a protected class under D.C. antidiscrimination law. Yet no investigation of these tweets was instigated after they were brought to your attention, after the precedent of investigating my tweets had already been established. Instead, a month after they were first published, they were quietly deleted without apology.

- Just last month, law professor Josh Chafetz tweeted: "The 'protest at the Supreme Court, not at the justices' houses' line would be more persuasive if the Court hadn't this week erected fencing to prevent protesters from coming anywhere near it." He added, "When the mob is right, some (but not all!) more aggressive tactics are justified." Later, he tagged Georgetown Law in a tweet saying that the law school was "not going to fire me over a tweet you don't like."

Prof. Chafetz was surely right about the last point. You and your colleagues on main campus were also right in choosing not to launch investigations of Profs. Fair and [Feldman]. All of these tweets were protected under Georgetown's free-expression policy. But now they would all merit at least an "investigation" to determine whether they violate the IDEAA's theory of hostile educational environment that was selectively applied in my case. Apparently it's free speech for thee, not for me.

It's all well and good to adopt free-speech policies that track the gold standard, the University of Chicago Principles of Freedom of Expression—and more broadly that same university's 1967 Kalven Report, which states that "the neutrality of the university . . . arises out of respect for free inquiry and the obligation to cherish a diversity of viewpoints"—indeed, it's essential. But it's not enough. If university administrators aren't willing to stand up to left-wing activists, Georgetown's enacted free speech and expression policy is a mere "pixel barrier."

What's worse, the problem isn't limited to fearful administrators. The proliferation of IDEAA-style offices (more typically styled Diversity, Equity, and Inclusion) enforce an orthodoxy that stifles intellectual diversity, undermines equal opportunity, and excludes dissenting voices. Even a stalwart T-14 law school dean bucks these bureaucrats at his peril.

Since I accepted your offer of employment, I've come to learn that Georgetown is by no means a follower in these trends. Instead, it's a leader. In contrast to the Jesuitical values that you're fond of reciting, this institution no longer stands for tolerance, respect, good faith, self-reflective learning, and generous service to others.

On the GULC website it reads: "Our motto 'Law is but the means, justice is the end' sums up the core commitment of Georgetown Law." But your and IDEAA's treatment of me suggests that neither the due process of law nor justice actually prevails.

I cannot again subject my family to the public attacks on my character and livelihood that you and IDEAA have now made foreseeable, indeed inevitable. As a result of the hostile work environment that you and they have created, I have no choice but to resign.

Sincerely,
Ilya Shapiro

Sources

The research process was quite different for this book than for my last one, *Supreme Disorder: Judicial Nominations and the Politics of America's Highest Court*. Although I didn't spend time in archives or reviewing primary historical documents for that project, I did piece together copious historical and journalistic accounts, as well as academic research.

In contrast, *Lawless* has much more of a ripped-from-the-headlines feel, being based on my "lived experience" with Georgetown and expanding to cover a moving target of outrages and policy failures. I did have a few parts—especially on the growth of bureaucracies, DEI, and critical legal studies—that required more traditional research, but for the most part I looked at recent journalistic accounts, blog posts, and op-eds, all stuff that's easily "googleable." Accordingly, and again very different from *Supreme Disorder*, there are relatively few footnotes in this book, which in any event I wanted to be more about the narrative than a literature review.

Instead, I'll refer you generally to the excellent work of Aaron Sibarium at the *Washington Free Beacon* and David Lat at his *Original Jurisdiction* Substack, as well as Nate Hochman's coverage of the "Shapiro beat" for *National Review* and FIRE's rich compendium of cases, news coverage, and student/faculty surveys. Jay Greene and James Paul's "Diversity University" report also provided a wealth of data and food for thought. Beyond that, I recommend the books, studies, monographs, and journal or feature articles listed in the bibliography below. Suffice it to say that this is not an exhaustive list of resources on the subject.

Academic Leadership Institute. "The History of Diversity in Higher Education." University of Michigan, June 25, 2021.

American Association of University Professors. "The 2022 AAUP Survey of Tenure Practices." May 2022.

Anderson, Craig B. "Political Correctness on College Campuses: Freedom of Speech v. Doing the Politically Correct Thing." *SMU Law Review* 46, no. 1 (1993): 171–224.

Bibas, Stephanos. "The Corruption of Apology." Persuasion, July 27, 2022.

Bonica, Adam, Adam Chilton, Kyle Rozema, and Maya Sen. "The Legal Academy's Ideological Uniformity." *Journal of Legal Studies* 47, no. 1 (January 2018): 1–43.

Brennan, Jason, and Phil Magness. *Cracks in the Ivory Tower: The Moral Mess of Higher Education.* New York: Oxford University Press, 2019.

Busch, Elizabeth Kaufer, and William E. Thro. *Title IX: The Transformation of Sex Discrimination in Education.* New York: Routledge, 2018.

Butcher, Jonathan, and Mike Gonzalez. "Critical Race Theory, the New Intolerance, and Its Grip on America." Heritage Foundation, December 7, 2020.

Cass, Ronald A., and John H. Garvey. "Law School Leviathan: Explaining Administrative Growth." *University of Toledo Law Review* 35, no. 1 (Fall 2003): 37–44.

Delgado, Richard, and Jean Stefancic. *Critical Race Theory: An Introduction.* 2nd ed. New York: New York University Press, 2012.

Dobbin, Frank. *Inventing Equal Opportunity*. Princeton, NJ: Princeton University Press, 2009.

Dobbin, Frank, and Alexandra Kalev. "Why Diversity Programs Fail." *Harvard Business Review*, July–August 2016.

Fortgang, Tal. "Conformity, Inequity, and Exclusion." *National Review*, April 13, 2023.

Foundation for Individual Rights and Expression. *The Academic Mind in 2022: What Faculty Think About Free Expression and Academic Freedom on Campus.* March 2023.

Frey, K., and S. T. Stevens. *Scholars Under Fire: Attempts to Sanction Scholars from 2000 to 2022.* Foundation for Individual Rights and Expression, 2023.

Ginsberg, Benjamin. *The Fall of the Faculty: The Rise of the All-Administrative University and Why It Matters.* New York: Oxford University Press, 2011.

Greene, Jay P., and James D. Paul. "Diversity University: DEI Bloat in the Academy." Heritage Foundation Backgrounder No. 3641. July 27, 2021.

Heriot, Gail, and Maimon Schwarzschild, eds. *A Dubious Expediency: How Race Preferences Damage Higher Education.* New York: Encounter Books, 2021.

Kors, Alan Charles, and Harvey A. Silverglate. *The Shadow University: The Betrayal of Liberty on America's Campuses.* New York: Free Press, 1998.

Lukianoff, Greg, and Jonathan Haidt. *The Coddling of the American Mind.* New York: Penguin Books, 2018.

Lukianoff, Greg, and Rikki Schlott. *The Canceling of the American Mind.* New York: Simon & Schuster, 2023.

Majeed, Azhar. "Defying the Constitution: The Rise, Persistence, and Prevalence of Campus Speech Codes." *Georgetown Journal of Law and Public Policy* 7, no. 2 (2009): 481–544.

Manzer, Robert. "The American University's Path to Illiberalism." American Enterprise Institute, April 20, 2023.

Martin, Jay. *The Dialectical Imagination.* New York: Little, Brown, 1977.

McGinnis, John O. "Law, Betrayed." *City Journal,* Spring 2023.

Melnick, R. Shep. *The Transformation of Title IX: Regulating Gender Equality in Education.* Washington, DC: Brookings Institution Press, 2018.

National Association for Law Placement. *Pulse Survey Results: Survey on Member Diversity, Equity, & Inclusion Efforts and Initiatives.* August 2020.

National Center for Education Statistics. *The Condition of Education 2013.*

———. *Report on the Condition of Education 2021.*

———. *Report on the Condition of Education 2023.*

Nierman, Evan, and Mark Sachs. *The Cancel Curse: From Rage to Redemption in a World Gone Mad.* New York: Skyhorse, 2023.

Rufo, Christopher F. *America's Cultural Revolution.* New York: Broadside Books, 2023.

Rufo, Christopher F., Ilya Shapiro, and Matt Beienburg. "Abolish Bureaucracies and Restore Colorblind Equality in Public Universities." Manhattan Institute Issue Brief, January 18, 2023.

Sibarium, Aaron. *The Takeover of America's Legal System.* New York: Free Press, 2022.

Skrentny, John David. *The Ironies of Affirmative Action: Politics, Culture, and Justice in America.* Chicago: University of Chicago Press, 1996.

Strossen, Nadine. *Hate: Why We Should Resist It with Free Speech, Not Censorship.* New York: Oxford University Press, 2018.

Xu, Kenny. *An Inconvenient Minority: The Attack on Asian American Excellence and the Fight for Meritocracy.* New York: Diversion Books, 2021.

Yenor, Scott. "How Texas A&M Went Woke." The American Mind, February 2023.

Acknowledgments

I never intended to write a book about cancel culture, law schools, or anything else of the sort—let alone have a personal reason for doing so. Nor was I intending to write any book so soon after my last one. Indeed, I joked that my biggest takeaway from the last go-around was never to write a book with a preschooler and a toddler in the house. But man plans and God laughs, so I ended up writing this one with two infants in the house.

Our "cancellation babies," Ollie and Lina (short for Galina, my mom's name), have been such a blessing and delight, providing an unexpectedly fun background against which to work on this project. Our "big boys," Jacob and Charlie, now in third and first grade, respectively, also provided a respite from the grind and a reminder that there are more important things in life than chapter deadlines—and that life goes on past cancellation campaigns.

With all of that activity and the professional demands on my time, I literally couldn't have produced this book without the support and encouragement of my wife, Kristin. She was heavily pregnant—with twins!—when I worked out my contract and was recovering from giving birth—to twins!—as I got going. Then she went back to work herself (as a real lawyer), so my mother-in-law, Diane Feeley, stepped up until we could get an au pair. Meanwhile, my father-in-law, Roger Feeley, made sure the house didn't fall apart and oversaw the construction of an addition that could hold our growing household. I have no idea how people raise kids without one set of grandparents not just available but living on-site. Diane and Roger are the nicest, most helpful people I've ever met, and I'm incredibly lucky to be married to their daughter.

This book also couldn't have been written without outstanding research support from Hunter Snowden, a legal intern ("law school associate") with the Manhattan Institute through almost my entire writing process, who produced thorough memos on an array of topics. Hunter did all that while completing his final year of a JD/MBA program at Emory, which included not just exams and graduation but shoulder surgery. I'm glad we planned around all that at the outset, because his work makes me look incredibly knowledgeable.

MI legal fellow Tim Rosenberger and legal intern Austin Severns came on board toward the end of the writing process and helped with final research and revisions. Tim was the head of the Stanford Fed Soc chapter during the juice-squeezing incident, so he also brought personal experience to bear. Two other MI staffers, Jason Peña and Derek Lux, helped out at the very end and very beginning, respectively, of their terms as legal-policy project managers. And three other recent law school grads, Gideon Rappaport and Tal Fortgang of NYU and Luke Bunting of Georgetown, were excellent sounding boards and wrote up some thoughts that I was able to incorporate. Tal has since joined MI as an adjunct fellow; he's wonderful to work with.

Speaking of MI, I'm indebted to my longtime friend and now colleague Jim Copland for facilitating my transition to this venerable institution and for showing me the ropes as I adjusted to a new think tank. I'm also grateful to Reihan Salam, Ilana Golant, and other senior staff, not just for bringing me on after I left Georgetown but for being so supportive of this book project.

My old friend Keith Urbahn was again invaluable as an agent; I thank my lucky stars that he takes time away from working with political celebrities and other prestige clients to handle my affairs. The process for this book contract was radically different than the last, but Keith, Matt Carlini, and their colleagues at Javelin provided exceptional advice and service. Would-be authors ask me whether an agent is really necessary if they feel confident in being able to negotiate a fair advance; my response is that literary agents do so much more than haggling over money. Doing it all yourself may be penny-wise but is certainly pound-foolish.

Eric Nelson and Hannah Long approached me soon after I resigned from Georgetown, when I was exhausted and not particularly interested in reliving "The Troubles" (as some friends have taken to calling that indelible period of my life). I'm grateful to them for convincing me that this book needed to be written, and for their hard work—and that of the entire HarperCollins team—in getting this to the finish line despite various bumps along the way.

I also have to thank all the folks who stood up for me during my Georgetown saga, from those four days of hell through the four months of purgatory and into my resurrection as a free man. Kmele Foster is a mensch, as are Rich Lowry—I joked that he made every *National Review* staff member write something about my case—and Paul Gigot. Others who provided helpful media coverage include Robby Soave, Tim Carney, John Davidson, and Dan McLaughlin. Princeton's Robby George and (now) Yale's Keith Whittington are islands of sanity, and their respective institutions—the James Madison Program and the Academic Freedom Alliance—pillars of truth as my alma mater descends into a sophistic maelstrom. Thanks also to Scalia Law's Todd Zywicki, who read my manuscript and made great comments. There are many more friends and strangers who offered support and celebration.

Then there's FIRE. I'd long counted many of its staff as friends and worked with them on briefs. Never did I think I'd become one of its clients. But when the cancellation campaign against me reached a fever pitch, FIRE was right by my side. Greg Lukianoff, Nico Perrino, Adam Steinbaugh, Daniel Burnett, Robert Shibley, and Ronnie London—we're talking the C-suite here!—worked closely with me on crisis management, public relations, and legal strategy. FIRE even connected me with my truly outstanding counsel, Jesse Binnall. I'd like to think that being associated with my case elevated Jesse's practice to new heights, which he richly deserves. And FIRE kept putting Georgetown's feet to the flames with letters and press releases. I was tickled by one of its blog posts that pointed out that the investigation of my 45-word tweet was taking longer than 12 round-trips to the moon or the gestation period of a bulldog, Georgetown's mascot. When FIRE stood up for me, it stood up for all scholars' rights and indeed for the principles that have made our nation free, open, intelligent, and prosperous.

I was also fortunate to participate in the Stanford Academic Freedom Conference in early November 2022, just as I began writing this book and less than a week before my twins' birth grounded me for several months. The conference, organized under the auspices of the Classical Liberalism Initiative at Stanford's Graduate School of Business—after the Hoover Institution pulled out—was partly a support group for the canceled and partly an exploration of best practices and strategies for fighting back against illiberalism in academia. It got media coverage because of the participation of Peter Thiel and Jordan Peterson, but what I found particularly valuable was interacting with people from diverse personal and professional backgrounds who were facing similar issues in their various disciplines. The overall goal was to identify ways to restore academic freedom, open inquiry, and freedom of speech and expression on campus and in the larger culture, to enable the search for truth and knowledge to flourish.

We can't take these principles for granted. My parents took me out of the Soviet Union more than 40 years ago because they didn't want me to grow up under a regime that tried to control one's every word and thought. I then moved myself from Canada to the United States because I prefer "life, liberty, and the pursuit of happiness" over "peace, order, and good government." Yet sadly, far too many Americans are blasé about their freedoms, which are now threatened by a growing culture of ignorance and illiberalism. When the freedom of conscience is forced to bend at the wheel of other, "equally important" values, we lose our shining city on a hill and destroy everything that human civilization has achieved. To paraphrase John F. Kennedy, it's the peace of the grave or the security of the slave.

My father, Leonid, died as I was completing this book, having never really gotten over my mother Galina's untimely passing a quarter century earlier. I hope I can continue making both of them proud and vindicating their decision to seek a better, freer life for our family.

Index

About the Author

ILYA SHAPIRO is a senior fellow and director of constitutional studies at the Manhattan Institute. Previously he was executive director and senior lecturer at the Georgetown Center for the Constitution, and before that a vice president of the Cato Institute and director of Cato's Robert A. Levy Center for Constitutional Studies. Shapiro is the author of *Supreme Disorder: Judicial Nominations and the Politics of America's Highest Court*, coauthor of *Religious Liberties for Corporations?*, and editor of eleven volumes of the *Cato Supreme Court Review*. He has contributed to a variety of academic, popular, and professional publications, including the *Wall Street Journal*, *Harvard Journal of Law & Public Policy*, the *Washington Post*, and the *Los Angeles Times*. He has testified many times before Congress and has filed more than five hundred amicus curiae "friend of the court" briefs in the Supreme Court. He holds a JD from the University of Chicago Law School. Shapiro lives with his wife and four children in Falls Church, Virginia.